salutary reminders that when the student is willing, teachers are everywhere."
—D. Patrick Miller, author of *The Book of Practical Faith*

"This book is a gift! A delightful resource! Creative, practical, and wise! The 37 practices offered here will serve as valuable guides for anyone intent on the spiritual path."
—Macrina Wiederkehr, OSB, retreat guide and author of *A Tree Full of Angels*

"*Spiritual Rx* offers bounteous and splendid seeds for a more complete life, each one containing worlds to be cultivated through contemplation. Informed by years of research and their unique database documenting the landscape of spiritual disciplines, Frederic and Mary Ann Brussat present an expansive and accessible compendium while always displaying their trademark quality and enthusiasm for every detail of practice."
—Shaun McNiff, author of *Trust the Process* and *Art as Medicine*

"If there's a better spiritual practice book than *Spiritual Rx*, we don't know what it is. Co-authors Frederic and Mary Ann Brussat give seekers sound advice for setting up their own individualized spiritual practice, present a wide variety of religious traditions as sources, and then offer an astonishing range of exercises from which readers can choose. They combine a broad diversity of cultural forms—books, films, art, and music—with well organized spiritual subjects, culminating in a clear and useful work that has something for everyone."
—Denise Breton and Christopher Largent, authors of *The Paradigm Conspiracy* and *Love, Soul and Freedom*

"The Brussats have done it again: given us an invaluable guide to spiritual practices and resources. *Spiritual Rx* is as comprehensive as it is light-hearted. It presents age-old wisdom in contemporary garb, through the best of modern movies, writings, music, and meditations. Thanks to the Brussats for sharing with us, so usefully and playfully, their expertise."
—Drew Leder, M.D., author of *Games for the Soul* and *Spiritual Passages*

"*Spiritual Rx* splendidly defines and illustrates the essential practices of daily spiritual life. It is a sourcebook of practical wisdom from all the world's spiritual traditions, and can be a guide to those just embarking on

the path as well as those already on the journey. Without offering a 'quick fix' to solve all problems, it is literate, gentle, and inspiring as it prescribes the possibilities of wholeness in our daily life."
—Margaret Kornfeld, D. Min., President of the American Association of Pastoral Counselors and author of *Cultivating Wholeness*

"If you're tired of inner-development books that are long on abstractions but short on practicalities, *Spiritual Rx* is the perfect antidote . . . a treasure chest chock-full of soul medicine."
—Maggie Orman, editor of *Prayers for Healing*

"*Spiritual Rx* is not only medicine for what ails you, it is great preventative medicine as well. Read this book, but more than that, experiment with the practices, teachers, and resources you find here. Your life and your connection to the Sacred will be all the healthier for your efforts."
—Debra K. Farrington, author of *Romancing the Holy*

"*Spiritual Rx* is a useful spiritual resource that can be followed systematically or sampled at random for its gems of wisdom and insight. People of any faith, or none, will find its message inspiring and reassuring. A timely contribution to the spiritual awakening that characterizes the times in which we live."
—Diarmuid O'Murchu, author of *Reclaiming Spirituality*

SPIRITUAL Rx

Also by Frederic and Mary Ann Brussat

100 Ways to Keep Your Soul Alive:
Living Deeply and Fully Every Day

100 More Ways to Keep Your Soul Alive

Spiritual Literacy:
Reading the Sacred in Everyday Life

SPIRITUAL R_X

PRESCRIPTIONS FOR LIVING A MEANINGFUL LIFE

BY FREDERIC AND MARY ANN BRUSSAT

NEW YORK

Copyright © 2000 Frederic and Mary Ann Brussat

The authors gratefully acknowledge these sources for permission to reprint the following:
Poetry by Jelaluddin Rumi and commentary by Coleman Barks from *The Essential Rumi* translated by Coleman Barks, HarperSanFrancisco, 1995. Copyright © by Coleman Barks. Reprinted by permission of the author.
Poetry from *House of Light* by Mary Oliver. Copyright © 1990 by Mary Oliver. Reprinted by permission of Beacon Press, Boston.
Haiku reprinted from *Seeds from a Birch Tree: Writing Haiku and the Spiritual Journey* by Clark Strand. Copyright © 1997 by Clark Strand. Published by Hyperion.

Library of Congress Cataloging-in-Publication Data

Brussat, Frederic.
    Spiritual Rx : prescriptions for living a meaningful life / by
Frederic and Mary Ann Brussat.—1st ed.
        p.   cm.
    Includes bibliographical references.
    ISBN 0-7868-6450-8
    1. Spiritual life.   I. Brussat, Mary Ann.   II. Title.
BL624.B76   2000
291.4'4—dc21   99-22001
                                                                        CIP

FIRST EDITION

Designed by Gillian Redfern-Rones

10   9   8   7   6   5   4   3   2   1

To our Scattered Sisterhood:

Marjorie Allen

Joy Carol

Ieva Graufelds

Kathy Kastilahn

Cora Louise Michael

GRATITUDES

We are blessed to have a career path that overlaps the path of spiritual practice. Our experiences on this grand journey have been informed and inspired by many teachers—writers, filmmakers, artists, musicians—many of whom we pay tribute to in this book. We are grateful to all of them for enriching our lives in so many concrete ways.

We also are blessed to have the generous support of the members and friends of the nonprofit organization we direct, who have enabled us to focus our attention on the wide variety of resources available for people on spiritual journeys. Most recently, we've found colleagues and a home for our reviews at the *Spirituality & Health* web site (www.spiritualrx. com) and magazine. Editor Bob Scott is gifted in the spiritual practices of hospitality, imagination, and listening; we're thankful for his leadership and friendship. Thanks as well to publisher Deidre Taylor and the Parish of Trinity Church Wall Street.

Dear friends have given us thoughtful feedback and creative ideas as we have developed the concepts and prescriptions in this book. We caught a passion for art and music as vehicles for spiritual reflection from Pat Repinski and Dave Rich, and they offered great suggestions for those sections. Linda Cutting, Ron Melrose, John Ortiz, and Evan Pritchard also contributed music choices, and Frank and Jean Bunts had ideas for the art. Each of them encouraged us to stretch into new fields of appreciation. We thank Belleruth Naparstek and Jerry Epstein for permission to use imagery exercises they have created. Jerry also helped with those sections of the book by reviewing all the exercises and lending advice from his vast experience of using imagery as a bridge to the inner world. We send our heartfelt appreciation to Colette Abouker-Muscat in Jerusalem for her exercises and her instruction in this practice.

Special kudos for kindness go to our editor friends Kathy Kastilahn and Sonia Solomonson of *The Lutheran,* who read the entire manuscript, asked thoughtful questions, and peppered the margins with their personal reactions to the material. We should all have such encouragement! We should all have friends like Joy Carol, too. Working side by side with us in the office, she has been our model for enthusiasm; she is very well named.

Looking back from this moment, we thank our agent Ned Leavitt for his efforts in placing this book, and his associate Libby Stephens for her attention to our concerns over the months while we were writing. Looking ahead, we are grateful to our editor Leigh Haber, publisher Bob Miller, and the rest of the team at Hyperion for all their editorial, production, publicity, and marketing expertise.

Just as we were putting the finishing touches on *Spiritual Rx,* we received the first tapes of a television series that is also organized around the Alphabet of Spiritual Literacy. It is most gratifying for us to have this endorsement of the Alphabet and to see it so beautifully extended into another medium. We salute director David Cherniack and producer Jim Hanley of Sleeping Giant Productions in Toronto for their sensitivity, creativity, and spiritual wisdom.

Our families and other friends are graces in our lives in more ways than we can acknowledge here, but we do want to mention a few. Cora Louise Michael and Ieva Graufelds have been models of love for us and compassion for others. We have come to rely on Marjorie Allen's weekly nurturing through shiatsu and conversations about spiritual practice. Alice and Roger Deakins's hospitality has given us a sense of what it means to have a large extended family.

Finally, we must express our gratitude to our cat Bebb. Although he has now joined his brother, Boone, on the other side, this little being stayed with us until we finished *Spiritual Rx.* He knew he was the prescription we needed! He was always a delight in our lives and a great teacher—of joy, play, wonder, and, in the end, mystery.

Blessed be the Holy Spirit who helps us make our ideas into sentences and supplies the words we cannot find ourselves.

CONTENTS

SPIRITUAL Rx

A man in prison is sent a prayer rug by his friend. What he had wanted, of course, was a file or a crowbar or a key! But he began using the rug, doing five-times prayer before dawn, at noon, mid-afternoon, after sunset, and before sleep. Bowing, sitting up, bowing again, he notices an odd pattern in the weave of the rug, just at the qibla, *the point, where his head touches. He studies and meditates on that pattern, gradually discovering that it is a diagram of the lock that confines him in his cell and how it works. He's able to escape. Anything you do every day can open into the deepest spiritual place, which is freedom.*

—COLEMAN BARKS

INTRODUCTION

THE PATH OF PRACTICE

The word "prescription"—abbreviated as "Rx"—has some interesting associations when applied to the spiritual life. As in medicine, a prescription can be a cure, remedy, or solution recommended to correct a disorder, imbalance, or problem. It can take the form of advice or information, which in spirituality is called wisdom. Finally, prescription is semantically related to precept or guideline. This meaning can be extended to include a spiritual rule or a set of activities undertaken as part of one's daily discipline. This book, then, consists of remedies, wisdom, and recommended activities for all those taking up the spiritual life.

Our prescriptions are organized under the Alphabet we introduced in our book *Spiritual Literacy: Reading the Sacred in Everyday Life*. There, beginning with Attention and proceeding to Zeal, we identified 37 practices that are markers of the spiritual life. Spiritual literacy is the ability to recognize the presence of the sacred in our everyday experiences. These spiritual practices both support this perspective and enable us to act upon it. They help us move into deeper relationships with God, our true selves, other people, and the whole Creation. They are how we live a spiritual life every day.

Practice has always been the heart and soul of the world's religions, and it is also the distinguishing characteristic of today's less organized spirituality movements. It can be something as simple as lighting a candle or a ritual as complex as a Native American vision quest. It can involve the spontaneity of a Christian's flash prayers in the street or the rigorous structure of a Muslim's five-times-a-day prayer. It is Africans and Sufis expressing their yearning for God through dance, Jews studying the Torah, Buddhists doing mindfulness meditation, and Hindus looking for divine signs in common objects.

The variety of practices matches the diversity of human personalities. Many connect with the Holy through the mind while others emphasize the body or the emotions. Some prefer group worship; others, private prayer. A person's daily practice might include elements of ethical training, emotional transformation, motivational change, physical exercise, community building, study of sacred texts, and acts of service. Practices attend to every mood and moment.

Many of us, however, were raised to think of spiritual practice as little more than a short grace before meals, saying bedtime prayers, and going to a weekly worship service. The problem with seeing practice this way is that it becomes just another entry on our already crowded To Do lists, one of those frequently unexamined routines of our daily lives. Practice degenerates into an onerous obligation similar to taking out the garbage or flossing our teeth.

A far more useful and rewarding approach is to view practice not as an activity we do but as the path we travel on our spiritual journey. It is our way of experiencing spiritual reality. Practice is and always has been here; it is a path with no beginning and no end. We just have to step into it. And, although practice does not require that we leave the realms of reason and sense perceptions, it gives us a much broader base to operate from.

This means that everything we do is practice. As the Zen Buddhists put it, how you do anything is how you do everything. Walking down the hall mindfully is as important as sitting on the mat in meditation. How a Christian acts at work on Monday is as significant as attendance at church on Sunday.

You don't step on the path of practice for a few minutes a day, then jump off to go about the rest of your life. If you want to see how you are doing, look at how you behave during a breakfast disagreement with your partner, in a traffic jam on the way to the office, in the line at the bank when someone skips ahead of you, in your reaction to a homeless person begging for money, or at your club when you are asked to do something that violates your conscience. This path also encompasses the joy you feel in a job well done, the elation that washes over you while making love, the affection you have for your pet, and the communion you experience in a circle of close friends.

Spiritual practices (plural), then, are the concrete acts we perform on the path of practice. Before we move on to a discussion of the 37 specific practices in our Alphabet, here are a few tips to keep in mind about the path in general.

FEEL WELCOME: THIS IS COMMON GROUND

Whether you are affiliated with one of the world's religions or are more comfortable with a free-floating spirituality, whether you are conservative or liberal, experienced or just beginning, there is room for you on the common ground of practice. A chief characteristic of the path of practice is its inclusivity. Everyone belongs.

JUST BEGIN

Anywhere is a good place to begin on the path of practice. Many have gone ahead of us and left notes along the way. Start slowly and take baby steps. There's no rush. With practice, each day is a new beginning. We're always on the way.

GIVE IT TIME

When you see practice as a way of life, you don't have to worry about making time to practice. All your activities are covered by the path. So be intentional about them. Dedicate your deeds to God and the greater good.

BE DISCERNING

Not all spiritual practices are for everyone. Know yourself, and look for the ones that are right for you. Watch for signs in your daily life pointing you toward a particular practice. Listen for a call from God, or, if you prefer, from your own intuition, telling you what to do.

BE NATURAL

Doing spiritual practices requires energy, dedication, and sincerity, but these activities do not have to be depleting, ponderous, or strained. As you move along the path of practice, you need to find a rhythm and a pace that matches your natural style and way of life.

BE FLEXIBLE

The path of practice is filled with many twists and turns. It calls for a certain flexibility of action. You may do a particular practice for years or get what you need from it in a few days. Try not to be rigid or unbending, for this saps your spirit and deters you from enjoying the surprises along the way.

LEARN FROM OTHERS

You are not the first on the path of practice or the only one to try a particular spiritual exercise. Listen to those with more experience. Tap into the resources of a tradition or find a teacher. Aim to be good at what you do.

LET GO

You are not in charge of this path. The harder you try to make things happen, the quicker you'll find yourself caught in the trap of disappointment. Surrender yourself to practice, and don't worry about where it is taking you. Go with the flow.

DON'T BE CONCERNED ABOUT EXTERNALS

Make sure that your being on the path is not dependent on or subservient to external conditions. It doesn't matter whether you're in the right or wrong place, whether the weather is good or bad, whether you're depressed or optimistic. You can practice any time and any place no matter what the conditions.

DON'T HAVE EXPECTATIONS

Taking up the path of practice is a way of weaning ourselves from expectations. Walking this road is not about going to heaven, gaining enlightenment, or achieving permanent inner peace. It is about dealing with whatever shows up in the present moment.

REALIZE NOTHING IS THE SAME

Spiritual practices involve plenty of repetition, and most of us are allergic to tedious or boring efforts. On the path of practice, however, nothing is ever exactly the same. Subtle changes are always taking place, revealing new variations on old themes. With practice you become attuned to them.

WELCOME BAD DAYS

Don't beat up on yourself for bad days when nothing seems to go right. In the big picture, even bad days have a purpose. They test our stamina and fuel our resolve. And they help us appreciate the easy days.

BE PERSISTENT

Be persistent in doing your spiritual practices. Don't let minor set-backs or even major catastrophes crimp your style. If you do stop, just start again. Remember that everything on the path helps you learn how to keep doing your practices.

BE FREE

Experiment, expand your horizons, open up new doors along the path of practice. Don't be frightened to explore a different field. If you meet with obstacles along the way, turn them to your advantage. If they steer you down a detour, accept that this longer route may have quite interesting scenery. Let your intuition and your imagination take you into new territory.

DEAL WITH YOUR DEMONS

Sometimes diligence in your practices becomes a signal to your demons that it's time to show up to see if they can drag you down or even stop you in your tracks. Accept them as fellow travelers along the path, know in your heart that they can also be your teachers, and stare them down, if necessary.

WORK WITH WHO YOU ARE

Practice yields a rigorous and rewarding form of self-knowledge. We can't escape who we are; we carry it around with us all the time. The challenge is to honor the best and the worst in ourselves. Work with it all.

REMEMBER PRACTICE IS PERFECT

Don't be concerned about making progress on the path. You may notice a positive force field of energy associated with your movement, but you don't know how far it reaches. Don't be a perfectionist about your practices either. What's important is that you keep at them, not that you get to a particular level or skill. Practice does not make perfect; it is perfect.

ENJOY THE COMPANY

The path of practice constantly reminds us how much we need the support and companionship of others. A community of practice offers us a chance to share our stories and to learn from others' experiences. Everyone we meet encourages us to grow by inspiring us or challenging us. Love and appreciate them all.

Don't Make Comparisons

After you have spent some time on the path of practice, you are less interested in comparing yourself to others and less likely to make judgments about them. Practice teaches us to treat each other as equals. It also holds us accountable for our actions.

Don't Set Goals

Don't do your spiritual practices with specific goals or objectives in mind. This invariably sets you on the path of achievement, where the ego wants to take center stage and bow to thunderous applause. The path of practice is its own reward.

Avoid Making a Production

According to spiritual teachers in all traditions, the greatest danger of all is to make your practices into vanity productions whereby you feel superior to others and even put them down. You have no special claims on this territory. The path of practice is the humble way.

Come Down off the Mountain

Our practices can be rejuvenated by dramatic mountaintop experiences that give us fresh energy and bold perspectives. But eventually we must return to the realities of our everyday lives. The path of practice is the ordinary way. It *is* daily life.

We have been using the term "path" here and, most likely, you are imaging it as a road—perhaps a dirt one winding through the countryside that eventually turns into a paved highway or a city street. You may see sharp turns and intersections, roads taken and not taken. Or you may recall the restrictive way the religions tend to describe the path—as the straight and narrow, or the steep and difficult climb up the mountain.

Those attributes may indeed be part of the path of practice, but we don't want to limit it to those images. Think of practice as a very broad boulevard. Although there are places along it when you can be still and alone, it is also packed with people and beings, animate and inanimate, visible and invisible, of our time and all times.

Part of the path may go in a direct line, but the route is hardly linear. It is constantly changing, from lines to circles to spirals to lines bursting forth in new directions and then circling back on top of the whole complexity of it all. There are no obvious intersections and one-and-only choices because everything is connected and overlapping.

What's more, this ground of practice is not dirt or stone or cement at all. It's more like a carpet made up of many colored strands, all interwoven, a diversity within a unity. The path of practice is composed of specific practices, the multiple threads of the spiritual life. It is to them that we now turn.

Work. Keep digging your well.
Don't think about getting off work.
Water is there somewhere.

Submit to a daily practice.
Your loyalty to that
Is a ring on the door.

Keep knocking, and the joy inside
will eventually open a window
and look out to see who's there.

—*JELALUDDIN RUMI*
translated by Coleman Barks

FINDING YOUR PRESCRIPTION OF PRACTICES

Rachel Naomi Remen tells a story in *Kitchen Table Wisdom* about a cancer patient who, despite all the best intentions, was having trouble with his daily imagery meditation. In a training program, he had been encouraged to imagine thousands of tiny sharks with sharp teeth hunting cancer cells in his body. He didn't relate to this imagery, however, and found it hard to do consistently. The image he preferred, deemed not "vicious" enough by others in the training program, was of a catfish, a bottom feeder that never sleeps and is known for its ability to sort waste products from the good material in an aquarium. As a child he had kept catfish as pets and to him they represented unconditional love, devotion, and vigilance. He created his own imagery exercise around catfish caring for his body. This was a practice he could remember to do because it was as unique to him as his DNA.

You have to find the "catfish practices" for your spiritual life. If you participate in a religious community, their rituals and traditions may be very meaningful. You may learn of other possibilities from your friends, through your reading, or from attending lectures and workshops. To make practice your way of life, then, you need to choose activities that you will actually do, day after day, even if your combination of them turns out to be totally unique to you.

So how do you put together a good set of spiritual practices? We propose that all of the tried-and-true ones used in the world's religions are available to you, although a particular tradition may emphasize some more than others. Buddhists, for example, are very familiar with the practices of attention and compassion, whereas Protestant Christians are apt to focus on faith, grace, and justice. Roman Catholic Christians easily recognize devotion, hospitality, and mystery as spiritual practices, while Native Americans emphasize connections, teachers, and wonder.

Your choices are influenced by the tradition you grew up with, your cultural heritage, your personality and personal history, your career and family situation, your stage of life, and the challenges you are facing. Over the years, you may try many different practices, sometimes simultaneously. To do so, however, you need resources and perhaps instruction, and this is where it begins to get confusing.

The current spirituality scene can be overwhelming. The sheer volume of information available on the various approaches makes it hard to identify the best ones for you. There is a plethora of teachers able to inspire and direct you, but how do you evaluate them? It is as if the path of practice is passing through a forest and the farther in you go, the more crowded it becomes with trees, bushes, underbrush, and all kinds of creatures. Now you can't even see the path because of the thickness of the vegetation. We've certainly noticed this trend in our work as book and media reviewers. There are plenty of books to read, films to watch, and things to try—but which ones are for you?

Spiritual Rx is designed to help you find your "catfish practices." It is offered to those just embarking on the path of practice as well as for those well along the way who feel they need a little tune-up. We cover 37 key practices that are common in the world's spiritual traditions. For each of them, we recommend the best teachers, videos, daily exercises, rituals, and projects that will give you a good idea of whether this particular practice satisfies the requirements of your spiritual life. Does it help you sense the sacred presence all around you? Does it reinforce your connections with others—the breadth of your world, and with your inner life—the depth of your being? Does it enable you to understand your obligations, tap your gifts, and express your commitments more directly? Let's go through the different sections of our coverage of each practice to see how this works.

DAILY CUES, REMINDERS, VOWS, BLESSINGS

Each chapter opens with four brief statements designed to catch key aspects of the spiritual practice. We are constantly challenged on the path of practice to move from the abstract to the concrete, to express our spirituality through specific deeds and thoughts. Using the daily cues and reminders, and affirming the vows are good first steps. The blessings remember the Source of our common path.

THE BASIC PRACTICE

Spiritual practices are activities you do to deepen your relationship with the sacred. They also mean that you relate in a particular way to your inner self, other people, and the world around you. Some practices require setting aside a special place and time, but most of them can be done in the midst of your daily life.

"We are what we practice," Jewish writer Avram Davis reminds us. "If we become angry a lot, then essentially we are practicing anger. And we become quite good at it. Conversely, if we practice being joyful, then a joyful person is what we become." We are practicing all kinds of things all the time, but the decision to do spiritual practices is intentional. These activities have meaning and purpose, and they influence how we live our lives. They are usually routes to greater self-understanding and increased participation in communities.

In these sections of *Spiritual Rx*, we define the 37 basic and essential practices of the spiritual life. We may identify them by their other names and note how they fit into the teachings of the world's religions.

All of the practices have an action element. They are about doing particular things. We give a few beginning instructions so you have a better idea of what each one involves. Recommended resources and more detailed suggestions follow.

CATALYSTS, CONTRASTS, AND COMPANIONS

These sections of *Spiritual Rx* recognize that people come to the spiritual life in many ways and for different reasons. Some experience an awakening that takes them by surprise, and they are never the same again. People who were raised in one of the world's religions may decide at some point on their journey that they want to dip into the spiritual river that flows through all the traditions. But most of us, frankly, are drawn to spirituality because, as a doctor might say, certain symptoms are "presenting."

You might feel that something is missing in your life, something you desperately want. You could be longing for inspiration. Or community. Or quality time. You could be in pain and in need of healing. You could be feeling happy and grateful and compelled to give something back to the universe. You could be facing a crisis and know that how you handled such situations in the past won't be enough this time. You could be burned out. You could be worried about your loved ones or frightened about the very real dangers in the world. You could be sensing that your life could be more meaningful but not know how to go about making it so.

Spirituality won't solve all your problems, but it will help you deal with them. The first step is to examine your symptoms—what is really happening in your life—to see what they reveal about the best spiritual practices for you. Before we discuss just how you do this, a few words on the process we went through developing this aspect of *Spiritual Rx*.

On our *"Spiritual Rx* Prescriptions" chart, we identify symptoms for which we would prescribe a particular spiritual practice. We struggled with what to call them, symptoms being an overly clinical term even for a book with Rx in the title. First, we had two columns, the practice and its "opposite." The opposite of compassion is judgment. The opposite of enthusiasm is apathy. If you are judgmental, you should practice compassion. If you are apathetic, we would prescribe enthusiasm.

But the religions of the world have been plagued over the centuries by conflicts arising from such dualistic thinking—good versus evil being the most common expression. It is too easy to distance yourself from the *other* quality when it is described as the *bad* way to be.

A more useful model is the Chinese symbol of the yin and the yang, a circle divided into two parts. The yin, or female side, is dark; the yang, or male side, is white. Inside each half circle is a small dot of its opposite—white in the dark, dark in the white. Each contains the other, and the whole composition reflects a harmony of opposites. Further, by tracing the outer borders of each half circle, we see that each part gives rise to the other through interaction.

As in the yin and the yang, opposites are not threats to the spiritual life but are aspects of it. These symptoms often act as catalysts, precipitating a desire to enter the path of practice or to move to a different phase of the journey. Instead of having symptoms positioned on a right/wrong continuum, we now see them in a circle. There are still columns on our chart, but the opposites have become contrasts, and a third column contains a list of companions. The spiritual practices, in the center, counter or balance the contrasts and enhance the companions. In reality, the qualities in the outside columns are extensions of one another and loop around in a circle, like the yin and the yang, with the practices centered on top of it all.

All the contrasts and companions may be encountered in the course of living the spiritual life. Some attitudes and actions do block practice, and you will want to clear them out of your way. Violence and injustice are two examples. But even here the looping lines tell an interesting story. Take anger, which we tend to quickly dismiss as being undesirable. Extend that anger around the circle and it changes into outrage, which when directed toward the results of violence turns into a desire for nonviolence, or the practice of peace.

Other symptoms are signs pointing you in the direction you need to go. By seeing how much you are living in the past, you discover the importance of living in the present. By understanding the targets of your greed, you can redirect your attention to that for which you are grateful. By noticing how cynical you have become, you recognize your longing for meaning.

Many negative experiences have gifts associated with them, and profound lessons come from embracing and taming them. Therapists are operating from this understanding when they prescribe a symptom, encouraging someone to talk about feelings of alienation, for example, or having a person who is afraid of elevators ride in them to overcome the phobia.

Further, others benefit when we work with our symptoms, even negative ones. By claiming our negative impulses, rather than denying them, we learn to care about people like ourselves who are fearful, depressed, indifferent, or wasteful. When we face our pain, we are less likely to inflict it or project it upon others. Spiritual practices such as compassion, justice, and mystery actually use our personal suffering as medicine to strengthen us for the healing of the world.

Symptoms can also be positive experiences that motivate you to take up a particular spiritual practice. How do you sustain a burst of creativity? Try the practices of imagination or wonder. Having felt the freedom of being released from your guilt by God, you are reinforced in the practice of forgiveness of others. Free-spiritedness goes hand in hand with play. A yen for adventure can be a sign that you would enjoy questing.

Even if no particular symptom is presenting in your life, you may still want to expand your repertoire of spiritual practices. Perhaps you find yourself asking questions like these: Could I use a mentor to improve the attention I give to my relationships? How can I fine-tune my listening skills? What new ways can I use to show my devotion to God? What can I do for peace and justice? How can I be more hospitable to other people and ideas in this pluralistic age? Spiritual practices can help you with all these challenges.

There is no set protocol that predetermines the prognosis if you apply certain spiritual practices to your life situations. Practices overlap and support each other. Different symptoms may trigger a number of responses. You can find out what you need only when you try this yourself. Spirituality is, after all, not about goals, creeds, and dogmas; it's about experience.

Pema Chödrön, a Buddhist nun, teaches a meditation practice in which you use your own feelings as the means of awakening compassion for others. She writes: "You can feel like the world's most hopeless basket case, but that feeling is your wealth, not something to be thrown out or improved upon. There's a richness to all of the smelly stuff that we so dislike and so little desire. The delightful things—what we love so dearly about ourselves, the places in which we feel some sense of pride or inspiration—these also are our wealth."

Our symptoms—the contrasts and the companions—are our wealth. They are stepping-stones to spiritual practice. Use the "*Spiritual Rx* Prescriptions" chart as a quick reference guide to common attitudes and habitual behaviors that you either have or desire. See which ones speak most directly to your condition. They will point you toward the spiritual practices that resonate with you right now. Then read the "Catalysts, Contrasts, and Companions" sections under those practices.

PERSPECTIVES

After we define the practices and identify the related symptoms, we add in some other points of view. Often the people quoted have also written books on this aspect of spirituality.

TEACHERS

We recommend that you begin to work with each spiritual practice by studying with a teacher. In most cases, this will mean reading a book. Some people will also be able to attend lectures or workshops given by the teachers.

With a few exceptions, our teachers are people who are writing today, and each of them is an important voice in the current spiritual renaissance. They represent all the major religious traditions as well as the free-floating spirituality movements that are not affiliated with any institutions. We give you samples of their ideas and point you to their most significant works. At the back of this book, you will find full bibliographic information on these and the other resources we mention.

Obviously, we believe these are the books you should read first for a

SPIRITUAL RX
PRESCRIPTIONS

Enhances	Practice	Balances/Counters
awareness	**attention**	distraction, stress
simplicity, pleasure	**beauty**	clutter, habitual life
contentment	**being present**	living in past or future
caring	**compassion**	judgment, pain
holistic way of life	**connections**	separations, dualisms
self-discipline	**devotion**	lack of commitment
energy	**enthusiasm**	apathy, boredom
trust	**faith**	hardened heart, difficulties
freedom, reconciliation	**forgiveness**	vengefulness, bitterness
receptivity, surrender	**grace**	shame, need for control
satisfaction	**gratitude**	greed, entitlement
optimism	**hope**	despair, impatience
tolerance	**hospitality**	hostility, criticalness
creativity	**imagination**	rationalism
happiness	**joy**	sadness, sorrow
equality, dignity	**justice**	oppression, fanaticism
generosity	**kindness**	selfishness
discernment	**listening**	disregard for others
intimacy	**love**	fear
understanding	**meaning**	cynicism, shallowness
balance	**nurturing**	deprivation, codependency
empathy, flexibility	**openness**	close-mindedness
serenity, equanimity	**peace**	anger, violence, worry
free-spiritedness	**play**	earnestness, predictability
adventure, risk-taking	**questing**	timidity, certitude
worth, awe	**reverence**	wastefulness, ennui
wholeness	**shadow**	Pollyannaism, projections
contemplation	**silence**	chaos
wisdom	**teachers**	pride
healing, growth	**transformation**	resistance to change
harmony, solidarity	**unity**	loneliness, individualism
idealism	**vision**	pragmatism
sensuousness	**wonder**	indifference
not knowing	**mystery**	tidy and logical systems
fulfillment, ecstasy	**yearning**	being stuck in status quo
authenticity	**you**	low self-esteem, grandiosity
passionate life	**zeal**	unlived life

better understanding of each spiritual practice. In addition, our teachers have all had teachers themselves, and they mention their influences and sources. You will never run out of resources to explore! But most of the teachers agree on one point: It's more important to do practices than to read about them.

VIDEOS

On an episode of the television drama *Northern Exposure* that first aired in the early 1990s, Leonard, a Native American shaman, decides to conduct some research on what he terms "white medicine." He asks the citizens of Cicely, Alaska, to tell him any myths or stories that have had a major impact upon their lives and still influence their activities. He is quite discouraged by what he hears until he listens as Ed, the town movie buff, resolves a personal problem by referring to scenes in the classic film *Citizen Kane*. Leonard decides this screenplay is exactly the kind of healing story he has been looking for.

Movies can be medicine. Their stories reflect our lives, and their characters reveal us to ourselves. Like myths, they re-create common dilemmas and expose universal truths. From watching them, we learn what can happen when we take certain actions, or fail to do so. In the "Videos" sections of *Spiritual Rx*, we prescribe movies that reveal how the characters have been influenced by a particular spiritual practice.

You usually get more out of a video when you view it with a purpose. If you watch a comedy expecting to be entertained, you will invariably notice the funny parts. The same goes for watching movies to learn about the path of practice. Read our description of the film to see what to watch for. Sometimes we are interested in a subplot, a subtle theme, or even one scene. But since movies are intensely focused experiences, even a brief moment in one can be an aid on your spiritual journey.

SPIRITUAL EXERCISES AND RITUALS

Even when you take an open-ended and flexible approach to your spiritual practices, you need to do them regularly, preferably daily. This just makes good sense when you first begin working with one; over time, it feels like the most natural and fulfilling way to go. In these sections of the book, we suggest daily exercises that will help you get to the essence of the practice. Most of them are quite simple. They involve noticing, naming, remembering, feeling, and reframing.

This is also where you will find instructions for some of the classic spiritual disciplines of the world's religions: mindfulness breathing, hymn singing, blessing prayers, *lectio divina,* observance of a Sabbath, pilgrimage, vision quest, silent retreats, and more. We explain their value and traditional use.

There is no need to go it alone on the path of practice. In fact, that is not even recommended. Therefore, we also outline rituals and ceremonies to be done by a group. Again, most of these are not complicated, but they do require that you gather with intention and perform symbolic acts that enable you to connect with other people and your emotions. This process, in turn, increases your appreciation of the spiritual practice.

PRAYERS OR MANTRAS

Repetition of a mantra or short prayer is another proven method used to stay centered on the path of practice. In some Eastern religions, mantras are recognized as words of divine origin with the power to move the individual from one state of consciousness to another. They are chanted in Sanskrit, regarded as a sacred language, and are given to devotees by a guru through an initiation. The sound itself, the cadence, and the transmission from a teacher combine to increase the mantra's impact.

We are recommending a more informal type of prayer and mantra practice, but one that has centuries of experience behind it in both the East and the West. A simple phrase is repeated silently during a period of meditation and also as you go about your daily business. The mantra becomes a constant companion, reminding you of your relationship with the Divine and helping you to navigate through all the distractions your mind may be prone to while you are walking down the street, waiting for the elevator, watching the computer retrieve a page, brushing your hair, or engaging in any other activity that doesn't require concentration. You may also use prayer beads, reciting the mantra as your fingers reach each new bead.

This type of remembrance of the Divine has been practiced in all the traditions. We note some of the more popular mantras in the chapter "Devotion." In each of the other chapters we introduce a brief phrase that you can use as a mantra or as a breath prayer. For the latter you say one part of the prayer as you inhale and another part as you exhale. Breath prayers can be whole sentences you want to reflect upon or just a few words that serve as reminders of your intentions. Try using these prayers as a preface to some of the other suggested activities.

IMAGERY EXERCISES

Next we offer imagery exercises designed to reinforce each spiritual practice. Imagery work involves finding and creating pictures and the sounds, smells, and textures associated with them in the realm of your imagination. These days it is being used extensively for health and healing, but it will support any kind of inner growth, learning, and insight. Imagery is a bridge to our inner life and a direct link to experiences of Spirit. It is the language of the invisible realm.

It is also a language your body understands. Because of the mind/body unity, imagery work is accompanied by physical reactions. You will notice that many of our exercises contain instructions to "feel" and "sense." Imagery is never only in our heads. These exercises give you a way of embodying your spiritual practices.

We have collected them from imagery teachers and also written new ones based on inspirational texts. Some are more "guided" than others, but in all cases you are encouraged to work with spontaneous images that come to you. Don't worry that you might not be "good" at this. It is best not to force it or look for results. Sometimes it just takes time to get used to receiving input in this way. Or the exercise may be visually oriented and you may be someone who responds more intensely to the other senses. Try the practice exercises in the chapter about "Imagination," and keep at it. For more instructions on doing imagery and a list of recommended books, see the "*Spiritual Rx* Resource Collection" at the back of this book.

JOURNAL EXERCISES

One of the most popular enrichment tools for a spiritual journey is the journal. Writing regularly in a journal encourages you to become a "watcher," to check up on your own behavior and to monitor your attitudes. All the spiritual traditions teach that it is difficult to change, to grow in wisdom, unless you first recognize who you are and how you habitually act. Some of our journal exercises encourage this kind of self-assessment.

Other exercises give you an opportunity to work through one of the key concepts of a practice, such as writing a here-and-now exercise for "Being Present" or identifying your gifts, skills, and vocation for "You." A third type of exercise is designed to reveal your feelings about current and past experiences with the practice. All the exercises can help you assess its value for you at this time of your life.

Of course, you can also use your journal to keep track of your reactions to the ideas in this book. See the *"Spiritual Rx* Resource Collection" in the back for some ideas as well as a list of our favorite books on journals.

DISCUSSION QUESTIONS, STORYTELLING, SHARING

Although many of the suggestions in these sections can also be done in your journal, they were designed with a different audience in mind. It is important that we create communities along the path of practice, and storytelling is one of the best ways to do so. These questions and exercises encourage the sharing of personal stories with family, friends, or members of a small group.

One benefit of group interaction is that it gives us a greater understanding of the diversity of spiritual experiences. Through hearing about what has happened to others, we develop our capacity to empathize and to recognize all the lessons that can come to us from different directions. Groups also provide a context for fleshing out some common attitudes toward a practice, especially those characterized by controversy and disagreement. For example, responses to a question like "Should repentance be a prerequisite for forgiveness?" reveal the complexity of the spiritual life.

HOUSEHOLD, GROUP, AND COMMUNITY PROJECTS

Here we outline ways to involve family and friends in projects to deepen your appreciation of a spiritual practice. Some of these can be done in your home, such as making a visual family tree to understand "Connections" or hosting an Outrageous Feast as part of the practice of "Play."

Other projects take you out into your community or encourage engagement with the wider world. We often suggest that you contact organizations doing work that reflects a spiritual practice. Rather than give you specific names and addresses, we would refer you to local religious and civic organizations, such as the Council of Churches or the United Way. The Encyclopedia of Associations, published by Gale Research, is available in the reference section of most libraries; it includes descriptions of thousands of national and international nongovernmental organizations.

FICTION, POETRY, OR CHILDREN'S BOOKS AND SPOKEN-WORD AUDIOS

The world is simply brimming with teachers, and we could not fit them all into the "Teachers" sections. And, frankly, sometimes we receive the wisdom indirectly. Novels, short stories, poems, and children's books reveal many aspects of the spiritual life. Spoken-word audios, often featuring teachers in dialogue with an interviewer or workshop attendees, give us more insights. You'll find some of our favorites described in these two sections of *Spiritual Rx*.

ART AND MUSIC

"The task of art is to take hold of the shining, the radiance, the manifestation, of that which as spirit weaves and lives throughout the world," Austrian philosopher Rudolf Steiner wrote. Certainly art and music are sources of some of our greatest pleasures along the path of practice. Contemplating paintings of religious subjects and listening to sacred music have long been part of liturgical settings and rituals. The arts prepare us for prayer, and they trigger our emotional responses to moments of spiritual communion.

We have built on this understanding of the value of the arts in *Spiritual Rx*. We have matched each of the practices to an artist, a particular piece, or a genre that illustrates its contribution to the spiritual life. Sometimes the art requires or mirrors the process of a practice, as listening to Bach's *Goldberg Variations* demands "Attention" and Louise Nevelson's art reflects "Hospitality." In other cases the piece evokes the practice for us. Pete Seeger's music inspires us to work for "Justice." Vincent van Gogh's paintings immerse us in "X—The Mystery."

We admit at the outset that our choices are totally idiosyncratic (though, surprisingly, we did agree with each other about them), so we have merely hinted at the thinking behind them. We hope you enjoy the selections and are stimulated to make your own.

SEE ALSO

Practices lead to more practices, and some are closely related to others. We've noted a few links at the end of each chapter. You may discover more by reviewing the *"Spiritual Rx* Prescriptions" chart.

PASSAGES IN *SPIRITUAL LITERACY*

For our book *Spiritual Literacy*, we collected more than 650 passages from a wide variety of contemporary writers—spiritual teachers, novelists, poets, naturalists, filmmakers, social activists, and more—that illustrate spiritual perspectives on everyday experiences. We organized them into chapters on things, places, nature, animals, leisure, creativity, service, body, relationships, community, and "A Day in the Spiritual Life," which begins with waking up and ends with getting a late-night snack.

We knew at the time we were arranging all this material that we could also organize it according to what practice in the Alphabet of Spiritual Literacy each excerpt demonstrates. We have done that now. At the back of this book, we identify the most helpful pages of *Spiritual Literacy* for you and your group to read and discuss as you work with each practice.

THE *SPIRITUAL RX* RESOURCE COLLECTION

Also at the back of this book is a complete list of the books, videos, music, and art selections, and other recommendations given in the practices chapters. We hope you'll turn to these handy reference pages frequently when you are selecting resources for your travels along the path of practice.

This is also a work-in-progress for us. The resources and exercises recommended here represent points on the path of practice. Farther along the road we are sure to become enthusiastic about other books. We will think of different exercises, be touched by new movies, find another artist or musician. Fortunately, there is a place where we can stay in touch with you.

Spiritual Rx is also a World Wide Web site: www.spiritualrx.com. Every week we post reviews of recommended books, audios, feature films, and videos for people on spiritual journeys. A database of more than 2,000 of these reviews can be searched using several criteria, including asking for new resources that match a particular practice in the Alphabet of Spiritual Literacy. The area called "The *Spiritual Rx* Resource Collection" contains a gallery with images of the art mentioned in this book and links to sources for the books, videos, and music. In the "Exchange" area, you are invited to chat with other users about your experiences with spiritual practices.

We hope you will visit the site and join us as we travel farther along the path of practice. We will share our excitement about our new discoveries, and we will enjoy hearing about yours.

THE PRACTICES

☎ ATTENTION ☎

> ### DAILY CUE, REMINDER, VOW, BLESSING
>
> The ring of a telephone is a cue for me to practice attention.
>
> •
>
> When I watch a musician, I am reminded of the
> importance of focused attention.
>
> •
>
> Greeting a family member, friend, or colleague, I vow to be
> attentive to his or her needs today.
>
> •
>
> Blessed is God who gives us attention as a tool for
> discovery and caring.

THE BASIC PRACTICE

Attention is also known as mindfulness, concentration, recollection. It is a primary practice, and not just alphabetically. We must stay alert or we risk missing critical elements of the spiritual life—moments of grace, opportunities for gratitude, evidence of our connections to others, signs of the presence of Spirit. The good news is that attention can be practiced anywhere, anytime, in the daily rounds of our lives. It leads to awareness.

Begin by doing one thing at a time. Keep your mind focused on whatever you happen to be doing at the moment. It is through the mundane and the familiar that we discover a world of ceaseless wonders. Train yourself to notice details.

CATALYSTS, CONTRASTS, AND COMPANIONS

Most of us have exhibited the symptoms of lack of attention at one time or another. It's actually harder to stay awake than we might think. Perhaps we are easily distracted by trivial pursuits, attracted to any media message, ready to jump into any conversation, or susceptible to periods of endless surfing through the information and choices available to us. Eventually, we end up living in a haze of stimulation without any grasp of its significance. We are operating on automatic pilot. Because nothing really registers on our consciousness, we feel drained of energy.

Sometimes, however, not paying attention has just the opposite effect: Everything registers, and we find we don't know what to do with it all. We are so bombarded with stimuli that we can't focus on anything. We feel scattered. We are, to put it simply, stressed.

For both lack of energy and stress, attention is a good corrective prescription.

PERSPECTIVES

To be awake is to be alive.
–HENRY DAVID THOREAU

The quality of one's life depends on the quality of attention.
–DEEPAK CHOPRA

Just remember that those things that get attention flourish.
–VICTORIA MORAN

TEACHER
● For clear and profound teachings on mindfulness, we recommend you begin with the writings of Thich Nhat Hanh. He is a Buddhist monk, poet, international speaker, and writer who now lives in a meditation community in France. *The Miracle of Mindfulness: A Manual on Meditation* covers the philosophy and practicalities of this practice, taking us step by step through exercises to be done while listening to music, drinking a cup of tea, washing the dishes, taking a bath, and more. In his little book *The*

Long Road Turns to Joy, Thich Nhat Hanh gives detailed instructions for walking meditation.

Present Moment, Wonderful Moment, another popular book, suggests the use of mindfulness verses, called *gathas,* in daily life. Thich Nhat Hanh gives 49 of them, divided into four general areas: verses for starting the day, for meditation, for eating mindfully, and for other daily activities, such as greeting someone, throwing out the garbage, turning on the television, and driving a car.

Reflecting upon each verse, Thich Nhat Hanh reveals the multileveled meanings of attention, often connecting the personal with the planetary. For example, this is the verse to be recited while washing your hands: "Water flows over these hands. May I use them skillfully to preserve our precious planet." This one is to be said as food is being served: "In this food I see clearly the entire universe supporting my existence."

VIDEOS

• *The Scent of Green Papaya* by Vietnamese writer and director Tran Anh Hung is one of the best films ever made about the spiritual practice of attention. The story opens in Saigon in 1951 as Mui, a ten-year-old servant girl, comes to work for a merchant family. She has already mastered the art of approaching the world with mindfulness. This is evident when she stops to watch a drop of papaya sap on a green leaf and looks with wonder at small insects moving across the floor. She relaxes into her chores, whether scrubbing the tile floors or preparing vegetables for the stir-fry. Later, as a young woman, Mui takes her attentive service into the home of a young composer, where it yields intimacy and eventually love.

• The importance of mindfulness in relationships is the theme of *Jerry Maguire,* a movie about a self-absorbed American sports agent. One day he looks inside and sees nothing but emptiness. He writes a corporate mission statement suggesting that his firm be less concerned about commissions and more interested in their clients. Quickly out of a job, Jerry decides to start his own company, but only an idealistic bookkeeper, whom he eventually marries, and one football player client are willing to go with him. Still, they are enough to effect Jerry's awakening. From them he learns that attention is a necessary ingredient for a meaningful marriage and for work that matters.

Spiritual Exercises and Rituals

● Mindfulness breathing is an important practice in contemplative traditions and in most relaxation and health-building regimes. Here are the basic instructions.

Breathe in deeply, focusing your mind on that one activity. Breathe out completely, emptying your lungs, with similar awareness. When you notice that your mind wanders—and it probably will—bring it back to the breath. If you notice a muscular discomfort, return your attention to the sensation of rhythmic breathing. When thoughts arise, simply acknowledge them: "I am having an angry thought." "I am thinking of something beautiful." "I am remembering." "I am planning." Be mindful of your breath and be mindful of your mind.

Do this exercise every day while sitting, for as long as you find helpful. Then bring this kind of focused awareness into other settings, being mindful of both breath and thoughts during a walk or while drinking your tea.

● The Hebrew word *kavvanah* can be translated as "directed intention" or "focused attention." It is especially recommended in Judaism as a preparation for religious acts and during prayer. By focusing the mind upon the words of prayer, the individual becomes aware of the presence of God. Try to do this with a prayer you use regularly.

● A bell is a traditional object used to call us to attention. In Buddhist practice, the sound of a bell signals the beginning and end of a period of meditation. We use a bell in our home to remind us to get up from our desks and move around, to shift our attention from the head to the body. Create a similar daily ceremony using a bell.

Prayer or Mantra

In some religions, the scope of the practice of attention is broadened to include attentiveness to God. A breath prayer or mantra that recognizes this type of practice, yet that is also appropriate for any mindfulness exercise, is suggested by Jesus' words to his disciples in the Garden of Gethsemane.

Breathing in: Remain here, mind . . .
Breathing out: and keep awake with me.

IMAGERY EXERCISE

Rabbi Dov Baer of Mezritch, a Hasidic sage, says: "When you gaze at an object, you bring blessing to it." Here is an imagery exercise based on this kind of attention.

Close your eyes. Breathe out three long, slow exhalations. Find yourself in a familiar room in your home. Look around and observe the layout and general color of the room. Sense any smells or sounds in the room.

Breathe out one time. Now focus on one object in the room. It can be large or small. Follow your gaze to this object, seeing the blessings flowing along the beam of your attention. Then open your eyes.

JOURNAL EXERCISES

● The descriptive writing in your journal gives you insights into the quality of your attention. Read through your journal looking for entries that take you back to a specific place, time, or conversation.

● Write a description of something or someone in the room with you: the objects on your desk, a sleeping cat, a bowl of fruit, your partner. Remember, it is not as important how well you write as how well you observe, so concentrate on recording vivid details. What shade of blue is the shirt? How strong is the smell and what is it similar to? How does the light illuminate your subject? For this journal entry, just describe a specific perception; don't reflect on what it means.

DISCUSSION QUESTIONS, STORYTELLING, SHARING

● Share a story about a time when paying attention enriched your understanding of a relationship, an event, or the natural world.

● Talk to someone involved in martial arts—visit a class if possible—about how heightened attention is a benefit of practice.

● Give an example of something that has flourished because of the attention you have lavished upon it.

HOUSEHOLD, GROUP, AND COMMUNITY PROJECTS

● The poet and doctor William Carlos Williams used to carry a notepad around with him in which he listed "Things I noticed today that I've missed until today." Make his practice into an ongoing project in your home or group. Every morning, remind yourself that during the day you are going to notice something new or see a familiar sight in a new way.

That evening, describe your discovery to family or friends. If you are doing this project as a group, allow time for reporting at your meetings.

• Make a visual record of your expanding awareness of the world. Once a week, perhaps on your Sabbath, find or draw something to represent one of your observations and paste it on a wall calendar. Over time you will find yourself becoming more attentive as you gather material to include.

FICTION, POETRY, OR CHILDREN'S BOOK

Spiritual literacy relies upon the practice of attention. We often say that finding the sacred in daily life is a little like doing one of those picture puzzles in children's books that give a list of objects or faces hidden in a picture. Once we locate the images, we always see them there! Check out picture puzzle books and practice finding things. The *I Spy* books with riddles by Jean Marzollo and photographs by Walter Wick are good ones. *I Spy Gold Challenger!* collects some of the best puzzles in the series.

SPOKEN-WORD AUDIO

Thich Nhat Hanh explains a wide variety of attention practices on *The Art of Mindful Living,* a two-cassette, three-hour audio recorded at a family meditation retreat. He is especially good with children. At one point, he encourages them to do "hugging meditation." The idea is to make the hug feel very real, not just a brief pat on the back. They should hug their parents and friends mindfully, breathing in and out deeply a few times before they let go, being aware of the happiness they feel when they hold someone in their arms.

ART

One of the best ways to expand our attention's capacity is to study photographs. Often we miss important and meaningful details in the flow of sights passing before our eyes. Photography fixes an image—stops the world—so that we have time to notice what we might not have noticed before. Seeing what has previously been "invisible" to us is an essential part of the spiritual life.

Each book in the *A Day in the Life . . .* series presents photographs taken by an international team of photographers during a 24-hour period in one country (America, Australia, India, Ireland, Israel, Italy, Japan, Soviet Union, and others). Looking at these pictures, ask yourself, "What detail here caught the photographer's eye?"

To expand this exercise, take a camera with you for a day and practice framing pictures through the lens. It is not necessary to put film in the camera to have it act as an aid to your attention. If you do use film, however, take time after you get it developed to study your pictures. What did your camera's eye pick up? Think of your photographs as mirrors of your attention.

Music

Johann Sebastian Bach's *Goldberg Variations* consists of an aria in G Major, 10 groupings of three variations, and a restatement of the aria. Listening for the differences in style, rhythm, phrasing, and emphasis in the 30 variations requires concentration. After you focus on what elements distinguish each variation, the repeated aria sounds amazingly full and rich. Once we pay attention to details, what we knew to be real takes on greater meaning and depth.

See also:

Beauty. Being Present. Grace. Gratitude. Listening. Silence. Wonder.

BEAUTY

THE BASIC PRACTICE

The Navajo blessing "May you walk in beauty" catches the essence of this spiritual practice. Beauty is both a path you travel and what surrounds you on the path. In the splendor of the Creation, we see its outer forms. In morality and benevolence, we recognize its inner expressions.

Start this practice with the assumption that beauty is everywhere just waiting for you to notice it. Allow yourself to feel its effect upon your soul. Some experiences will stop you in your tracks and take your breath away.

Others will be more subtle but equally sublime. Then make your actions reflections of the beauty all around you.

CATALYSTS, CONTRASTS, AND COMPANIONS

Clutter gets in the way of beauty. If we have too many things and tasks in front of us, we may not notice what is beautiful about them. The contrast is simplicity; by paring away excesses, we make an opening for splendor.

Routine and rigid thinking also restrict our appreciation of beauty. If we are stuck in a rut, we never discover the refreshment waiting just around the corners of our daily schedule. If we have a narrow understanding of aesthetics, we are limited in our ability to recognize beauty's varied manifestations.

Beauty is startling, stimulating, and soothing. Try this practice when you need to be pulled out of your habitual way of seeing and being. Its cultivation produces pleasure.

PERSPECTIVES

Never lose an opportunity of seeing anything that is beautiful for beauty is God's handwriting.
–RALPH WALDO EMERSON

Beauty saves. Beauty heals. Beauty motivates. Beauty unites. Beauty returns us to our origins, and here lies the ultimate act of saving, of healing, of overcoming dualism. Beauty allows us to forget the pain and dwell on the joy.
–MATTHEW FOX

It's the beauty within us that makes it possible for us to recognize the beauty around us.
–JOAN CHITTISTER

TEACHERS

● What is considered to be beautiful varies from culture to culture, from generation to generation, and often from one period of our lives to another. A good way to expand your appreciation of beauty is to study aesthetics from a cross-cultural perspective, the specialty of Yi-Fu Tuan, professor of geography at the University of Wisconsin-Madison. His book *Passing Strange and Wonderful* is a fascinating exploration of the significance of beauty for individuals and cultures.

"The more attuned we are to the beauties of the world, the more we come to life and take joy in it," writes Tuan. He begins with a discussion of the "building blocks" of aesthetic experiences, the five senses. Beauty is discovered in the warmth of a coffee cup, eating, listening to music, walking through an aromatic garden, observing the stars, and many other examples.

The author then examines how beauty is perceived by Australian Aborigines, the Chinese, medieval Europeans, and modern Americans. This wide-ranging survey encourages us to look at even the most common sights—a commercial strip by the highway, for example—for what they reveal about our aesthetics. He concludes with a consideration of the link between the beautiful and the good, expressed as moral beauty.

● Martin Marty and Micah Marty in *When True Simplicity Is Gained: Finding Spiritual Clarity in a Complex World* are teachers of the wedding of beauty and simplicity. Micah Marty, a photographer, recommends that we approach our lives using the methodology of his craft: Focus on what is important and remove superfluous clutter. To demonstrate, he presents some stunning photographs taken at Shaker Village of Pleasant Hill, Kentucky. Here members of this nineteenth-century movement sought to live the ideal of a simple, God-centered life. Beauty is reflected in pictures of a spiral staircase, wool in a basket, a gate and a latch, a deacon's bench, a mixing bowl, and many other objects and scenes.

Martin Marty, a historian of religion, provides meditations to complement the photographs, reminding us that simplicity is not a commodity to buy or a system to learn but a profound spirituality rooted in community and God. The 40 brief essays are each linked to a scriptural passage and unfold in response to a classic prayer by John Wesley, Jakob Bohme, Thérèse of Lisieux, Reinhold Niebuhr, Elizabeth Seton, George Fox, and others.

The elder Marty suggests that we read each meditation title as the completion of the statement "When true simplicity is gained, it brings with it . . ." We fill in focus, repose, freedom, dazzlement, priority, sufficiency, perspective, reordering, direction, and more. Those who appreciate simplicity, he writes, "bring the beauty of the sacred into ordinary life and ordinary concerns into the holy place."

VIDEOS

• *Enchanted April* is a portrait of many kinds of beauty: physical beauty, inner beauty, the beauty of place, and beauty in relationships. Four Englishwomen rent a medieval castle in Italy for a month. Although they come from different classes and stages of life, they share a need to put aside their burdens and find themselves again. Their vacation becomes a time of soulful renewal.

Beauty can have that effect; it engages our senses and calls us out of ourselves long enough for us to see life in a new way. By the end of the film, each woman has discovered an aspect of herself long neglected. All of them exhibit an inner radiance to match the sensuous delights of the scenery around them. With beauty as the catalyst, they become friends and also reconnect with their loved ones.

• In *Beyond Rangoon*, Laura, an American tourist in Burma, watches as Aung San Suu Kyi, the leader of the pro-democracy movement, walks toward some soldiers during a street demonstration. Despite the guns pointing directly at her, she passes gracefully through their line. Her act of courage, reflecting inner beauty, inspires and empowers Laura for the challenges that lie ahead of her during a trek through the countryside.

• Two other movies explore the shadow side of beauty—what it can do to those who possess it and those who are enchanted by it. *The Accompanist* is a French film about an opera singer who uses her beautiful voice and body as a means of dominating her husband and a working-class pianist. *The Object of Beauty* reveals how the possession of a Henry Moore bronze figurine affects three people with different values. Both films can lead to an examination of your need for beauty.

SPIRITUAL EXERCISES AND RITUALS

• Beauty is an important part of worship in all the world's religions. Albert Rouet writes in *Liturgy and the Arts*: "Liturgy is beautiful because it dares to make the least action beautiful, whether carrying a chalice, going up to read, purifying a ciborium, standing up, or giving the sign of peace." The next time you participate in a service, pay attention to how the ritual acts express beauty.

• Add a beautiful element to a spiritual practice you do regularly. For example, during daily prayer, light a candle. On your Sabbath, bring in fresh flowers to decorate your dining table.

• Each week affirm your commitment to simplify your life by giving away or discarding one excess possession.

• Create a blessing ceremony for some of the beauties in your group's life. Everyone brings one object to the circle. In turn, say, "This is beautiful to me because . . ." The group responds: "We bless your beauty."

PRAYER OR MANTRA

Sacred writings are filled with tributes to beauty. Use this one from Rumi during a period of meditation in the morning and during breaks throughout the day. Notice any increased awareness that accompanies the repetition of the mantra.

> Breathing in: Every moment . . .
> Breathing out: a new beauty.

IMAGERY EXERCISE

This exercise, "Walk in Beauty," is based on a Navajo prayer.

> Close your eyes. Breathe out three long, slow exhalations.
> See and sense beauty before you. . . . See and sense beauty behind you. . . . See and sense beauty above you. . . . See and sense beauty below you. . . . See and sense beauty all around you.
> Breathe out one time. See and feel yourself walking in beauty. . . . Know that it is finished in beauty. How are you feeling?
> Breathe out again and open your eyes.

JOURNAL EXERCISES

• There is no single standard for beauty, even though our culture often tries to promote one. See how many different images of beauty you can find this week, or in seven journal entries, as you describe (1) a beauty experienced in childhood, (2) a beauty experienced at school or work, (3) a beauty in nature, (4) a beauty in your home, (5) a surprising beauty, (6) something most people consider to be beautiful, (7) something few people consider to be beautiful.

• Read Gerard Manley Hopkins's poem "Pied Beauty" (included in most collections). Write about the beauty of (1) a dappled thing; (2) the gear, tackle, and trim of a trade; (3) something counter; (4) something original; (5) something spare; (6) something strange; and (7) something fickle.

DISCUSSION QUESTIONS, STORYTELLING, SHARING

● In German the word "beautiful" is related to "shining." A beautiful person is one whose inner brilliance permeates his or her entire being. Tell your family or friends about your most memorable encounter with a person who was shining.

● Share a story about a beautiful place that comforted, restored, or inspired you.

● Recall a time when a work of art revealed to you the intrinsic beauty in something you had considered ugly or disagreeable. What does this experience reveal about the nature of beauty?

● Did your parents encourage your appreciation of beauty? What did they do? How is this quality honored in your home now?

HOUSEHOLD, GROUP, AND COMMUNITY PROJECTS

● Have a makeover. Better still, make it possible for others, perhaps some of the residents of a local nursing home, to have makeovers. First, think about what would make you feel more beautiful: a haircut, a manicure, different makeup, a new outfit?

● Beautify your home. Start by clearing out any clutter and things you are not using. Then choose one area to give special attention. Perhaps you will clean and polish the wood furnishings or scrub all the tiles. As you are working, admire the textures, colors, and structure of each item.

● Organize a community beautification project for a local park, schoolyard, street, or highway. Pick up litter, mow the grass, trim the bushes, plant flowers, or arrange rock gardens.

FICTION, POETRY, OR CHILDREN'S BOOK

One of the true patrons of beauty is American poet Walt Whitman. His classic "Song of Myself," originally published as part of *Leaves of Grass*, is filled with ringing affirmations of the beauty of the body, the natural world, the soul, and relationships of all types. In some of these verses, Whitman seems utterly transported by his subject.

SPOKEN-WORD AUDIO

In *Beauty Without Nature: Refounding the City*, James Hillman, the father of archetypal psychology, talks about the aesthetics of the structures and processes of urban life. It's not necessary to go outside the city into nature to discover beauty, he argues. Things made by human hands—skyscrapers, airports, market halls, hotels—can also nourish the soul.

ART

One Hundred Flowers is an impressive collection of Georgia O'Keeffe's paintings of enlarged flowers. Here are huge blossoms—the originals are up to six feet tall—filling the canvas. With their close-up scale, bold colors, and sensual shapes, these works startled the art world; one reviewer said they make the viewer feel "as if we humans were butterflies."

Talking about how she came to do the flower paintings, Georgia O'Keeffe told Mary Lynn Kotz of *ArtNews*: "That was in the 20s, and everything was going so fast. Nobody had time to reflect . . . There was a cup and saucer, a spoon and a flower. Well, the flower was perfectly beautiful. It was exquisite, but it was so small you really could not appreciate it for itself. So then and there I decided to paint that flower in all its beauty. If I could paint that flower in a huge scale, then you could not ignore its beauty."

MUSIC

Joe Cocker's pop song "You Are So Beautiful" is a simple testimony to the power of beauty. The lyric repeats the title and says little else. Still, there seem to be layers of feeling behind the words. Cocker uses his distinctive voice to convey a palpable yearning not only for the object of his desire but for beauty in general. Listen especially for how his voice cracks on the final phrase.

SEE ALSO:
Attention. Kindness. Meaning. Reverence. Wonder.
X—The Mystery. You.

BEING PRESENT

DAILY CUE, REMINDER, VOW, BLESSING

Having the first cup of coffee, tea, or milk in the morning is my
cue to be here now.

•

When I sit on a bench, I am reminded of the joys of simply being
present to my surroundings.

•

Whenever I experience or witness sickness, I vow to appreciate
every moment of my life.

•

Blessed is the Invisible Lover who is ever present with us.

THE BASIC PRACTICE

The word "present" in the spiritual life always has a double meaning.
There's present, as in here, in attendance. And there's present, as in now,
a moment of time. What is the spiritual practice of being present? Being
here now.

The world's religions all recommend living in the moment with full
awareness. Zen Buddhism especially is known for its emphasis on "now-
ness." Hindu, Taoist, Jewish, Muslim, Christian, and other teachers urge
us to make the most of every day as an opportunity that will not come to
us again.

Also under the rubric of this Alphabet letter is the traditional spiritual exercise called practicing the presence of God. This means recognizing that God is here now moving through our everyday activities, no matter how trivial they might seem.

CATALYSTS, CONTRASTS, AND COMPANIONS

The contrasts to being present are living in the past and living in the future. We do the former when we hold on to regrets. We constantly review things that have already happened, trying to explain them in terms of our own or someone else's actions. Often this kind of thinking leads to guilt or blaming.

We live in the future when we make assumptions or fantasize about what could happen and then become attached to those expected outcomes. This habit usually results in disappointment. Whether we are consumed with positive expectations (optimism) or negative projections (pessimism), we are not living in the moment.

When you find yourself constantly reacting to your experiences in one of these ways, when you always want to be otherwise and elsewhere, it is time to be present. The companion of this practice is contentment.

PERSPECTIVES

Every moment is enormous, and it is all we have.
–NATALIE GOLDBERG

The present is holy ground.
–ALFRED NORTH WHITEHEAD

The present moment is never unbearable if you live in it fully. What is unbearable is to have your body here at 10 A.M. and your mind at 6 P.M.; your body in Bombay and your mind in San Francisco.
–ANTHONY DE MELLO

TEACHERS

Interestingly enough, two of the best teachers of being present lived in the seventeenth and eighteenth centuries. They are authors of classic Christian devotional works, but their main point—that God is encountered only in the present moment—is one that those of other traditions can appreciate as well.

● Jean-Pierre de Caussade (1675–1751) was a French Jesuit priest and spiritual director. God is everywhere and ever present, he writes in *The Sacrament of the Present Moment*. To feel God's presence, we must surrender ourselves through love and obedience to the stirrings of grace in all our activities.

De Caussade challenges us to read "the book of life," the record of divine action in the world, because we each have a purpose "in the plot of the holy scripture which unfolds every day." God speaks to us specifically in what happens to us from one moment to the next, one way this morning, perhaps a different way this afternoon.

● Brother Lawrence of the Resurrection (1614–1691) worked for 15 years as a monastery cook in Paris. His ideas on a practical method of maintaining a loving awareness of God's presence are collected in *Writings and Conversations on the Practice of the Presence of God*. Every moment is important, he says, because it is an opportunity to have a conversation with God. "It is not necessary to have important things to do," he adds. "I flip my little omelette in the frying pan for the love of God."

● This theme, that we can discover the sacred through our ordinary day-to-day existence, is explored by two contemporary teachers in *The Sacred Portable Now: The Transforming Gift of Living in the Moment*. Daniel Singer is a teacher of the Alexander Technique, a mind/body discipline, and Marcella Bakur Weiner is a professor and a psychologist in private practice. Their book is designed to provide "tools to negotiate a spiritually fulfilling experience of living a full and active life." For example, time spent waiting in line at a bank machine can become a "noticed moment" of deep awareness of self, others, and the sacred. They also recommend being self-witnesses, putting thoughts in the proper perspective, doing only what is necessary, going at the appropriate speed, and reconnecting with our ability to physically sense ourselves and the world through such basic actions as standing and walking.

VIDEOS

● The German film *Wings of Desire* portrays the appeal of the present moment. Damiel, an angel in Berlin, is spending eternity observing and testifying to the feelings and activities of humans. But, he confesses to another angel, he longs to be able to say "now, now, and now" rather than "since always" and "forever." He wants to enter into history if only to hold an apple in his hand. When he falls in love with a beautiful trapeze artist, he decides to take the plunge, declaring it's "now or never!"

His first act as a man is to get a cup of coffee. He stands at the coffee truck and drinks the strange liquid. He rubs his hands together and feels their warmth. He observes all the vibrant colors around him. His contented expression says it all: He has given up eternity for this moment, and it is enough.

• *Le Huitieme Jour* (The Eighth Day), a French film, has a wonderful scene when the characters engage in this spiritual practice. Harry is a salesman whose workaholism has cost him his family. He is depressed and disenchanted with life until he meets Georges, a young man with Down's syndrome, who has a real knack for living in the present and appreciating the parade going on all around him. In the key scene, the two friends are in the country and about to return to town. Georges suggests they take a moment—60 seconds exactly—to lie in the grass. The camera lingers with the contented expressions on their faces. Later Harry is able to share this way of being with his young daughters.

• For every story of someone who lives fully in the present, there are other films about people who don't. *Plenty*, a video movie based on the play by David Hare, is the story of a woman obsessed with the past. During World War II, Susan worked for the British in Nazi-occupied France. After the liberation she declares: "We will improve our world. There will be days and days like this." For years, then, she keeps trying to reexperience that feeling. Her life in postwar England pales in comparison, and the only thing her idealism yields is disappointment. Her honoring of a past experience limits her ability to appreciate life now.

SPIRITUAL EXERCISES AND RITUALS

• For the next week, monitor your language for signs that you are not living in the present. The key phrases to listen for: if only, could have, should have, would have, could be, should be, must be, will be, going to, and assuming that. One phrase catches it all: If [I did or experienced something in the past] then [this will happen in the future]. When you hear yourself using these phrases, substitute words in the present tense.

• Evan Pritchard, the author of *No Word for Time: The Way of the Algonquin People*, observes that watching the clock with its relentless movement into the future can keep people from sinking into the present moment. He suggests these exercises. For one day, don't look at a clock or watch. Do every task for as long as it takes for you to feel intuitively that it is finished.

● Attend a yoga or Tai Chi class. The focus on precise movements and positions heightens your sense of presence.

PRAYER OR MANTRA

"Be Here Now" by George Harrison from his album *Living in the Material World* is part pop tune, part chant, making it a good mantra.

> Breathing in: Be Here . . .
> Breathing out: Now.

IMAGERY EXERCISE

African-American spirituals often testify to the palpable presence of God in daily life. Some images from those songs are used in the following exercise.

Breathe out three times. Sense and see the precious Lord's hands taking your hand. Know that God is holding you and the whole world in his hands.

Breathe out three times. Sense God at your hands. Sense God at your feet. Sense God's presence all around you. Sense God's light shining through you. Let your light shine.

Then open your eyes.

JOURNAL EXERCISES

● Do a here-and-now exercise. Record in your journal what you are experiencing at this very moment: what you are seeing, smelling, hearing—the reports of your senses—as well as how you are feeling—an emotional reaction. You might do this through writing a description, making a list of impressions, or drawing a sketch.

● Free intuitive writing puts you in touch with the present, often on a very deep level. To try it, open your journal to a blank page; relax and clear your mind. Then write or draw whatever comes to you, even if it doesn't seem to make any sense. Some people find that writing very fast, using their nondominant hand, or writing without looking at the page releases this kind of spontaneous thought.

DISCUSSION QUESTIONS, STORYTELLING, SHARING

• During a visit with a friend, act as if it is to be your last meeting. See how this awareness affects the quality of your presence. Before parting, or soon afterward, review this aspect of your encounter. Did your friend notice anything unusual about it? Talk about what you can do to bring the same quality of experience to all your meetings.

• At the next gathering of your group, try just being together for one hour. Don't worry about saying anything or doing anything in particular (including keeping silent). See what happens.

• Go around the circle and each make a "now" statement. Talk about something you are dealing with today. Avoid the temptation to explain how you got into this situation with a story about your childhood or what you have learned from experience (in the past). Don't talk about what you would like to see happen next or predict an outcome (in the future).

HOUSEHOLD, GROUP, AND COMMUNITY PROJECTS

• Watch children at play; they know how to be in the moment! If no children live in your home, volunteer to be with children at a nursery school, day care center, library, or elsewhere.

• It is easier to be present in some kinds of activities than in others. Examples are gardening, playing or singing music, or putting together a puzzle. Choose one of these to do as a family or a group one evening this week.

• There is a Jewish tradition, notes Naomi Levy in *To Begin Again*, that a single visit to someone's sickbed takes away one-sixtieth of the person's illness. "The ancient sages understood that just being in the presence of another human being can lift a person up." Visit someone who is sick as a family, if appropriate. Arrange through a congregation, hospital, or nursing home for your group to participate in a visitation program.

FICTION, POETRY, OR CHILDREN'S BOOK

• Haiku is a poetic form that traditionally consists of three lines of syllables (five-seven-five) and presents one image, usually from common life, happening in a specific place during a particular season. Haiku is always about being present. In *The Essential Haiku*, editor Robert Hass presents treasures from the Japanese haiku masters Basho, Buson, and Issa. Some of them are reprinted in *Spiritual Literacy* on pages 142, 202–204, 263, and 375.

● *Seeds from a Birch Tree: Writing Haiku and the Spiritual Journey* by Clark Strand contains contemporary examples, many written by students. The author, who has been writing and teaching haiku for 20 years, suggests ways to "find" haiku by taking haiku walks, keeping a diary of your poems, and sharing them in a small group. He offers this method of reading haiku: Repeat the poem until you can recite it without looking at the page. As you say it silently to yourself, imagine the scene it describes. Watch what is happening, according to the haiku. Try this with a haiku from Hass's or Strand's collections or with this one by Strand: "back from the mountains / a yellow handrail guides me / down the subway stairs."

SPOKEN-WORD AUDIO

A Buddhist understanding of the timelessness of the now is presented in *The Teachings of Zen Master Dogen*, consisting of excerpts from *Moon in a Dewdrop* read by poet Gary Snyder. Dogen (1200–1253) was the founder of the Soto School of Zen Buddhism in Japan.

ART

American abstract expressionist Jackson Pollock, best known for his action paintings, described his works as "energy and motion made visible." For his "drip" paintings—see the numbered pieces of 1947 to 1950—the artist tacked a canvas to the floor, then walked around it flinging, pouring, dribbling, and smearing the paint to create an elaborate all-over work of overlapping lines and free-wheeling shapes. He said he used this technique so as to "literally be in the painting" during the process of creation.

MUSIC

Each movement of Beethoven's *Symphony No. 6 in F Major, Op. 68*, known as the *Pastoral Symphony*, is a present moment distinct in its sounds, moods, and gifts to the listener. In the first movement, titled "Awakening of Cheerful Feelings on Arrival in the Country," the composer uses a recurring melodic theme to convey the sense of being surrounded by one beautiful impression after another. The second movement, "Scene by the Brook," is a marvelous evocation of the tranquility experienced when meditating by water; near the end, we hear the distinct calls of a nightingale, a quail, and a cuckoo. The last three movements bring a "Merry Gathering of Country Folk," interrupted by a dra-

matic "Thunderstorm," and then a restoration of calm in "Shepherds'
Song: Happy, Thankful Feelings After the Storm."

SEE ALSO:
Attention. Connections. Gratitude. Nurturing.
Reverence. Silence.

☙☙ COMPASSION ☙☙

THE BASIC PRACTICE

Compassion is a feeling deep within ourselves—a "quivering of the
heart"—and it is also a way of acting—being affected by the suffering of
others and moving on their behalf. Buddha and Jesus are the best-known
exemplars of compassion, and it is the central ethical virtue in the two
religions that developed from their teachings.

The spiritual practice of compassion is often likened to opening the
heart. First, allow yourself to feel the suffering in the world, including
your own. Don't turn away from pain; move toward it with caring. Go

into situations where people are hurting. Identify with your neighbors in their distress. Then expand the circle of your compassion to include other creatures, nature, and the inanimate world.

CATALYSTS, CONTRASTS, AND COMPANIONS

The practice of compassion increases our capacity to care. It reinforces charity, empathy, and sympathy. It is very good exercise for your heart muscle.

But when you move toward others with compassion, you are likely to bump into some common attitudes, just waiting to close your heart again. The usual suspects are judgment and all its associated "isms": racism, sexism, ageism, classism, and nationalism.

On a personal level, your compassion is sabotaged by feelings of ill will toward others: spite and malice. These feelings, and others arising out of emotional wounds and personal pain, are actually symptoms indicating that you need to have compassion for yourself.

PERSPECTIVES

Those who follow compassion find life for themselves, justice for their neighbor, and glory for God.
–MEISTER ECKHART

The feeling of wishing to save the world comes very often out of a wish to escape from having compassion on your own darkness, for what is inside yourself. If you don't start there, you will never have true compassion.
–HELEN M. LUKE

True compassion does not come from wanting to help out those less fortunate than ourselves but from realizing our kinship with all beings.
–PEMA CHÖDRÖN

TEACHERS

● Sharon Salzberg, a Buddhist and one of the founders of the Insight Meditation Society in Barre, Massachusetts, is a primary teacher of this spiritual practice. Her book *Lovingkindness: The Revolutionary Art of Happiness* is a classic in the field. *A Heart as Wide as the World* provides more encouragement through numerous stories about compassionate people.

To cultivate compassion, Salzberg explains, we must acknowledge the true nature of suffering in the world: "Compassion allows us to bear witness to that suffering, whether it is in ourselves or others, without fear." Then, having refused to deny pain, we open ourselves to it: "To be compassionate is to sense from within what it must be like to experience someone else's experience." This empathy becomes a bridge to others. "And when we actually understand how it feels to suffer—in our selves and in others—we are compelled to live in a way that creates as little harm as possible."

• Compassion also leads to service. In *Compassion in Action: Setting Out on the Path of Service,* Ram Dass and Mirabai Bush explain that traveling the road of compassion requires you to learn the art of listening, start small right where you are, reflect on your motives, and look for a match between your talents and the needs of others. The authors have served as chairpersons of the Seva Foundation, an international development organization.

• In *A Spirituality Named Compassion,* priest and mystic Matthew Fox approaches the subject from the perspective of the Creation Spirituality tradition in Christianity. He defines compassion as a sensitivity to all aspects of the Creation, an appreciation of the interconnectedness of all living beings, and a passion for making justice and doing works of mercy.

VIDEOS

• *Ulee's Gold* shows us how the spiritual practice of compassion opens the heart of a middle-aged beekeeper. Ulee uses his solitary work to isolate himself from the loss he feels as a widower and a Vietnam veteran. Jimmy, his son, is serving a prison sentence for armed robbery, and his daughter-in-law, Helen, ran off two years ago. Ulee is the sole caretaker for their children, teenage Casey and her younger sister, Penny.

When Jimmy asks his father to find Helen and take her into his home, Ulee reluctantly agrees. Over time, though, he allows himself to be touched by Helen's suffering as she undergoes drug withdrawal. He begins to express his nurturing side, lets go of some of his rigid ideas, and even accepts help from a neighbor. When Jimmy's partners-in-crime threaten to harm his family, Ulee is able to see even these enemies as suffering souls needing his compassion.

• The Brazilian film *Central Station* also depicts the process whereby an individual wakes up to a feeling of kinship with other people through compassion. Dora is a cynical and selfish former schoolteacher who writes letters that she never mails for illiterate people in the Rio de Janeiro railroad station. Then one of her customers is killed by a bus and the woman's son, nine-year-old Josue, comes to Dora for help. Her first idea is to sell him to some people in the adoption business, but eventually she decides to return him to his father in the country. During the long bus journey, she experiences a change of heart. At a rural pilgrimage site, she earns money writing letters again, but now she identifies with the people and their yearning for connection. She also discovers that she feels real concern for Josue's well-being and tenderness for life itself.

● Two other movies explore the complicated dynamics of compassion. *City of Joy* is based on Dominique Lapierre's book set in the slums of Calcutta, India. Through the emotionally affecting stories of an American doctor and an Indian rickshaw driver, it explores how compassionate service brings us face to face with our limitations and our need to work in community.

● *Hidden in America* is a sensitive drama about a doctor who wants to help an unemployed man and his two hungry children. The Emmy Award–winning screenplay raises a difficult question: How do you show compassion to someone who is too proud to accept any assistance?

SPIRITUAL EXERCISES AND RITUALS

● Tonglen meditation practice means "taking in and sending out." In *Start Where You Are,* Buddhist nun Pema Chödrön describes it as a way to "let ourselves feel what it is to be human" and by doing so to "widen our circle of compassion." In the first stage of the practice, you rest in a state of openness or stillness. In the second, you work with texture through breath awareness, visualizing that you are breathing in dark, heavy, and hot (claustrophobia or fixation) and breathing out white, light, and cool (spaciousness, freshness) through every pore in your body.

The third stage works with a specific instance that you are aware of. You breathe in the pain of a person, animal, or distress you are personally feeling, and you breathe out something to relieve the pain—a good meal, kindness, confidence.

In the fourth stage, you breathe in the pain of all those suffering like the one you have just cared for—all hungry people, all hurting animals in the world, all those feeling inadequate. You breathe out whatever will lighten their load. Chödrön advises always working both with the immediate suffering of one being and with the universal suffering of all. In this way, your practice is both heartfelt and visionary.

● Create a Compassion Collage. Gather pictures of people, places, and things for which you feel compassion. You may take photos yourself, cut them out of magazines and newspapers, copy them from books, or find them in the direct mail appeals from service organizations. Look for strong pictures to which you have an emotional response, no matter how painful. Include examples of the suffering of animals, nature, and things. Add words or symbols to represent others areas of concern: "Earthquake" to remind you to feel compassion for victims of natural disasters, "Incest" to recall those suffering from sexual abuse, "Prison" for political prisoners and those who have committed crimes, "Garbage" to note the suffering caused by wasteful consumption. Leave one area of your collage blank for what has not yet touched your compassionate heart. Keep the collage in a place where you can contemplate it at least once every day. One or more images may become the focus of prayer or a catalyst for the tonglen meditation described above.

PRAYER OR MANTRA

This self-instruction in the form of a mantra is based on Jesus' words in Luke 6:36.

> Breathing in: Be compassionate . . .
> Breathing out: as God is compassionate.

IMAGERY EXERCISE

The following exercise uses a method described in *The Spiritual Exercises of Saint Ignatius of Loyola.*

Read the Parable of the Good Samaritan in the Bible—Luke 10:29–37. If you like, also read biblical commentaries in order to better understand the attitudes the different characters represent.

Imagine the scene of the story: the road to Jericho, the injured man, the people passing by. Walk into the scene. Be the man set upon by thieves. Be a priest or a Levite walking away from him. Be the Samaritan. You may also choose to remain an observer of the events. Notice your location and how you are feeling.

Replay the sequence of events in the story, lingering with any parts of it that touch you. Being there now in the story, what do you say? What do you do? How do you feel about what is happening?

End this exercise with a prayer of gratitude for this experience of compassion.

JOURNAL EXERCISES

● Identify an area where you need to be compassionate to yourself. Write about how you will go about this.

● Make a list of "missed opportunities" to show compassion to poor, sick, lonely, alienated, or hurting beings. Look for any patterns in your behavior or inaction. Identify an obstacle or rationalization that has kept you from being more compassionate.

DISCUSSION QUESTIONS, STORYTELLING, SHARING

● Share an example of a situation when your willingness to be compassionate was tested. What do you usually do when you meet someone in need of help? What kinds of questions do you ask yourself? What conditions do you set?

● Tell a story about a moral mentor you have known—someone who inspired you with his or her compassionate activity.

HOUSEHOLD, GROUP, AND COMMUNITY PROJECTS

● Go on a fast. If you are inexperienced in this practice, begin with a one-day fast. Eat only fruits and vegetables and drink at least eight glasses of water. Or skip a meal a day for one week. Use the time you would have spent preparing and eating food for quiet reflection on the experience of being hungry. Feel compassion for the millions of people around the world who do not have enough to eat.

● Volunteer to serve meals at a soup kitchen, to carry meals to shut-ins, to read to people in the hospital, or to do any other activity that puts you close to suffering.

FICTION, POETRY, OR CHILDREN'S BOOK

Raymond Carver's *Cathedral* is a collection of short stories about individuals confronted with unexpected disasters—marriages that break down, jobs that vanish overnight, tragedies that drive people to drink, to isolation, to states of incalculable sadness. In "A Small Good Thing," a woman orders a $16 birthday cake for her young son, but he is hit by a car and dies. The baker, upset that the mother has failed to pick up the cake, harasses her. Angry and anguished, she and her husband go to the bakery. The surprise ending of the story reveals the meaning of compassion.

Spoken-Word Audio

Awakening Compassion: Meditation Practice for Difficult Times by Pema Chödrön is a six-cassette audio retreat. Chödrön explains *lojong*, or "mind training," a Tibetan Buddhist practice designed to open the heart to life as it is and awaken compassion for all beings. One part of the practice is tonglen meditation. The other involves working with 59 maxims that help to loosen the grip of the ego on the mind and show us how to transform bad circumstances into the path of enlightenment.

Art

● Two of Pablo Picasso's most famous paintings evoke compassion. *Guernica*, painted in 1937 for the Spanish Pavilion at the Paris World's Fair, reflects the artist's visceral response to the destruction caused by the Spanish Civil War. *Weeping Woman*, from the same year, is considered to be a postscript to *Guernica*.

● For more subtle reflections of compassion, see the chalk drawings of German expressionist Käthe Kollwitz, such as *Plowing* and *Municipal Lodging*.

Music

Benjamin Britten's *War Requiem* was first performed in 1962 at the dedication of the new Coventry Cathedral built next to the ruins of the cathedral destroyed during World War II. In this choral work, Britten alternates the language of the mass with tenor and baritone solos taken from the antiwar poetry of Wilfred Owen, who died on the battlefield in World War I. Compassion is a constant companion of this powerful music.

See also:

Attention. Connections. Gratitude. Justice. Nurturing. Reverence. Shadow.

CONNECTIONS

THE BASIC PRACTICE

Separateness is an illusion. That's what we learn through the spiritual practice of connections. Everything is interrelated—in time, space, and our very being. Both religion and science reveal this truth—Hinduism's image of Indra's net, Buddhism's understanding of interbeing, the experiences of the mystics, the teachings of ecology and physics, even the Internet.

One definition of spirituality is "the art of making connections." There

---

are certain givens: The one is made up of many. One thing always leads to another. Everything is related to everything else. You practice connections, then, by consciously tracing the ties linking you with other beings. Any point is a good starting place—your family line, your work, your backyard. Watch for the moments when the separations disappear. And don't be shy about naming mystical experiences as such when you have them.

CATALYSTS, CONTRASTS, AND COMPANIONS

The practice of connections reinforces a holistic way of life and our awareness of how the spiritual, emotional, and mental aspects of our being interpenetrate and nourish each other. It enables us to see the big picture.

We need to engage in this practice when we have a tendency to compartmentalize our experiences, to put them in neat little boxes instead of seeing them as parts of a whole. This is a cultural as well as a personal habit. The history of the world is plagued by dualing dualisms: mind versus body, humans versus nature, God versus the world, science versus religion, country versus city, male versus female. The spiritual practice of connections erases such arbitrary and unnecessary distinctions.

PERSPECTIVES

The point of all spiritual practice is to wake up from the dream of the separate self.
–STEPHEN MITCHELL

The thoughts of the Earth are my thoughts . . .
The voice of the Earth is my voice.
–NAVAJO ORIGIN LEGEND

There are no backwaters. There is only one river, and we are all in it. Wave your arms, and the ripples will eventually reach me.
–SCOTT RUSSELL SANDERS

TEACHERS

● Rabbi Lawrence Kushner is our favorite teacher of the spiritual practice of connections. In all of his books, he proves to be a good prospector for meaning in ancient and modern religious texts and stories. *Invisible Lines of Connection* is about the signs of the sacred he discovers in his everyday experiences with his family and friends and in his work at Congregation Beth El in Sudbury, Massachusetts. Computer games, photographs, movies, an eye malady, jury duty, sailing, shopping at a discount store, dancing the hokey pokey, relating to his wife, children, parents, and brother—all become ways to see that we are "players in a sacred story."

Again and again Kushner identifies lines "throughout all Creation, just beneath the surface, joining each person to every other person and to every other thing in a luminous organism of shared responsibility." God, then, is "the 'One' through whom everything is connected to everything else."

● Indigenous cultures also have much to show us about the connections over time and space and between all beings. In *Other Ways of Knowing: Recharting Our Future with Ageless Wisdom,* John Broomfield gathers ancestral teachings about human nature that recognize a cyclical understanding of time, a multidimensional present, and the reality of communication between humans and other species. He draws insights from Native American, Australian Aboriginal, Siberian, Polynesian, and other cultures. For example, "In place of our objectified, materialist view of the Earth, the way of the shaman offers spirit connections with all animals and inanimate forms." This way of knowing acknowledges a web of life that "weaves body, mind, and spirit."

VIDEOS

● In a world of increasing isolation, many of us want to reconnect with the people and the aspirations that are important to us. *Field of Dreams* is a Capraesque film about a man who does just that. Ray Kinsella, an Iowa farmer with a wife and young daughter, hears a mysterious voice telling him to build a baseball field in his cornfield. Even though this means putting his family in financial jeopardy, Ray follows orders, believing, as the voice puts it, "If you build it, he will come." Actually, many people come.

This stirring film uses baseball, the national pastime that has unified Americans for generations, as a point of entry for explorations of a variety of connections—between a deceased father and his son, a fan and the players of the sport, and a doctor and a significant moment in his past. It is these kinds of ties that give life depth and breadth.

● *The Secret of Roan Inish* is about an affinity for a type of geography, a landscape, or a particular place. Ten-year-old Fiona is sent to live with relatives on the Irish coast. She listens intently as her grandfather talks about the ancestral home they had to abandon on the nearby island of

Roan Inish. Later, when Fiona visits there, she feels drawn to its gulls, seals, abandoned buildings, and ghostly inhabitants. This lyrical film speaks to the spiritual longing for home and the ways connections are conveyed through family stories.

● Many people exercise their feelings of kinship with the natural world by developing deep relationships with animals. *Never Cry Wolf* is set in the Arctic wilderness of Canada. Tyler, a biologist, arrives to study some wolves believed to be preying upon the caribou herds. At an isolated campsite, he observes a white wolf, his mate, and three cubs. Tyler forms a genuine bond with these canines based on a deep respect for their individuality, loyalty to family, and intelligence. Then during an expedition to learn the truth about the wolves and the caribou, he has a mystical experience of oneness with nature. With a new awareness of the interrelatedness of life, Tyler realizes the importance of protecting wildlife.

SPIRITUAL EXERCISES AND RITUALS

● Christians believe that they belong to a communion of saints—a community of believers that transcends time and space. Other religious traditions emphasize the influential role of ancestors or spirit guides in people's lives. Think about the invisible presences to whom you feel connected. Dedicate one of your activities during the day to those who have gone before you and those who will come after you. For example, send a check to an organization working to preserve a treasure from the past that you want to be available to future generations.

● Express your connection to a special place—your home, your neighborhood, a favorite location for retreat. Carry a picture or a drawing of it in your wallet or a pebble found there in your pocket.

PRAYER OR MANTRA

This prayer is from the *Chinook Psalter,* quoted in *Prayers for Healing* edited by Maggie Oman.

> May all things move and be moved in me
> and know and be known in me.
> May all creation dance for you within me.

IMAGERY EXERCISE

Thich Nhat Hanh, the Vietnamese Buddhist monk, uses the term "interbeing" to describe the interconnection of all Creation. "When you touch one," he writes, "you touch many, and when you touch many, you touch one." Imagery is one way to know yourself as part of the multitudes. This exercise is based on Thich Nhat Hanh's description of eating a tangerine, found on page 235 of *Spiritual Literacy*.

Breathe out three times. See yourself holding a round orange tangerine that changes into a blossom on a tree. Sense how the tree is bathed in the light of the golden sun and then covered with soft, cool rain. Notice how the blossom becomes a small fruit that grows into the tangerine. See, feel, and smell the tangerine in your hand.

Breathe out one time. Imagine yourself peeling the tangerine and eating a piece of it, knowing that as you do so, you are being part of the sun, the rain, the tree, and all of Creation. Then open your eyes.

JOURNAL EXERCISES

● One of the most common demonstrations of connections is the experience of a synchronicity or a meaningful coincidence, when we realize that two apparently random things have happened together for a purpose. It might be meeting someone at just the right moment, a dream that comes true in waking life, or a communication with the dead. Describe one of these experiences and assess its impact on your life's direction.

● The butterfly effect is a term used to describe how an interconnected universe responds to particular actions; if a butterfly is hurt here, the effect is felt even in distant galaxies. Write about one of your deeds that has had far-reaching consequences. Try to predict how another action might reverberate in a distant place.

DISCUSSION QUESTIONS, STORYTELLING, SHARING

● In this ecological world of interdependence, we are all on the same team and anything done for one is done for all. What experience, practice, or resource has recently deepened or nourished your sense of being part of a team?

● Have you ever had a mystical experience when you felt the boundaries between you and the world dissolving and you were one with the universe? Where were you and what happened?

HOUSEHOLD, GROUP, AND COMMUNITY PROJECTS

● In some cultures, families create home shrines to honor their ancestors. A "family tree" wall of photographs, a table of framed photographs, or a collection of photo albums also salutes these connections. Tell stories about your ancestors as you look at the pictures.

• Saint Francis of Assisi is a good role model for the spiritual practice of connections. He treated all parts of the natural world as relatives. Have members of your household choose something from nature to relate to: Brother Sun, Sister Moon, Uncle Tree, Aunt Rock, Cousin Pond. Share your perceptions of these relationships.

• Explore the Internet. Every site offers you "links" to related information; click with your mouse on a phrase in an article or directory, and you are transported to a new destination, another address where you will find even more links. This way of accessing material challenges the fragmentation of data in our increasingly complex world; link by link individual users are reestablishing the connections.

• Participate in a project that demonstrates your connection to something that is far away from you—such as raising money for the restoration of the Amazon rain forest.

FICTION, POETRY, OR CHILDREN'S BOOK

E. M. Forster's novel *Howards End* is about two families in Edwardian England that have an indelible impact upon each other. The overarching theme of the story is the attempt to reconcile the divisions that tear our souls apart and keep us from seeing life whole—splits between rich and poor, city and country, male and female, mind and heart. Margaret, one of the main characters, thinks: "Only connect! That was the whole of her sermon. Only connect the prose and the passion, and both will be exalted, and human love will be seen at its height. Live in fragments no longer."

SPOKEN-WORD AUDIO

The Faithful Gardener by Clarissa Pinkola Estés is a beautiful parable about the connections throughout God's garden. The author's Hungarian uncle arrives in America with an abiding belief in the land as a living being. After a large portion of woodlands is destroyed to make way for a highway, he clears the land near the road and leaves the ground plowed but unseeded. He then tells Clarissa about a little fir tree whose story reflects the circle of life. It grows up in the forest, occupies a place of honor during the Christmas celebrations, surrenders itself in a fireplace, and returns as nourishing ashes to the garden. "I am everywhere now," it exclaims.

ART

American pop artist Claes Oldenberg's giant steel *Clothespin* reminds us that connections are made through ordinary, everyday things. By exaggerating its size, the artist encourages us to value this household object. It is a simple tool that can secure a sock to a clothesline, but it is also a symbol of an embrace, reminding us of how we connect with other people.

MUSIC

There is something about fingers touching strings, particularly classical and flamenco guitar music, that captures the essence of the spiritual practice of connections. Listen to a guitar fingering stylist like Peppino D'Agostino to see what we mean. On his album *Close to the Heart*, good examples are "Higher Connections," "Samba Marina," and "London Skies."

SEE ALSO:

Compassion. Forgiveness. Hospitality. Justice. Peace. Unity. Zeal.

 DEVOTION

DAILY CUE, REMINDER, VOW, BLESSING

The sound of a bell, a church chime, or the stroke of a clock
is a cue for me to pray.

•

When I see a candle, I am reminded to focus my devotion
on God.

•

When I hear reports of natural disasters, I vow to remember all
suffering beings in my prayers.

•

Blessed is the Beloved who is worshiped and served
through our devotion.

THE BASIC PRACTICE

A devotional life is one lived in the presence of the Lord. The world's religions tutor us in an amazing variety of ways to practice. To name just a few: Sufis dance. Buddhists chant. Roman Catholics pray with a rosary. Protestants sing hymns. Orthodox Christians meditate on icons. Hindus gather to receive blessings in temples. Taoists do breathing exercises. Jews wrap themselves in a prayer shawl. Native Americans bring up the sun. Muslims make a pilgrimage.

Whether our devotional practices are formal liturgies or informal gestures, they recognize that everything is linked to the Divine. There can be no bracketing of our existence into holy and unholy precincts.

Begin, then, by cultivating your own garden of devotion. Pick as many seeds to plant as you desire. Water them with love. Be vigilant in your caretaking. Add new plants to the garden for variety. And be happy knowing that this garden pleases God.

CATALYSTS, CONTRASTS, AND COMPANIONS

Devotion is not something that is done once a week, just on religious holidays, or only in response to a particular event in your life. Special devotions may be called for at those times, but as a spiritual practice, devotion needs to be part of your daily routine.

Devotion then helps you build self-discipline. Being constant in your prayers prepares you for other disciplines needed in your life. On the other hand, if you lack commitment and don't tend to follow through in the long run, your devotional life will suffer as well.

PERSPECTIVES

My life is an instant, a fleeting hour. My life is a moment, which swiftly escapes me. O my God, you know that on Earth I have only today to love you.
–SAINT THÉRÈSE OF LISIEUX

May my body be a prayerstick for the world.
–JOAN HALIFAX

A leaf, a flower, a fruit, or even
Water, offered to me in devotion,
I will accept as the loving gift
Of a dedicated heart. Whatever you do,
Make it an offering to me—
–THE BHAGAVAD GITA

TEACHERS

● Edward Hays is a Catholic priest and prolific author who writes in the areas of contemporary spirituality, personal prayer, liturgy, and ministry. He has pioneered new approaches and imaginative takes on the devotional life in his many books.

One of our well-worn favorites is *Prayers for a Planetary Pilgrim: A Personal Manual for Prayer and Ritual.* It is divided into sections containing morning and evening prayers for each of the four seasons; psalms for the twenty-first century; cosmopolitan prayers modeled on Buddhist, Native American, Islamic, Hindu, Judaic, and Taoist traditions; rituals for a planetary pilgrim; and suggestions for equipment and exercises. Hays also provides solid advice on creating a personal prayer shrine and using devotional aids such as sacred objects, prayer pebbles, and prayer flags.

Everything in this devotional book is eminently fresh and practical. Hays's other books are also highly recommended, especially *Prayers for the Domestic Church.* When our beloved cat Boone died, we used one of the blessings from that book. When we bring in our Christmas tree, we say another. Here is one of his mini-blessings: "(When Making a Telephone Call to a Loved One) May my words be rich in love and may this call bring peace and joy. (Upon Completing the Call) Blessed are you who gives to us such gifts that enrich our hearts."

• Another popular Christian teacher of devotional practice is Richard J. Foster. In *Prayer: Finding the Heart's True Home,* he sets out to name our experiences of prayer so that we can be more intentional about them. He believes that people pray in far more ways and far more often than they realize. In this comprehensive volume, he tallies up the incredible variety of approaches we use to communicate with God.

The book is divided into three sections depicting how prayer can take an inward trek of personal transformation (Prayer of the Forsaken, Prayer of Examen, Prayer of Tears, etc.), an upward turn toward intimacy with the Creator (Prayer of Adoration, Sacramental Prayer, etc.), or an outward arc of serving others (Petitionary Prayer, Intercessory Prayer, etc.). Foster, a Quaker, adds emotionally honest reflections on his own devotional practices to make the point that seizing upon the sanctity of the ordinary is essential to a rich inner life.

• *The Gift of Prayer: A Treasury of Personal Prayer from the World's Spiritual Traditions* is one of the best collections of prayers available. This anthology was assembled by the editors of *Fellowship in Prayer,* an interfaith journal. From ancient and modern sources, there are prayers of contemplation, meditation, healing, blessing, and forgiveness. Here are two examples. From Latin America: "O God, to those who have hunger give bread; And to us who have bread give the hunger for justice." A Jewish prayer: "In that which we share, let us see the common prayer of humanity. In that in which we differ, let us wonder at the freedom of humankind."

VIDEOS

● *Baraka* is a spellbinding nonnarrative film that delivers an unforgettable collection of snapshots from the global family album. Some of the most moving images portray the devotional activities of people around the world. We see them gathering at sacred sites and performing rituals that have retained an intimacy with the natural world.

The most startling and powerful scenes show us the shared distresses of Earth and humankind—poor people scavenging for food in garbage dumps, the befouled atmosphere around the Kuwaiti oil fires, the trees felled in the rain forest. *Baraka* (taken from the Sufi word meaning "blessing" or "essence of life") is a tutorial for the spiritual practice of devotion, showing us how to do it and why.

● Francis of Assisi remains one of Christendom's most appealing models of the devotional life. Franco Zeffirelli's *Brother Sun, Sister Moon* tells the story of this man's spiritual renewal. Like other explicitly religious films, this one aims for the heart and not the head.

Francesco Bernardoni returns home to Assisi in A.D. 1200 nervously exhausted from the wars. Thanks to a series of divine epiphanies, he breaks from his rich parents and their wealthy community. He retreats to the countryside to begin a simple life of sacrifice. The rest of the film charts his efforts to incarnate the servanthood of Christ through his poverty and service to the dispossessed.

SPIRITUAL EXERCISES AND RITUALS

● Create an altar for your personal prayer, ritual, and meditation. Include objects found in nature, flowers, candles, art, and photographs that increase your focus on the sacred. See *Altars Made Easy: A Complete Guide to Creating Your Own Sacred Space* by Peg Streep for more ideas on altar ware, statuary, prayer aids, offerings, and scents.

● Try movements such as bowing, kneeling, falling prostrate, or dancing as embodied prayers—a style of devotion practiced in all the traditions. Celeste Snowber Schroeder's *Embodied Prayer: Harmonizing Body and Soul* contains good exercises to get you started.

● Experiment with flash prayers. These are short, instantaneous, intercessory prayers. The next time you hear the siren of an emergency vehicle, say "God be with those in crisis and with those going to help."

● Create a prayer book in a loose-leaf format with different sections containing specific reminders of the different emphases of your devotional life. A section for prayers of praise and thanksgiving might include favorite scripture passages, lists of your blessings, and pictures of sacred art. A section for intercessory prayers could hold the needs of family and friends you have agreed to pray for, requests for the sick and the suffering around the world, prayers for world leaders, and the like. Include recent photographs, greeting cards, newspaper or magazine clippings, drawings, quotations, business cards, and other items.

PRAYER OR MANTRA

Over the centuries, certain words or short phrases have taken on a sacred character because of their use as repetitive prayers or mantras. Here are a few examples of traditional mantras.

Buddhism: Om Mani Padme Hum (the jewel in the lotus of the heart)

Christianity: Lord Jesus Christ, Son of God, have mercy on me, a sinner (known as the Jesus Prayer); Maranatha (Come Lord); Hail Mary (Mother of God)

Hinduism: Om (the sound of ultimate reality); Hare Krishna Rama (three holy names of God); Aum Namah Sivaya (Adoration to Siva)

Islam: La illaha Allah (There are no gods but the God); Allahu Akbar (God is the most great)

Judaism: Barukh attah Adonai (Blessed art thou, O Lord); Shalom (Peace)

IMAGERY EXERCISE

Catholic priest Anthony de Mello developed a series of exercises for use as prayers; they are collected in *Sadhana: A Way to God*. This one, titled "A Place for Prayer," recognizes that where we pray often influences our prayer.

After some time spent quieting yourself, withdraw in imagination to some place that is likely to foster prayer for you: a seashore, a riverbank, a mountaintop, a silent church, a terrace that gives on to the starry sky, a garden flooded by the light of the moon . . . See the place as vividly as possible . . . All the colors . . . Hear all the sounds (the waves, the wind in the trees, the insects at night) . . . Now raise your heart to God and say something.

JOURNAL EXERCISES

● Since 1992, priest and novelist Andrew Greeley has kept a daily prayer record in a file on his computer; he has published several volumes of these journals. Addressing God as "My Love," he shares his intimate feelings, dreams, creative efforts, and scholastic interests. Keep a running record of your dialogues with God in your journal.

● There are hundreds of images and names for God in sacred litera-ture and even more mentions of attributes of the Divine. Muslims rec-ognize 99 names for Allah. To what aspects of God are you devoted? Make a list of the ways you have addressed God over the years; this gives you a good indication of the nature of your relationship. Then brainstorm a list of new names for God. Use at least one new one each week in your prayers.

DISCUSSION QUESTIONS, STORYTELLING, SHARING

● Brother David Steindl-Rast points out the importance of finding cues to prayer. He tells of two sisters who had a clock that struck every 15 minutes. With each stroke of the clock, one would say, "Remember God's presence," and the other would add, "Let us always be grateful." Talk in your group about what kinds of things spark your prayers.

● What benefits have you derived from worshipping in a community? What parts of the service are most satisfying to you?

● Prayers of action, according to Richard J. Foster, are "each activity of daily life in which we stretch ourselves on behalf of others." Using this definition, talk about your prayers of action this week.

HOUSEHOLD, GROUP, AND COMMUNITY PROJECTS

● Find ways to expand the devotional activities in your household. Use a variety of graces at meals. Incorporate blessing prayers into such activities as leaving for school, going to the grocery store, or washing the car.

● Form a prayer group. *A Circle of Prayer: Coming Together to Find Spirit, Caring and Community* by Holly Bridges includes tips on organizing and maintaining a circle.

FICTION, POETRY, OR CHILDREN'S BOOK

One of the important elements of the spiritual practice of devotion is using different names and images to enable us to draw closer to the Holy One. Two children's books explore this process.

● In *Old Turtle* by Douglas Wood, the created beings on Earth argue about God, describing the Divine in their own images: a wind who is never still, a great rock that never moves, a snowy peak, a swimmer, a runner, the shining sun, and more. Then Old Turtle intervenes to say that God is above all things and within all things and simply "is." When human beings arrive on the scene, there is more discord, until the beauties of nature remind them why they were created.

● *In God's Name* by Sandy Eisenberg Sasso celebrates religious diversity. Different seekers come up with their own names for God, including Source of Life, Creator of Light, Shepherd, Maker of Peace, My Rock, Healer, Redeemer, Ancient One, Comforter, Mother, Father, and Friend. Eventually all the people come together and realize that there is no single right name for God.

SPOKEN-WORD AUDIO

Contemplative Prayer by Thomas Keating is an audio workshop with a member of the Cistercian Order. He demonstrates how individuals can open themselves to God through solitude, silence, and prayer. Keating is convinced that intimacy with God enables us to move beyond the illusions, addictions, and enslavements of the false self. He provides helpful tips on the practice of Christian meditation, the tradition of divine reading, and group prayer.

ART

Icons have been used for centuries by Orthodox Christians as aids to meditation and worship. To believers, icons are windows into the sacred; they provide bridges to Jesus Christ, links with the saints, and reminders of significant events in the history of salvation. *Praying with Icons* by Jim Forest provides a succinct and profound overview of this devotional art. It contains color plates and black-and-white photographs of icons along with prayers that can be used with them.

MUSIC

A wide variety of sacred music is attracting a worldwide audience. Gregorian chants have hit the best-seller charts, and Hindu and Buddhist meditation music is very popular. *B'ismillah: Highlights from the Fez Festival of World Sacred Music, Volume I,* contains Pakistani chants, Egyptian odes, flamenco-style Christian songs, and Sufi dance music. *Hamdulillah: Highlights from the Fez Festival of World Sacred Music, Volume II,* showcases spiritual songs from Iran, medieval Muslim and Andalusian songs, Moroccan Jewish traditional music, and Islamic songs of Central Asia.

SEE ALSO:
Compassion. Gratitude. Nurturing. Silence. Transformation.
X—The Mystery. Yearning.

ENTHUSIASM

THE BASIC PRACTICE

The word "enthusiasm" is derived from the roots *en*—in or within— and *theos*—God. It means having God within or being one with God. People with this gift carry a special kind of energy. They bring warmth and feeling to their relationships and vigor and freshness to their activities.

To practice enthusiasm, make others aware when you are excited about something. Throw yourself into your projects. Be known for your eagerness, your curiosity, your willingness to give it all you've got. Proclaim your passions. Hold nothing back. Sing your heart out.

CATALYSTS, CONTRASTS, AND COMPANIONS

Enthusiasm is invigorating. It helps you get up and go. It is a good prescription, then, when you are feeling lethargic and listless, when your energy seems frozen.

Enthusiasm counterbalances apathy and boredom, two common blocks to an engaged spiritual life. A sluggish spirit just doesn't care about anything. The world isn't interesting enough; there's a dreary sameness to all your activities.

When fatigue or another of these conditions has you dragging through your days, when you find that you've replaced wonder with whatever, go for enthusiasm. If you can't muster it from within, surround yourself with enthusiastic people.

PERSPECTIVES

Enthusiasm is the greatest power.
For one endowed with enthusiasm
nothing in this world is impossible.
–THE RAMAYANA

Do not judge whether what you are doing is impressive or mediocre, spiritual or mundane. Just do it with enthusiasm. Just give yourself to whatever you do with this full knowledge: "God is within me. All actions that I perform are an offering to Him."
–SWAMI CHIDVILASANANDA

Enthusiasm is one of life's greatest qualities, but it must be practiced to become a dominant factor in one's life. . . . There is real magic in enthusiasm. It spells the difference between mediocrity and accomplishment.
–NORMAN VINCENT PEALE

TEACHERS

● Many religions recommend the emulation of saints as teachers of desirable qualities. In *Passion for Life: Fragments of the Face of God*, Joan Chittister, a Benedictine sister, profiles 30 individuals from all eras and different traditions who "have lived in circumstances similar to ours and have shown us how to live in them well, with character, with courage, with passion for the right, the true, and the holy." They are "so possessed by an internal vision of divine goodness that they give us a glimpse of the face of God in the center of the human." In other words, they have enthusiasm.

In this inspiring book, the words of Joan Chittister and the profound icons painted by Robert Lentz combine to show how saints—religious and lay, chosen by a traditional process or acclaimed by the people—speak to our times. Mary Magdalene and Hildegard of Bingen remind us that God has a feminine voice. Mother Jones models perseverance through her work as a labor organizer, and Dorothea Day exemplifies clarity of purpose in her ministry with the poor. Mahatma Gandhi, Dr. Martin Luther King, Jr., and Martin of Tours show us what it means to be nonviolent. Amos of Israel and Oscar Romero of El Salvador prove that prophets can emerge from our midst.

• "Bodhisattvas are beings who are dedicated to the universal awakening or enlightenment of everyone. They exist as guides and providers of succor to suffering beings and offer everyone an approach to meaningful spiritual life," writes Zen priest, leader, and translator Taigen Daniel Leighton in *Bodhisattva Archetypes: Classic Buddhist Guides to Awakening and Their Modern Expression*. He explains the qualities of seven major bodhissatva figures, including the Prince of Wisdom, the Heart of Compassion, and the Earth Mother. He then identifies modern exemplars of these archetypes, including Bob Dylan, Margaret Mead, Albert Schweitzer, Toni Morrison, and Gary Snyder. He concludes: "The bodhisattvas are not glorified, exotic, unnatural beings but simply our best qualities in full flower." Included in that bouquet is enthusiasm.

• A wonderful resource that identifies many other teachers of this spiritual practice is Robert Ellsberg's *All Saints: Daily Reflections on Saints, Prophets, and Witnesses for Our Time*. The editor-in-chief of Orbis Books comments on the lives and insights of 365 saints. Included are traditional saints such as Francis of Assisi, Thérèse of Lisieux, and Joan of Arc; lesser-known saints such as Juan Diego and Elizabeth of Hungary; contemporary prophets including Raoul Wallenberg, Dietrich Bonhoeffer, and Dom Helder Camara; and artists, poets, and scholars such as Flannery O'Connor, Walker Percy, G. K. Chesterton, Albert Camus, and E. R. Schumacher.

VIDEOS

• *The Accidental Tourist* is a quirky film about the unpredictability of love. Macon writes city guides for business travelers who only want to experience the familiar while away from home. He leads a rather boring life. When his wife leaves him, he moves in with his reclusive siblings, the kind of people who eat potatoes every night for dinner and alphabetize their canned goods. Then Macon meets Muriel at the kennel where he leaves his dog during a trip, and she offers to help walk and train his pet.

Muriel, a single parent, is a totally enthusiastic person. Before he quite knows what is happening, she has pulled Macon out of his cocoon and into her slipshod life. This romantic comedy demonstrates how an exuberant soul adds color and magic to the lives of all those she touches.

• Another comedy, *Sister Act,* makes the same point. In this movie, the enthusiastic one is Deloris, a lounge singer in Reno. After she witnesses a mob murder, the police decide to hide her in a convent. She has trouble adjusting to life there until she is asked to direct the choir. With inspired creativity, she translates the pop songs "My Guy" and "I Will Follow Him" into snappy devotional anthems. The nuns respond with their own zest for life, and soon the choir is packing audiences into the church. Deloris embodies enthusiasm, and it is catching.

• *Race the Sun* shows how enthusiasm can conquer apathy. A group of working-class students at a high school in Hawaii are down on themselves and down on life. Then their science teacher encourages them to build a solar-powered car for a 2,000-mile race in Australia. Her practice of enthusiasm propels them to rise to this challenge.

SPIRITUAL EXERCISES AND RITUALS

• Watch your reactions to people and events. On a continuum from "bored" to "ecstatic," where would you place yourself? Continue this exercise for a week, and notice what contributes to a change in the degree of your enthusiasm.

• When you are reading sacred literature, imagine that you are being filled with fuel for your enthusiasm. Make a "holy book" of passages that have this effect upon you.

• Select a favorite hymn to use in a worship service or ritual. Encourage participants to really let themselves go as you sing it together. John Wesley, the founder of Methodism, gave some very specific instructions for singing: "Sing lustily and with a good courage. Beware of singing as if you were half dead, or half asleep; but lift up your voice with strength."

PRAYER OR MANTRA

In the Bible, God surveys the Creation and sees that it is good. Repeat this mantra about anything that happens and whatever you encounter to affirm the goodness of the Creation.

> Breathing in: This is . . .
> Breathing out: good!

IMAGERY EXERCISE

This exercise, "God in My Breath," is a brief version of one Anthony de Mello presents in *Sadhana: A Way to God*. The intention is to bring God within—*en theos*.

Close your eyes and practice breath awareness for a while. . . . Reflect now that this air that you are breathing in is charged with the power and the presence of God. . . . Notice what you feel when you become aware that you are drawing God in with each breath you take.

Now while you breathe in, fill your lungs with the divine energy. . . . While you breathe out, imagine you are breathing out all your impurities . . . your fears . . . your negative feelings . . . your apathy . . . your boredom. . . . Imagine your whole body becoming radiant and alive through this process of breathing in God's life-giving Spirit and breathing out all your impurities.

Stay with this awareness as long as you can without distractions.

JOURNAL EXERCISES

● Do an enthusiasm examination of yourself. When do you feel filled with God? When do you feel most alive? What are you passionate about? Do you always feel free to express your enthusiasm? If not, what tends to stifle this spiritual energy?

● Write a profile of a person you would call a "living saint" who is infused with the spirit of God. How has this individual moved you? How do you feel in the company of this person? Try to come to terms with your reactions to "holy people" through this exercise.

DISCUSSION QUESTIONS, STORYTELLING, SHARING

● Walt Whitman said about his first reading of Ralph Waldo Emerson: "I was simmering and he brought me to a boil." What has brought you to a boil recently?

● Describe a specific incident when you were enthusiastic about a project. What was it? How did the people around you respond to your excitement? Did anyone try to take the wind out of your sails? How did you handle the situation?

● What do you do to revive your spirits when you are feeling sluggish, bored, or apathetic?

HOUSEHOLD, GROUP, AND COMMUNITY PROJECTS

● Create a scrapbook of Enthusiastic Souls, perhaps organized around saint days or birthdays. Using one of the resources described above, or other books about saints and heroes, read up on the lives of people you admire. Copy down meaningful lines from their writing. Find one way to honor this person—with a prayer, a reading, or a specific action.

● Make supporting other people's enthusiasms an ongoing activity in your household. Send thank-you notes to people whose commitments you admire, just as you would acknowledge a gift. Regularly share your passions with family and friends—give a favorite book with a note about why you love it, recommend a film, e-mail a meaningful quote. And when you spot enthusiastic people, cheer them on.

FICTION, POETRY, OR CHILDREN'S BOOK

● Too often children's innate enthusiasm is dampened by adult assessments of what is possible. But not in *The Carrot Seed*, a story by Ruth Krauss with pictures by Crockett Johnson, and *Wanda's Roses*, a story by Pat Brisson illustrated by Maryann Cocca-Leffler. In the first, a little boy plants a carrot seed. His mother, father, and older brother all say, "It won't come up." But he weeds around the seed and waters the ground, and one day he carts away a very big carrot, just as he always knew he would.

● In *Wanda's Roses*, a girl notices a thornbush growing in an empty city lot and, believing in her heart that it is a rosebush, decides to care for it. She really throws herself into this project, reading up on roses, clearing the trash away so the bush gets more light and air, and watering it. Soon all the adults in the neighborhood are talking about Wanda and the rose-bush, worrying that it will never flower. Then Wanda invites them to a party in her rose garden where they all enjoy the surprising results of her enthusiasm.

Spoken-Word Audio

The Mentor's Spirit: Life Lessons on Leadership and the Art of Encouragement by Marsha Sinetar salutes teachers, artists, parents, elders, or business associates who provide guidance, support, and inspiration in our lives. These "artists of encouragement" can also shine through books, movies, poems, and works of art. Sinetar believes that mentors—living or dead—serve as spurs to our "spiritual intelligence."

Art

The spiritual practice of enthusiasm arises out of deep passion and visceral energy. Both qualities are apparent in Sonia Delaunay's *Flamenco Singer*. Spheres of bright colors—reds, oranges, yellows, blues, greens—explode and radiate away from the central figure of the singer, some of the disks becoming spirals before moving off the canvas. The vibrational power of such a vocal performance must come from a place deep within, the source of all enthusiasm.

Music

● "Let cheerful anthems fill this house." So goes the opening of Edwin Hawkins's gospel standard "Oh Happy Day" as sung by The Sisters of Glory (Thelma Houston, Cece Peniston, Phoebe Snow, Lois Walden, Albertina Walker) on *Good News in Hard Times*. This is a particularly fine collection of gospel tunes, including a heartfelt version of the traditional "Will the Circle Be Unbroken," rhythmic vocal dialogues on the contemporary "How I Got Over," and a great percussion accompaniment for "He's Got the Whole World in His Hands."

● Almost any recording in the gospel music genre is a good example of enthusiasm. It is testimony music, expressing what it feels like to be filled with God. And although there are many fine single gospel singers, the most enthusiastic performances usually are by groups and choirs. For wonderful samples of the latter, listen to the Smithsonian Folkways recordings *African American Spirituals: The Concert Tradition (Volume 1)* and *African American Congregational Singing: Nineteenth-Century Roots (Volume 2).*

SEE ALSO:
Hope. Joy. Kindness. Play. Wonder. Zeal.

FAITH

THE BASIC PRACTICE

Faith defined as an acceptance of certain religious doctrines is an
essential element in Judaism, Christianity, and Islam. In Hinduism and
Buddhism, it is an attitude of devotion that opens a gateway to spiritual
practice.

In the broad scope of the spiritual life, we see faith not as something
you have but as something you are in—a relationship. It involves an
awareness of and an attunement to God's presence in our everyday
experiences.

Practicing faith, then, is like developing any relationship. You have to give it time and attention. It requires you to see, hear, feel, and constantly remember your partner—God. Have confidence in the relationship's viability, even when you are facing mysteries, doubts, and paradoxes. Trust in this faith, even to the point of staking your life on it.

CATALYSTS, CONTRASTS, AND COMPANIONS

Many people assume that the chief challenges to faith are disbelief and doubt, but the real stumbling block to faith is resistance to God, or the hardened heart. In the biblical traditions, the heart is used as an image for the deeper self, the true and total person. The hard heart is not open to the sacred. It is similar to eyes that do not see and ears that do not hear.

Difficulties can be catalysts to faith. During a dark night of the soul, sometimes all we can do is trust that this, too, will pass. Facing illness, death, or the myriad other challenges in our lives, we are strengthened by the knowledge that a Greater Power watches and waits with us. In the long run, it's the relationship that matters.

PERSPECTIVES

Faith is the fruit of hard, constant care and vigilance, of insistence upon remaining true to a vision; not an act of inertia but an aspiration to maintain our responsiveness to Him alive.
—ABRAHAM JOSHUA HESCHEL

Learning to trust—that is the great thing. You realize that you do have to do your work, you have to provide what you can, but also you have to learn to believe that Providence is going to provide all that you really need.
—BEDE GRIFFITHS

Seek not for perfect belief, but let your faith grow as you test and find what works for you, as you experience God in your life.
—PIR VILAYAT INAYAT KHAN

TEACHERS

● Marcus Borg provides a clear and stirring explanation of faith as relationship in *The God We Never Knew: Beyond Dogmatic Religion to a More Authentic Faith*. This teacher, who calls himself a "devoted but non-exclusivist Christian," speaks to seekers of many traditions when he advocates a subtle, flexible, intelligent, and mature framing of faith for this age of religious pluralism.

"Faith is the human response to God," Borg states simply. But his understanding of God moves beyond the simplistic supernatural theism of his childhood to panentheism—the belief that everything is in God and God is in everything. Faith is belief in, fidelity to, and trust in this reality in whom we live and move and have our being.

Faith grows over time: "It is not a requirement that we are to meet but a quality that grows as our relationship with God deepens." Borg's favorite metaphor for this is the "hatching of the heart." The spiritual journey is about "opening of the self to the reality of the Spirit." He discusses the important role of spiritual practices in this process, including sacraments, rituals, and laws; the collective sharing of sacred stories, images, sounds, and music; and individual acts such as prayer and deeds of compassion.

• Rabbi David A. Cooper is another guide to faith. He has studied the world's wisdom teachings extensively as part of his efforts to share the messages of his own tradition. In *God Is a Verb: Kabbalah and the Practice of Mystical Judaism*, he challenges us "to develop new connections and heart-openings with the Divine Source of Existence." He suggests that we think of God as a process and use an interactive word—the verb God-ing—to describe our relationship to the Divine. From the Jewish mystics, we learn that we are copartners with God in the ongoing creation of the universe.

Cooper models the life of faith as an integration of study, daily practices, and contemplative exercises. These equip us to do the spiritual work to repair our souls and the soul of the world and to raise holy sparks. In one of the most helpful sections of the book, he outlines the Jewish way to enlightenment. It consists of 12 paths designed to bring us to an intimate relationship with the Holy One.

VIDEOS

• *Thérèse* is a stylized screen portrait of Saint Thérèse of Lisieux (1873–1897), who is also known as the Little Flower of Jesus. A devout teenager, she longs to join her two sisters in a Carmelite convent. When the local church authorities deny her request because she is so young, she appeals to the Pope. Finally allowed to enter the order, she is radiant as she takes her vows as a bride of Christ.

Thérèse easily adapts to the rhythms and rituals of convent life, working in the laundry, praying, and relaxing with the other sisters. Her deep love for Jesus is tested in a grim and losing battle with tuberculosis. But even in moments of not knowing, she remains true to her commitment. In a scene just before her death, she gently fans a figure of Christ on the cross that she has placed on her pillow. For Thérèse this relationship is all she needs.

• How to be faithful in a relationship with God is also the theme of the movie *Chariots of Fire,* the true story of Eric Liddell, son of a Scots missionary, and Harold Abraham, a Jew attending Cambridge, who became champions at the 1924 Paris Olympics. Both of them use their faith as a catalyst to bring out the best that is within them. Harold taps into the anger he feels toward those who practice anti-Semitism to fuel his individuality. Eric's Christian faith compels him to take a moral stand and to see grace as a spur to his achievements on the track.

• When faith is regarded merely as an adherence to particular beliefs and customs, it can lead to spiritual pride and rejection of the validity of other paths. This is the shadow side of faith, a theme explored in *Black Robe.* In seventeenth-century Canada, Father Laforgue, a French-born Jesuit, is assigned a mission in the wilderness. On the 1,500-mile journey there, he is escorted by a group of Algonquin Indians. The priest, shocked by the Indians' vulgarity and sensuality, regards them as godless savages in need of conversion. They are told by a shaman that the black-robed man with the strange customs must be a demon. These distrustful attitudes result in great suffering for all parties.

In the end, however, Laforgue is humbled by his encounter with another way of life. He arrives at his mission to find the tribe there decimated by European diseases. Putting aside spiritual imperialism, he realizes that it is more important to love these people than to save them for Christianity. At this point, the film turns into a true reflection of faith as relationship.

SPIRITUAL EXERCISES AND RITUALS

• Set aside a time in the evening when you can speak freely without being overheard. After a few preparatory minutes of silence, talk out loud to God in a conversational way. You might begin with the question "How was my day?" Answer by reviewing your experiences hour by hour, noting with gratitude the times when you sensed God's presence, admitting those actions and thoughts that made you feel separated from God. Express your feelings; even talk about your problems.

Conversational prayer signals your interest in having a relationship with God. And it is usually not one way. The practices of attention and listening help you discover God's end of the conversation. Rabbi Cooper suggests you also use sacred texts, such as the Bible, sacred poetry, and collections of spiritual writing. After talking to God for a while, open your book of inspiration at random, read one paragraph, then close the book and sit quietly for a few more minutes. Later, write about your experience in your journal. As you work with this exercise over time, see if any patterns are obvious and identify any moments when you feel a special connection.

• Retreating to a cloister or a monk's cell is a traditional way to cultivate a deeper intimacy with God. Find a quiet, secluded place where you can be alone and not have to answer the door or the telephone. Use silence, meditation, and prayer to deepen your relationship with God.

PRAYER OR MANTRA

French priest Pierre Teilhard de Chardin captures an important aspect of faith in these lines from a prayer.

> Breathing in: Trust in . . .
> Breathing out: the slow work of God.

IMAGERY EXERCISE

This exercise, "A Clean Heart," is developed from Marcus Borg's metaphor of spirituality as the hatching or softening of the heart. It also recalls the plea from the heart expressed in Psalm 51:10.

Breathe out three times. See and sense yourself opening your chest and taking out your heart. Examine it carefully in the light, noticing any shell that has formed around it and any hardness of its surface. Smell your heart for signs of anything trapped inside.

Breathe out one time. If your heart is covered by a shell, break open the shell, releasing anything trapped inside. Where your heart is hard, gently massage it, telling it that you love it. Sense how your heart is getting softer and more flexible.

Breathe out one time. Clean your heart with whatever tools you need (a feather, a small brush, a broom). Notice if anything is written on your heart. Sense and know that a right spirit is being put into your clean heart. Holding your heart up to the light again, notice how it looks and feels. Then place your heart back inside and sew up your chest. When you are finished, open your eyes.

JOURNAL EXERCISE

Write a personal creed. To organize your thoughts, you may find it helpful to look at a statement of faith used in a religious liturgy. Or begin by listing "Beliefs I No Longer Have" and "Beliefs I Now Have." Other useful headings to use in preparing a creed are: Who Am I? What Is Happening in the World? What Are We Here For? What Is Valuable? What Can I Do Now? How Do I Know Spirit Is Moving in My Life?

DISCUSSION QUESTIONS, STORYTELLING, SHARING

● Go around the circle and have each person list three things he or she is faithful to.

● Talk about the different stages of your journey of faith. What was the religion of your birth family? When did you experience your first doubts? Did you ever fall away from your faith in God? What drew you back? What new experiences of faith do you look forward to?

● Share a story about a dark time in your life when your relationship with God and your sense of God's faithfulness to you were sources of strength.

HOUSEHOLD, GROUP, AND COMMUNITY PROJECTS

● Play trust games with your family and friends. For example, one person stands in the middle of a tight circle. He or she falls, eyes closed and body stiff, into the arms of one person and then is passed across and around the circle. Or one person is blindfolded and led through a forest or house that he or she is unfamiliar with.

● It takes tremendous faith to break an addiction and turn your life around. That has been the experience of many people in 12-step programs. Invite someone who participates in a program like Alcoholics Anonymous to talk to your group about faith's role in his or her recovery. If you are in a position to do so, support such programs in your community by making space available for meetings.

FICTION, POETRY, OR CHILDREN'S BOOK

A Prayer for Owen Meany by John Irving is a rare and wonderful testament to the fervor and resilience of faith. The narrator of the story is John Wheeler, a teacher in Toronto who introduces himself with the statement that he believes in God because of Owen Meany, his friend since childhood. Owen is a bit of a freak in their town. For one thing, he's very short. For another, even as a youngster, he is convinced that he is meant to be "God's instrument." Although he faces many tribulations over the years, Owen emerges from them unscathed. Eventually he foresees the date and circumstances of his own sacrificial death. Owen's kind of belief—that God has a plan for his life—is a cornerstone of faith.

SPOKEN-WORD AUDIO

The Legend of Baal-Shem by Martin Buber focuses on the simple, joyful faith of Israel ben Eliezer, also known as the Baal Shem Tov, the founder of the Eastern European movement of Hasidism in Judaism. He taught that "faith is the foundation of everything." Folk singer, composer, and actor Theodore Bikel reads an especially good collection of stories about this great Jewish sage that reveals his closeness to God.

ART

Georges Rouault, a French painter and devout Christian, once wrote: "One is never finished seeing and watching. Our eyes are the doors of our spirit and the light of our mind." Many of his creations are meditations on faith as a single-minded relationship with God. In *Joan of Arc*, Rouault shows the saint riding a prancing horse, holding up a banner, as the sun shines brightly upon them. The luminous colors in the painting are a testament to her ardor.

MUSIC

The Lark Ascending by Vaughn Williams is identified as a "romance for violin and orchestra." The solo violin mimics the lark's call while also becoming a bird in flight, circling around the orchestra, diving and then soaring to the heavens. This 15-minute piece conveys a deep relational quality between the one instrument and the whole orchestra that makes it a beautiful reminder of faith.

SEE ALSO:

Grace. Gratitude. Hope. Meaning. Questing. X—The Mystery.

FORGIVENESS

DAILY CUE, REMINDER, VOW, BLESSING

Shaking hands is a cue for me to practice forgiveness.

•

When I clean my room, I am reminded of the cleansing and restorative power of forgiveness.

•

When I put my foot on the gas pedal in my car, I vow to accelerate my practice of forgiveness.

•

Blessed is the Divine Healer who forgives us and asks us to forgive others.

THE BASIC PRACTICE

There are three kinds of forgiveness, all interrelated. There is self-forgiveness, which enables us to release our guilt and perfectionism. There is the forgiveness we extend to others and receive from them, intimates and enemies alike. And there is the forgiveness of God, which assures us of our worth and strengthens us for this practice.

All the spiritual traditions raise up the value of forgiveness, but many people still find it to be a nearly impossible ideal. Just try it. Look truthfully at one hurt you have not been able to forgive. Identify any associated feelings you might have, such as anger, denial, guilt, shame, or embarrassment. Imagine what it would be like to live without feeling this offense. Then let it go.

Other steps may be necessary for healing—a confession of your contribution to the conflict, making amends, changing behavior, a commitment to the community—but giving up your claims for, and sometimes against, yourself is where you have to begin.

CATALYSTS, CONTRASTS, AND COMPANIONS

We all know the obvious symptoms that could be relieved by forgiveness—feeling so wounded that we want revenge, constant brooding over a long list of petty grievances, feeling so guilty we don't know how to approach someone we have offended, worry that the hurt could happen again. Bitterness and stubbornness can also be signs that forgiveness is called for, especially when these attitudes are associated with a need to be recognized as the one who is right.

In contrast to these limiting behaviors, which usually erect walls between ourselves and others, forgiveness is freeing. It means that we can move out of our previous position and move on with our lives. Best of all, it enables us to be reconciled with our neighbors and with God so that once again we feel part of the greater community of the spiritual life.

PERSPECTIVES

Forgiveness is freeing up and putting to better use the energy once consumed by holding grudges, harboring resentments, and nursing unhealed wounds. It is rediscovering the strengths we always had and relocating our limitless capacity to understand and accept other people and ourselves.
–SIDNEY AND SUZANNE SIMON

Carry no conscious burden. This means do not owe anything to anyone. This means that you have not done anything wrong to people. If you have done something wrong, straighten it out. Take care of all your old problems. I believe correct virtuous fulfillment can remove a conscious burden.
–HUA-CHING NI

The practice of forgiveness is not only, or even primarily, a way of dealing with guilt. Instead, its central goal is to reconcile, to restore communion—with God, with one another, and with the whole creation.
–L. GREGORY JONES

TEACHERS

• Forgiveness is a specific act, an attitude, an art, and an ongoing process. All these aspects of this spiritual practice are explored in *A Little Book of Forgiveness: Challenges and Meditations for Anyone with Something to Forgive* by D. Patrick Miller. This teacher writes cogently about "a radical way of life that openly contradicts the most common and popular beliefs of this troubled world." He discusses forgiving others, forgiving yourself, and where forgiveness leads.

Miller sees this spiritual practice as a way of letting go of the past, of settling accounts, of doing good, and of moving into the future with hope. It is the first step on the path to wholeness where anger, resentment, and guilt no longer take center stage. "Forgiveness is not mere sympathy, nor condescension, nor forced generosity," he notes. "It is the ultimate declaration of equality, founded on the recognition that all crimes are the same crime, every failing the human failing, and every insult a cry for help."

• Our second teacher of forgiveness focuses on what it means to be assured of the forgiveness of God. "God does not stop loving us every time we do something wrong and neither should we stop loving ourselves and each other for being less than perfect," writes Rabbi Harold S. Kushner in *How Good Do We Have to Be? A New Understanding of Guilt and Forgiveness*. Here the author of *When Bad Things Happen to Good People* asserts that being human, we can't be perfect, but we can keep struggling. Rather than condemning us for our mistakes, God uses forgiveness to encourage us to step freely into the future with the assurance that "we can grow and change and need not repeat the same mistakes again." Once we have experienced this kind of acceptance, we in turn can offer it to the other people in our lives.

VIDEOS

• *Cry, the Beloved Country,* the film version of Alan Paton's classic novel, makes an eloquent statement about the transformative power of forgiveness. Stephen Kumalo, an Anglican clergyman from a rural Zulu village, travels to Johannesburg, South Africa, to find his son, Absalom. The two have been estranged, and now he learns the boy is in prison for killing Arthur Jarvis, an idealistic white man known for his altruistic work with blacks. Although Absalom insists the shooting was an accident, Kumalo is filled with remorse and seeks out James Jarvis, the dead man's father, a rich white supremacist from their province.

James, meanwhile, has realized the extent to which he was in conflict with his son. Among Arthur's papers, he found a scathing indictment of his family's racism. He and Kumalo recognize the bond of sorrow and suffering they share and their mutual need for forgiveness. Back home, they meet again and reach out to each other in a moving example of reconciliation.

• Victor Hugo's *Les Misérables* is another classic novel about forgiveness. It has been made into a Broadway musical and several films, the most recent being director Bille August's emotionally affecting version.

Jean Valjean, just out of prison after serving 19 years, steals some silverware from a bishop who has given him dinner. Caught by the police, Valjean is stunned when the bishop not only forgives him but makes it possible for him to remain a free man. In gratitude, he goes on to lead an exemplary life, becoming the mayor of a small town and the benevolent head of a factory.

He is pursued, however, by Javert, a police officer who is so filled with self-hate that he can only hurt others. Offered absolution himself, he cannot accept it. This story explores the very real power of forgiveness to change lives for the better and, when refused or denied, for the worse.

• Sometimes forgiveness comes as a grace when we least expect it. *The Mission* is set in eighteenth-century South America where the Jesuits have established missions to the Guarani Indians. Mendoza, a former mercenary and slave trader, experiences a release from the sins of his past when he comes to work with the Indians he has hunted.

He and the other priests later discover the difficulty of modeling a life of love and forgiveness. The survival of the missions is threatened by the pragmatic needs of their religious order, the predatory racism of European settlers, and political pressures from the colonial powers. Eventually the priests must make choices of conscience in a world not unlike our own—one convulsed with power struggles, greed, and violence.

SPIRITUAL EXERCISES AND RITUALS

• In many Christian worship services, there is a point after the Confession of Sins prayer called Passing the Peace. One worshipper turns to another and says, "The peace of God be with you." The reply is "And with you also." Use this or another saying in your rituals to indicate both the forgiveness of God and mutual forgiveness.

● A New Year's (Rosh Hashanah) tradition in Judaism enacts the renewal of forgiveness. People go to a river, stream, or the ocean and throw clothes, stones, or bread crumbs into the water to symbolize the casting off of their faults and failings. Incorporate this or a similar ceremony into your celebration of the New Year, a birthday, or an anniversary.

PRAYER OR MANTRA

This prayer uses the familiar words (your choice of the version) from the prayer Jesus taught his disciples known as the Lord's Prayer.

Breathing in: Forgive us our errors/sins/trespasses . . .
Breathing out: as we forgive those who error/sin/trespass against us.

IMAGERY EXERCISE

"Climbing the Waterfall" is based in part on a scene in the film *The Mission*. The intention is to experience being forgiven.

Breathe out three times. See yourself standing before a majestic waterfall. Find a large rope sack and place inside it, one by one, all the burdens and distresses of your life for which you feel guilty. Now begin to climb the slippery rocks alongside the waterfall, pulling the sack containing your burdens, distresses, and guilts. Feel and sense the weight of the sack, the sharpness of the rocks under your feet, the cold spray of water on your face. Knowing that this climb is your choice, how do you feel?

On the rock ledges at the side of the waterfall, meet people you have wronged. Apologize to each one for what you have done and ask him or her for forgiveness. Greet them, one after another, no matter how they respond to you. Know that with each greeting, a burden is being released.

Breathe out one time. Reaching the top of the waterfall, enter into a rain forest, taking your sack of burdens, distresses, and guilts with you. Notice how the sack looks and feels now. At a clearing in the center of the forest, meet the being who finally removes the sack from you. As this being helps you bury the remains of the sack, know that you are forgiven. How do you feel?

When you are ready, open your eyes.

Journal Exercises

● Make a "confession of sins." In your journal list instances when you have hurt, betrayed, lied to, ignored, or used another being. Note times when you have failed to do the right thing and left good things undone. At the bottom of your list, add a prayer for forgiveness.

● Write a letter to someone who has died asking for forgiveness or expressing your forgiveness. Write another letter in the voice of this person back to you, agreeing to or acknowledging your request.

Discussion Questions, Storytelling, Sharing

● Tell the story of one of your most vivid experiences of forgiveness.

● Do you think repentance—an admission of wrongdoing, a sign of remorse, or a commitment to change—should be a prerequisite for forgiveness? Why or why not?

● Are any acts unforgivable? If you think so, give examples and explain.

Household, Group, and Community Projects

● The need to resolve conflicts and forgive each other becomes very evident in the close confines of a home. Without discussing a particular grievance, talk together about some ways you can facilitate forgiveness. Some couples, for example, don't let the sun go down on an argument. Others use rituals to reinforce a desire for reconciliation. Here is a good one from Ardath Rodale: Pull a weed to remove a grudge; then plant a seed to indicate the sprouting of new love in your heart.

● Groups also need to reinforce intimacy by practicing forgiveness. Sharon Salzberg reports that Buddhist teacher V. Pandita says at the closing ceremony of his retreats: "If I have hurt or harmed you in any way, either intentionally or unintentionally, I ask your forgiveness. And if you have hurt me in any way, intentionally or unintentionally, I forgive you." This is a good way to end any meeting.

● Be representatives of the practice of forgiveness in political discussions in your community. For example, investigate alternatives to jail for criminals. Work for the abolishment of the death penalty. As Sister Helen Prejean asserts: "People are more than the worst thing they have ever done in their life."

FICTION, POETRY, OR CHILDREN'S BOOK

Life can turn dark in the twinkling of an eye. In a spiritual emergency, one way to rebuild our characters is with the practice of forgiveness. These are themes of Anne Tyler's novel *Saint Maybe*.

In 1965 Baltimore, Ian Bedloe belongs to an "ideal, apple-pie household." He and his parents are surprised, then, when his older brother, Danny, decides to marry Lucy, a divorcée with two small children. One evening Ian, feeling pressed into too much baby-sitting, expresses in harsh and judgmental terms his doubts about Lucy's loyalty to Danny. The consequences are catastrophic and, over the years, Ian must go through the different seasons of forgiveness as he struggles to make peace with the past.

SPOKEN-WORD AUDIO

Seventy Times Seven: On the Spiritual Art of Forgiveness by Joan Borysenko explores the connections between this spiritual practice and wholeness using illustrative material from Christianity, Buddhism, and Taoism; case histories of spontaneous healing; and findings on mind/body interactions. Borysenko reveals that forgiveness of self and others leads to meaning, beauty, balance, and right relationship. She emphasizes that it is often a factor in the healing of illness and the achievement of emotional wellness.

ART

Rembrandt's painting *The Return of the Prodigal Son* captures the climactic moment in Jesus' parable (Luke 15:11–32). We feel the compassionate dimension of forgiveness in the father's gentle embrace of his wayward son. On the side, the elder son looks on, obviously displeased with this surprising display of unconditional love. Sometimes it is not easy to accept or tolerate forgiveness.

MUSIC

Music can intensify our emotional responses so that we experience a breakthrough to a different level of awareness. That is why it often helps to listen to sad songs when we feel depressed. And that is why *Threnody to the Victims of Hiroshima* by Krzysztof Penderecki is recommended for the practice of forgiveness. This song of mourning and lamentation realized through an avant-garde musical score is a jarring sound-world of strange chords, ominous crescendos, and startling breaks. The effect is cathartic, just what is needed to set the stage for forgiveness.

SEE ALSO:
Connections. Hope. Love. Openness. Peace. Shadow.

# GRACE

THE BASIC PRACTICE

Grace is a gift of God. Because it comes to us at God's initiative, there are some things we can't do about grace. We can't earn it. We can't control it. We don't have to deserve it.

If grace is out of your hands, so to speak, how do you engage in the spiritual practice of grace? Accept that you are accepted. Practice receiving. Receive objects, love, help. Notice when presents and presence come to you without your effort.

CATALYSTS, CONTRASTS, AND COMPANIONS

Grace confounds certain very natural human tendencies. We want to believe we are in control. We assume there are specific moves we can take to ensure that we are rewarded. We expect God's gifts to be doled out according to some recognizable plan.

But grace does not work that way. Instead, it teaches us to surrender to God. Not only are we not in charge, we don't have to be. We just need to stay open to receiving the sacred.

Receptivity, in turn, requires that we give up shame—those persistent feelings that we are unworthy, that we don't deserve all that we have, that we're not as good as people assume, that we've messed up, that our whole life is a mistake. Grace doesn't listen to that litany. It isn't based on a scorecard. Grace happens.

PERSPECTIVES

Grace can never be possessed but can only be received afresh again and again.
–RUDOLF BULTMANN

Grace overcomes shame, not by uncovering an overlooked cache of excellence in ourselves but simply by accepting us, the whole of us, with no regard to our beauty or our ugliness, our virtue or our vices. We are accepted wholesale. Accepted with no possibility of being rejected. Accepted once and accepted forever. Accepted at the ultimate depth of our being.
–LEWIS B. SMEDES

I am just learning to feel
That I do not have to actually catch God,
But that someday God will catch me
And pour into my heart
A flood of ineffable Delight.
–SRI CHINMOY

TEACHERS

This spiritual practice involves noticing the "gracelets" in our daily lives, those signs of God's presence that indeed feel like gifts. Two of the most astute practitioners of grace are Madeleine L'Engle and Frederick Buechner.

● Madeleine L'Engle is a Christian writer who has sprinkled her books with tributes to a gracious God. She is the author of many novels, children's books, essays, poetry, prayers, and meditations on the scriptures. In her autobiographies she has shared details of her life in a family (*The Summer of the Great-Grandmother*) and as a partner in a long marriage (*Two-Part Invention*).

Glimpses of Grace: Daily Thoughts and Reflections by Madeleine L'Engle with Carole F. Chase is a collection of 365 brief readings from this prolific writer's diverse works. Her interests in children, science, theology, family, ritual, and ecumenism are richly demonstrated here. The many graces of life are described in beautiful and reverent prose: the wonders of the natural world, the love in someone's eyes, the power of art, the riches of the imagination. Many things, she tells us, bear messages from the Divine. For example, "Bach's music points me to wholeness, a wholeness of body, mind, and spirit, which we seldom glimpse, but which we are intended to know. . . . It is a gift, sheer gift, waiting there to be recognized and received."

● Frederick Buechner, a Presbyterian minister, has published novels, essays, sermons, portraits of biblical characters, as well as two collections, organized as dictionaries, of brief redefinitions of religious terms. He has also completed three parts of his autobiography: *The Sacred Journey, Now & Then,* and *Telling Secrets.*

Here's how he describes this spiritual practice: "Grace is something you can never get but only be given. There's no way to earn it or deserve it or bring it about any more than you can deserve the taste of raspberries and cream or earn good looks or bring about your own birth. A good sleep is grace and so are dreams. Most tears are grace. The smell of rain is grace. Somebody loving you is grace. Loving somebody is grace. Have you ever *tried* to love somebody?"

Buechner can find hints of grace everywhere, especially in his own experiences. It's not surprising, then, that a collection of excerpts from his writings, organized with a reading for each day of the year, is called *Listening to Your Life.* It is as good a teaching tool for this spiritual practice as you are likely to find.

VIDEOS

- The film that most beautifully and profoundly reveals the meaning of grace is *Babette's Feast*. Based on a short story by Isak Dinesen, this film won the 1987 Academy Award for Best Foreign Language Film. The setting is Denmark in the late nineteenth century. Babette, a French woman who has had to flee Paris, is given sanctuary in the home of two sisters who preside over a small, austere religious sect and spend their days in acts of charity. Babette quickly settles into their modest lifestyle.

Years later, after winning the lottery, Babette asks permission to prepare a sumptuous meal for the community's celebration of their founder's birthday. The sisters agree but since they have renounced earthly pleasures, they worry about the temptations that might come with the extravagant meal. They and the other members of their group vow to eat and drink in silence. But an unexpected guest shows up that night, and he articulates their joy and surprise in Babette's feast. We are vessels of God's grace, one to another, especially when we love, give, and express ourselves creatively.

- "Friendship," according to John O'Donohue, "is the grace that warms and sweetens our lives." That certainly is the case in *Good Will Hunting*. Will, the emotionally troubled protagonist, is a 20-year-old townie who works as a janitor at M.I.T. in Boston. After a scrape with the law, he is taken under the wing of a professor of mathematics who has discovered that Will is a math whiz with a photographic memory. As part of his rehabilitation, he must see a therapist every week.

An interesting relationship develops between these two underachievers. Will, an orphan, has walled himself off from all but a few people. Sean McGuire, the therapist, is still recovering from the death of his wife. Gradually, they help each other heal. Will is also fortunate to have the love and support of both his best friend and a sexy, smart, and sensitive girlfriend.

Blessed with these nurturers of his soul, Will is able to find his place in the world. They see in him things he is not able to see in himself. To put it simply, they grace his life and help him move forward with self-confidence.

SPIRITUAL EXERCISES AND RITUALS

- Get in the habit of acknowledging moments of grace in your life. When something happens unexpectedly; when a reward comes to you without your having worked for it; when you receive an opportunity you think you do not deserve; when you recognize an insight or a person's appearance as a gift, say "That's a freebie."

• Create a ritual for a grace-filled time, such as when someone returns home from school, a trip, or a stay in the hospital. Sing hymns and read stories about grace. Have a grab bag filled with small wrapped gifts at the door.

PRAYER OR MANTRA

This mantra is in the form of three affirmations. It uses Frederick Buechner's definition of grace.

1. There's nothing *you* have to do.
2. There's nothing you *have* to do.
3. There's nothing you have to *do*.

IMAGERY EXERCISE

Denise Levertov's poem "The Avowal," which appears on page 252 in *Spiritual Literacy,* is one of our favorite descriptions of grace. Here is an exercise based on its images.

Breathe out three times. See yourself as a swimmer floating faceup in the water. Sense how the water holds you without your effort.

Breathe out one time. See yourself as a hawk soaring above the Earth. Sense how the air holds you without your effort.

Breathe out one time. See and sense yourself in free fall, floating into the Creator's deep embrace. Know that you are being surrounded by the light of grace. Then open your eyes.

JOURNAL EXERCISES

• Reflect upon this New Testament passage from I Peter 5:10: "The God of all grace . . . will restore, support, strengthen and establish you." Then write about experiences of divine grace when God has done one of these things for you.

• In addition to recognizing grace when it happens to us, we need to be a grace in other people's lives. Don Quixote puts it well at the end of the play *The Man of La Mancha*: "I just wanted to add a measure of grace to the world." Write about specific ways you have added, or could still add, a measure of grace to the world.

DISCUSSION QUESTIONS, STORYTELLING, SHARING

● Share a story about a time when you have felt accepted although you thought you were unacceptable. Or identify an unearned gift in your life.

● A real obstacle to grace is our refusal to accept the help of others. Recall a situation when you did not want to rely upon the goodwill of someone else. What was the source of your refusal?

HOUSEHOLD, GROUP, AND COMMUNITY PROJECTS

● Play "clue" in your house this week. Everyone pretends to be a detective looking for clues of God's grace. Remember that grace comes through people, places, events, things, animals, work, and so on. Share your findings over a meal at the end of the week.

● Communities as well as individuals are recipients of grace. Catholic priest Henri J. M. Nouwen, in fact, once called the church "the garden of God's grace." Often a community's rituals are intended to be vehicles of grace. Create an oral history of grace moments in the life of your group on audio- or videotape.

FICTION, POETRY, OR CHILDREN'S BOOK

Susan Howatch has written a series of six novels about the dynamics of sin and grace in the lives of clergy and lay members of the Church of England. They are *Glittering Images, Glamorous Powers, Ultimate Prizes, Scandalous Risks, Mystical Paths,* and *Absolute Truths.*

In the last one, the year is 1965 and Charles Ashworth is Bishop of Starbridge. His establishment faith and his prophetic sense of ministry are shattered by the death of his wife. Suddenly he is forced to square off with hatreds, passions, and ghosts he has kept under cover for years. This novel reveals how God's grace can work wonders when our lives are shaken at the roots.

SPOKEN-WORD AUDIO

Enduring Grace: The Lives of Six Women Mystics from the Age of Faith, a lively lecture on two cassettes by Carol Flinders, reclaims from the dust of history inspiring portraits of Saint Clare of Assisi, Mechthild of Magdeburg, Saint Catherine of Siena, Julian of Norwich, Saint Catherine of Genoa, and Saint Teresa of Avila as "midwives of the Spirit." These European Catholics used their personal experiences of God's grace to en-lighten and enrich the lives of others. Their spiritual practices encourage us to regard inwardness, suffering, forgiveness, prayer, and the expression of the deep self as avenues through which grace flows both into and out of us.

ART

In the exquisite paintings of Pierre-Auguste Renoir, we sense the beauty of grace—a world of presence and presents. *Dance at Bougival* shows a couple very much in love relishing the marvels of the moment. *Woman with a Parasol* centers on a bright-eyed woman who is clearly enjoying an afternoon's respite in the sun as her toddler explores the surprises in the tall grasses behind her. *In the Meadow* captures the glow of two girls who have stopped by a path to look at the flowers. And *A Shepherd Boy* depicts a true moment of grace as a youth relaxes in a garden of flowers and waits for a bird to perch on his finger.

MUSIC

The Shakers in America were known for the graceful lines of their beautifully crafted furniture, which reflected the simple lifestyle of these communities. One of their hymns speaks about recognizing the gifts of grace: "'Tis the gift to be simple, / 'Tis the gift to be free, / 'Tis the gift to come down where we ought to be." A wonderful instrumental elaboration on this tune occurs in American composer Aaron Copland's *Appalachian Spring*. It starts with the lilting, easily recognized phrase—grace arrives in the familiar. Then come the variations—first the strings, next the winds, then the full ensemble. All together now: simple gifts and many graces abounding.

SEE ALSO:
Faith. Gratitude. Hope. Hospitality. Love. X—The Mystery.

░ GRATITUDE ░

DAILY CUE, REMINDER, VOW, BLESSING

Picking up a spoon to eat a meal is my cue to practice gratitude.

•

Every time I walk in the door of my home, I am reminded to count my blessings.

•

On my birthday, I vow to practice gratitude during the next year.

•

Blessed is the Beneficent One who is deserving of our constant gratitude.

THE BASIC PRACTICE

The spiritual practice of gratitude has been called a state of mind and a way of life. But we prefer to think of it as a grammar—an underlying structure that helps us construct and make sense out of our lives. The rules of this grammar cover all our activities. Its syntax reveals a system of relationships linking us to the Divine and to every other part of the Creation.

To learn the grammar of gratitude, practice saying "thank you" for happy and challenging experiences, for people, animals, things, art, memories, dreams. Count your blessings and praise God. Utter blessings and express your appreciation to everything and everyone you encounter. By blessing, we are blessed.

CATALYSTS, CONTRASTS, AND COMPANIONS

The continuum of words related to gratitude go from greed and jealousy; through taking things for granted and feeling entitled; to appreciation, acceptance, and satisfaction. The practice of gratitude would be an appropriate prescription whichever one of these words describes your attitudes.

The rules of the grammar of gratitude are not as simple as they seem at first glance, however. For example, often instead of rejoicing in what we have, we greedily want something more, better, or different. We can't be grateful because we are making comparisons and coveting other possibilities.

When this happens on a personal level, when it's our ego that is dissatisfied, then we are ungrateful. But when we want something more, better, or different for the glory of God or for the benefit of the community, this greed may be a manifestation of our devotion, our love, or our yearning for justice. And then we are grateful for these commitments.

PERSPECTIVES

Whoever does not express his gratitude to people will never be able to be grateful to God.
–MUHAMMAD

Jewish tradition gives us a goal: We should say one hundred blessings each day. When we try it, we discover that it's quite difficult to find one hundred things each day for which to be thankful. So difficult, in fact, that we spend most of our time looking.
–DANNEL I. SCHWARTZ AND MARK HASS

Saying thank you is more than good manners. It is good spirituality.
–ALFRED PAINTER

TEACHERS

• The best teacher of gratitude is Brother David Steindl-Rast, a Benedictine monk and author of *Gratefulness: The Heart of Prayer*. This paperback captures and conveys the multiple meanings of this capacious spiritual practice. "Gratefulness," he says, "is the inner gesture of giving meaning to our life by receiving life as gift." It is a basic attitude that begins with surprise—the sight of a rainbow, perhaps, or a narrow escape from death—and opens the door to joy. It moves in circles; the giver of a gift becomes the receiver of thanks.

Being thankful to God involves waking up to the blessings all around us. Steindl-Rast sees gratitude as the linchpin of a devotional life that is animated by faith, lifted by hope, and nurtured by love. At the end of the book, he presents an alphabet of key concepts for a life of praise. "Thanksgiving," he concludes, "comes from the heart where we are rooted in universal belonging."

● Another teacher of gratitude is clinical psychologist Timothy Miller. In *How to Want What You Have: Discovering the Magic and Grandeur of Ordinary Experience,* he talks about why it is so difficult for most of us to break the habit of looking enviously at what others have and taking for granted what is already ours. Miller has found in the world's religious traditions three principles to help us be happy with what we have. The first is compassion, the second is attention, and the third and most important is gratitude. He defines it as "the intention to count your blessings every day, every minute, while avoiding, whenever possible, the belief that you need or deserve different circumstances." Miller has some concrete tips for evoking more gratitude in daily life, including a gratitude game (picking an unremarkable object in your immediate surroundings and seeing how it evokes gratitude) and identifying habitual nongrateful thinking and statements.

VIDEOS

● *Awakenings* is a quintessential film about the spiritual practice of gratitude. Dr. Sayer, a shy neurologist, administers a drug called L-dopa to a group of chronically institutionalized patients suffering from "postencephalitis syndrome," a kind of sleeping sickness that has turned them into living statues, conscious but not moving. One of them, Leonard, has been entombed in his body for 30 years. After receiving the drug, his rigidity vanishes. Now able to move, talk, and touch, he announces without bitterness: "I've been away for quite some time. . . . I'm back."

As we watch Leonard rejoice in his daily activities, we realize the precariousness and the preciousness of the physical sensations we too often take for granted. For a brief time, Leonard truly enjoys the multiple enchantments of the world. Not being similarly present in our living is an act of ingratitude.

● Movies often depict the tragic consequences of greed, envy, and jealousy—all obstacles to an attitude of thankfulness. One of the most powerful depictions of envy is *Amadeus*, a drama about the life of the great composer Wolfgang Amadeus Mozart. Antonio Salieri, an Austrian composer, becomes obsessed with Mozart's effortless creativity and fame. Although he is himself a gifted musician, envy makes it impossible for him to enjoy what he has and the genius he is witnessing.

SPIRITUAL EXERCISES AND RITUALS

● Reverse any tendency you have to make comparisons. Quit talking about what you don't have compared to what you have; stop whining about how you are doing careerwise, relationshipwise, or any otherwise in comparison to how a friend or enemy is doing. The next time you start chattering about wanting something more, better, or different, don't listen to yourself.

● Say grace before all your meals. An especially good source of thanksgiving prayers from different traditions is *100 Graces* collected by Marcia and Jack Kelly during their travels to monasteries, abbeys, and retreat centers in the United States.

● Short blessing prayers are acts of gratitude in many religious traditions. They convey our recognition that the Creator of the Universe is known through whatever is being blessed. They are also intended to call God's light and love to a person, place, creature, or object. Rabbi Lawrence Kushner elaborates: "With each blessing uttered we extend the boundaries of the sacred world and ritualize our love of life." Say as many blessings as you can every day.

PRAYER OR MANTRA

This breath prayer is from a poem by German poet Rainer Maria Rilke.

> Breathing in: To praise . . .
> Breathing out: is the whole thing.

IMAGERY EXERCISE

Some of our most profound experiences of gratitude occur when we find ourselves in a beautiful place in nature. This exercise is adapted from one offered by Belleruth Naparstek in her book *Your Sixth Sense: Unlocking the Power of Your Intuition.*

Settling fully into your body . . . as you take a nice, deep, full, cleansing breath . . . and breathing out as fully as possible . . . now imagining a place . . . preferably outdoors . . . where you feel safe and peaceful . . . and looking around you . . . feeling whatever you're sitting against or lying upon . . . and listening to the sounds of the place . . . and smelling its rich fragrance . . . And feeling your heart fill with gratitude for such stunning beauty . . . each beat of your heart drumming out its strong, steady gratitude . . . saluting all the beauty all around you . . . each beat pulsing out its thanks . . . resonating outward in slow and gentle waves . . . reaching into every corner of this place . . . offering a blessing . . . and feeling the place respond with its own powerful, loving pulse . . . answering you that you are welcome . . . back and forth . . . pulse to pulse perfectly synchronized . . . where the giver becomes the receiver . . . and the receiver becomes the source . . .

And so, whenever you are ready . . . you can very gently allow yourself back into the room . . . knowing in a deep place that you are better for this . . . And so you are.

JOURNAL EXERCISE

Keep a Daily Gratitude Journal. Every day before you go to bed, write down five things that you can be grateful for that day. In *Simple Abundance,* Sarah Ban Breathnach describes this journal exercise as a transformative process: "As the months pass and you fill your journal with blessings, an inner shift in your reality will occur."

DISCUSSION QUESTIONS, STORYTELLING, SHARING

● King Faisal of Saudi Arabia displayed a flask of petroleum on his desk with a card saying "Allah's Bounty." What would you put on your desk as a constant reminder of gratitude?

● Share a story about an experience that at first seemed unpleasant, negative, or even traumatic, which you came to understand as a blessing.

HOUSEHOLD, GROUP, AND COMMUNITY PROJECTS

● Create a Gratitude Calendar for use in your household's daily or Sabbath devotional observances. Set up a schedule of blessing emphases in a date book, perhaps having a different focus for each month: (1) People We've Known, (2) People We Do Not Know but Admire (living and dead), (3) Artists, (4) Service Providers, (5) Spiritual and Other Communities, (6) Our Bodies, (7) Places, (8) Animals, (9) Nature, (10) Food and Drink, (11) Things, (12) Opportunities.

● Identify creative ways to show your gratitude to God and the world. Send letters of appreciation to teachers or writers whose work has touched you. Make Gratitude Awards for excellent household service (to a cooking pot, the dishwasher, the telephone) or faithful companionship (to a pet, your car). Thank your body by giving your feet a massage or blessing your skin with moisterizing lotion. Show your gratitude for the gifts of nature by incorporating some of them—houseplants, leaves, acorns, rocks, sand—into a table centerpiece. Hold dedication ceremonies for your home, garden, or a project at work.

● Be a blessing by performing a service to a neighbor or a shut-in—doing a chore, running an errand, or delivering groceries.

● Extend your gratitude into your community. In appreciation for the good service of a grocery store, a cleaner's, or a gas station, tell your friends about the place so that the business can grow. To thank public servants and community activists, attend meetings and fund-raisers or volunteer to help in their offices.

FICTION, POETRY, OR CHILDREN'S BOOK

The Lively Garden Prayer Book by William Cleary is a bright and gladsome collection of poems in which plants, beetles, dogs, cats, worms, aphids, and many other beings sing their praises to the Great God of Sky and Earth. There's even room in this backyard theology for poison ivy, tics, weeds, dung, and the "maggot's magnificat." The blessings range from A (Acorn) to Z (Zucchini).

SPOKEN-WORD AUDIO

Many people return from near-death experiences with a deeper appreciation for what they have. On *A Year to Live*, Stephen Levine describes his experiment of living one year as if it were his last. He keeps a journal, inhabits his body in new ways, and squares off against some of the demons that dim his appreciation of life—fear, desire, and the need for control. Best of all, Levine uses the practice of gratitude to "sharpen life and soften death."

ART

French impressionist Claude Monet's series of paintings of the water-lily pond on his property are blessings of the natural world and blessings to viewers. The artist's gratitude for a special place seems to pulse through these scenes, embracing the water, the floating flowers, the reflected sky and clouds. Monet painted this water garden extensively during the last 30 years of his life, catching it in different seasons and times of day, his appreciation of its pleasures apparent in every brushstroke.

MUSIC

Since becoming a member of the Orthodox Church in 1977, British composer John Tavener has endeavored to use music to praise the Creator. He calls his *Akathist of Thanksgiving* "a musical ikon to the glory of God." An *akathist* in this tradition is a hymn of thanksgiving or supplication. Tavener uses poetry written in the 1940s by Archpriest Gregory Petrov shortly before his death in a Siberian prison camp. The 10 sections of the nearly 80-minute piece, scored for choir, countertenor and bass soloists, and a string orchestra, each contain a series of "Glory to you" statements: "for each step of my life, each instant of joy," "for the diamond sparkle of morning dew," "for surrounding us with thousands of your creations," "for revelations asleep and awake," and, the inspiration for the piece, from the dying words of Saint John Chrysostom, "Glory to you for everything."

SEE ALSO:

Attention. Beauty. Being Present. Connections. Joy. Zeal.

HOPE

DAILY CUE, REMINDER, VOW, BLESSING

Turning on a light is my cue to practice hope.

•

When I plant a seed or a bulb, I am reminded to plant hope
in my heart.

•

Whenever I meet people who are thrashing about in gloom and
doom, I vow to hold up the banner of hope.

•

Blessed is the Spirit of Life who births hope in our hearts and
positive attitudes in our minds.

THE BASIC PRACTICE

Hope is a positive and potent spiritual practice with the power to pull
us through difficult times. It is usually described with light metaphors—a
ray, a beam, a glimmer of hope; the break in the clouds; the light at the
end of the dark tunnel. It is often discovered in unexpected places.

Hope can be learned with practice. Certain attitudes support it. One
is patience, an ability to tolerate delays, a willingness to let events unfold
in their own time. Another is courage, an attitude of confidence even when
facing the unknown. A third is persistence, the determination to keep

going no matter what happens. We have hope when we can say "All will be well," and we mean it.

CATALYSTS, CONTRASTS, AND COMPANIONS

Hope is the basic ingredient of optimism, a tendency to dwell on the best possibilities. It is a frequent companion of another spiritual practice—enthusiasm. It, too, is energizing. The greeting "Be of good cheer" puts it well.

But a more common—and very telling expression—is "Hope for the best, but expect the worst." The more likely outcome, it implies, is the worst. When we are without hope, we easily fall victim to such negativism. When the light of hope is absent, we are overcome by gloom and doom, despair and defeatism.

In terms of personal style, without hope we are easily frustrated and quickly discouraged. We may lack the stamina and nerve to continue struggling against adversity. We are fainthearted. We really do expect the worst.

PERSPECTIVES

Never despair! Never!
It is forbidden to give up hope.
–REBBE NACHMAN OF BRESLOV

To be alive is to live in a state of hope. Hope is a precondition of our mental health. Hope is the scaffolding of our existence. Hope is a reassertion of our belief in the meaning of human life and in the sense of the universe.
–HENRYK SKOLIMOWSKI

Hope begins in the dark, the stubborn hope that if you just show up and try to do the right thing, the dawn will come. You wait and watch and work: you don't give up.
–ANNE LAMOTT

TEACHERS

• Hope is an invaluable asset for political, cultural, and religious leaders. One of its most articulate spokespersons is Vaclav Havel, the playwright and human rights activist who was elected president of the Czech Republic in 1973. *The Art of the Impossible: Politics as Morality in Practice* is a collection of 35 speeches given from 1990 to 1996.

For Havel, hope is an orientation of the spirit grounded in the conviction that events and actions have meaning, regardless of how they turn out. Even a state of hopelessness has value: "Perhaps one could never find sense in life without first experiencing its absurdity." In a speech in Paris, he recalls the times under communist rule when he and other dissidents cultivated patience—"waiting as a state of hope." It's a stance he believes belongs in the world of politics today and our technocratic civilization.

At the Future of Hope Conference in Hiroshima in 1995, Havel confesses that there were times when all he had worked for seemed unlikely to succeed and he asked himself, "Why don't you just give up on everything?" Then he would realize that hope is a state of mind, even when it is pinned to a specific goal. "The only thing that can explain the existence of genuine hope is humanity's profound and essentially archetypal certainty—that our life on this Earth is not just a random event among billions of other random cosmic events that will pass away without a trace, but that it is an integral component or link, however minuscule, in the great and mysterious order of Being."

● Jim Wallis, founding editor of *Sojourner's*, a Christian magazine, shares Havel's understanding of hope as an animating force in politics. In *The Soul of Politics*, he examines the new movement to link spirituality and politics. It includes religious support for nuclear disarmament, efforts to provide sanctuary for Central American refugees, and projects to create housing for the homeless. "Between impossibility and possibility," writes the author, "there is a door, the door of hope." Those seeking environmental justice, racial reconciliation, gender equality, and economic innovation have walked through this door of hope. Wallis beckons his readers to join them.

VIDEOS

● *Places in the Heart* is an emotionally affecting film about living with hope. It is set in a small Texas town during the 1930s. When Edna's husband, the sheriff, is killed, this vulnerable and passive woman is suddenly faced with the challenge of taking full responsibility for her life and her children's future. She hires Moze, a black itinerant worker, to plant and harvest a cotton crop on her 40-acre farm. She takes on Mr. Will, a blind man, as a boarder. This extended family is bonded together during a tornado and in the biggest challenge of all—harvesting the cotton in time to win the bonus prize for the first crop, money desperately needed to pay the farm's mortgage.

This is a story about struggling through adversity and being sustained by hope. The closing scene of *Places in the Heart* takes place in a church during a communion service. It demonstrates in a palpable way how the hope for a better life, one of inclusiveness and reconciliation, extends even beyond the grave.

• Hope as a positive and animating force that enables us to follow our dreams is the theme of *Shades of Fear*. When Gabriel Angel, a buoyant young black woman from Grenada, sets sail for England on an ocean liner, she carries with her the blessings of family and friends. Her plan to become an aviator makes her spirit soar. All those who meet her aboard the ship— including an art forger, a doctor, a missionary, and an art history professor—are affected by her exuberance, ardor, and optimism.

• "The first and last task of the leader is to keep hope alive," John Gardner, an astute observer of politics, has written. This asset is seen in the life and work of Nelson Mandela in *Mandela: Son of Africa, Father of a Nation,* the official film biography of the first democratically elected president of the racially united South Africa.

The Xhosa tribesman was trained to be a leader at Christian schools. He studied law in Johannesburg and helped found South Africa's first black law firm. He went on to become a forceful presence in the African National Conference (ANC), initiating nonviolent campaigns against the the country's policy of apartheid. When the ANC was banned, Mandela went underground and organized a nationwide strike. He was imprisoned by the government for 27 years. During that time Mandela continued to incubate hope for his fellow black Africans. This inspiring and edifying screen portrait celebrates Mandela as a freedom fighter and a bearer of hope.

SPIRITUAL EXERCISES AND RITUALS

• Write affirmations to express your hopes for yourself and a better world. The sacred texts from all traditions contain assurances that give rise to hope. For example, "All things work together for good for those who love God." "Even though I walk through the darkest valley, you are with me."

• Make positive, optimistic statements as often as possible. Be cheerful. This is not being a Pollyanna; it is leaving a door open to hope.

● In *Soul Between the Lines*, workshop leader Dorothy Randall Gray suggests the following personal ritual. Write a hope on a piece of paper, fold it up, and bury it beneath a houseplant. As the plant grows, envision your wishes growing as well.

● The word "hope" in Hebrew means "to twist, to twine around," like strands in a rope. Hold a "Rope of Hope" ceremony. Tie three strands of yarn or twine together and begin a braid to be passed around the circle. All participants add another section to the braid as they describe projects they are involved in to bring hope to the world. Then gather in a group and symbolically "throw" the rope as a lifeline to those who need it. Say a prayer thanking God for the opportunities to bring hope to the world.

Prayer or Mantra

One of your affirmations can be used as a mantra. This one serves as a reminder of the source of hope.

> Breathing in: Hope is . . .
> Breathing out: in God.

Imagery Exercise

Any attitude can be reinforced by working with the image that you attach to it. When you recall the image, you resurrect the feeling. Here are several exercises based on common images of hope. Do whichever one speaks to you or adapt the format to your own image of hope.

Close your eyes. Breathe out one time. See yourself in a long tunnel with nothing but darkness behind and ahead of you. Moving forward, see a dot of light in the distance, which is getting larger the closer you move toward it. Walk out of the tunnel through the light. Then open your eyes.

Close your eyes. Breathe out one time. See a plant blooming in the desert. Then open your eyes.

Close your eyes. Breathe out one time. Find yourself standing outside on a very cloudy day. Looking around you, notice how all the plants, buildings, and objects are becoming lighter and brighter. Look up and see the sun in a cloudless sky. Then open your eyes.

JOURNAL EXERCISES

• Quickly write a list beginning with "I hope for . . ." Do a second list beginning with "I have hope in . . ." Try writing with your nondominant hand to access your less expressed feelings.

• The Chinese have a saying, "If you keep a green bough in your heart, surely the singing bird will come." How and where can you make a place for hope in your life? Describe specific opportunities.

• Write a reflection on the ways you have been a life-bringer and a bearer of hope to your family, friends, or community.

DISCUSSION QUESTIONS, STORYTELLING, SHARING

• Describe a situation when hope pulled you through.

• What do you think people mean when they say "Don't get your hopes up too high?" What would be a good response to this advice?

• Does the prospect of the future fill you with anxiety or hope? Talk about the people and the events that have contributed to your feelings.

HOUSEHOLD, GROUP, AND COMMUNITY PROJECTS

• Hold a family or household council to talk about your attitudes toward the future. Identify people who have nurtured your optimism. Then find ways to honor these mentors of hope—writing letters, adding their pictures to a household shrine, or making a contribution to an organization in their names.

• Practice patience within your group. Do not hesitate to table discussions or postpone decision making, especially if some of those present need more time to consider options. Periodically have an unstructured business meeting—with no outside time limits—and allow people to speak as long as they want.

• Plant trees. Many people plant trees in whose shade they will never sit during their lifetimes. This act reflects confidence and hope in the future.

FICTION, POETRY, OR CHILDREN'S BOOK

Barbara Kingsolver's novel *Animal Dreams* is about a woman named Codi who after 15 years of wandering returns to Grace, Arizona, to look after her widowed father, who is in the first stages of Alzheimer's disease. She takes a job teaching high school biology and resumes a relationship with Loyd, a Native American she dated as a teenager.

Codi is trying to figure out what to do with her life, and she has a suspicion that what she does will determine who she is. She wonders if she can be like her idealistic younger sister, Hallie, who is helping poor farmers in Nicaragua. In a letter, she says to Codi: "The very least you can do is to figure out what you hope for. And the most you can do is live inside that hope. Not admire it from a distance, but live right in it, under its roof."

For Codi, this happens when she and her students discover that a mining company has not only polluted the town river but is planning another ecologically disastrous move that will have dire effects on the community. Working with a ladies' sewing club, she finds a cause worthy of her commitment.

SPOKEN-WORD AUDIO

To keep hope alive in our communities, we need to be persistent and practice patience. This is what we learn from the example of Melody Ermachild Chavis. She is a Buddhist, a writer, and a private investigator who works on trials and appeals for death-row inmates. On *Starting in Your Own Backyard* she talks with New Dimensions Radio host Michael Toms about projects in her crime-ridden neighborhood designed to make it a better and a safer place. When a young man was shot to death outside her home, she made a shrine for him and later participated in a grieving ritual for those killed in the local drug wars. She describes a volunteer gardening project for African-American youth and a vigil held outside a gun store for all victims of violence. This courageous and compassionate woman holds the hope banner high.

ART

Ken Kiff's extraordinary *Flower and Black Sky* is a paean to the up-lifting power of hope. In a bleak and overcast world, a dying tree and a pale rock stand next to a single glowing flower that is radiantly alive. This startling image makes the heart sing!

MUSIC

Rock music is basically a hopeful medium, despite all the lyrics about personal woes and the messes and miseries of the world. When we need a boost, nothing is quite as effective as putting on a pounding rock song and joining in the defiant and hopeful chorus. To see what we mean, listen to these anthems of hope: "I Can See Clearly Now" by Johnny Nash,

"You Can Make It If You Try" by Sly and the Family Stone, "I Shall Be Released" by Bob Dylan, and "I Will Survive" by Gloria Gaynor.

SEE ALSO:

Connections. Faith. Forgiveness. Grace. Imagination. Love. Vision.

HOSPITALITY

Daily Cue, Reminder, Vow, Blessing

The sight of a welcome mat is a cue for me to extend hospitality to someone today.

•

When I see the hosts of a party looking after the needs of their guests, I am reminded of the graciousness of hospitality.

•

Whenever I pass a house of worship, I vow to practice hospitality toward different spiritual paths.

•

Blessed is the Eternal Womb who encourages us to be welcoming to all.

The Basic Practice

We are practicing hospitality when we welcome guests—including strangers and enemies—into our lives with graciousness. An open house reveals certain things about us: We are well disposed toward others, we focus on the positive, and we believe the universe is basically a friendly place. Sometimes hospitality requires that we cross boundaries and dismantle some of the barriers erected in our society to keep "the other" out. Sometimes it means entertaining ideas that might be alien to us.

To be hospitable, you need to accept pluralism as a natural condition in the world. Celebrate the diversity of the Creation. One particularly valuable spin-off of hospitality is interreligious dialogue. Spirit speaks in many languages, and this spiritual practice helps us receive these multiple messages.

CATALYSTS, CONTRASTS, AND COMPANIONS

Hospitality and hostility are both derived from the same root word—but they couldn't be more different. Whereas hospitality is about welcoming all, hostility thrives on insider/outsider conflicts. Practice the former to increase your tolerance of the various groups in our society and their distinctive lifestyles.

On an interpersonal level, hospitality is a good prescription to balance a tendency to be critical of and unaccommodating to others. People who are distrustful of the world, who become fearful and paranoid when strangers approach, or who are suspicious of ideas unlike their own will also benefit from this practice.

PERSPECTIVES

The German word for hospitality is Gastfreundschaft, which means friendship for the guest. . . . It means the creation of a free space where the stranger can enter and become a friend instead of an enemy.
–HENRI J. M. NOUWEN

I believe this is why truly spiritual people are in the habit of cultivating the nearly forgotten art of basic hospitality, perhaps because they realize that when we are able to make others feel comfortable, the pleasures of belonging are close at hand.
–PHILIP L. BERMAN

I welcome every creature of the world with grace.
–HILDEGARD OF BINGEN

TEACHERS

• Hospitality on the spiritual journey means staying open to the insights of the world's religions, traditions with which you are familiar and ones that at first might seem strange. Diana Eck is a good exemplar of this practice. She is a Harvard professor of comparative religions and Indian studies who has been active in the interfaith dialogue program at the World Council of Churches for 15 years. She is convinced that her encounters with people of other faiths have challenged, changed, and deepened her Christianity. Her book *Encountering God: A Spiritual Journey from Bozeman to Banaras* traces this process.

Eck grew up a Methodist in Bozeman, Montana. Experiences with Hindus in India helped her come to a richer appreciation of God, everyday spirituality, and the Holy Spirit. Jesus' hospitality and his aversion to exclusivism make up the cornerstone of Eck's belief in pluralism, which, as she puts it, does not mean giving up our commitments but opening them up to the challenges of mutual discovery, understanding, and transformation. "The pluralist accepts the fact that many voices will speak in the exploration of religious truth, each in its own terms, trusting the encounter of real dialogue to reach a deeper understanding of one another's faith and of our own."

• Judith A. Berling, professor of History of Religions at the Graduate Theological Union, Berkeley, studied the ancient tradition of religious diversity and hospitality in China. *A Pilgrim in Chinese Culture: Negotiating Religious Diversity* explores how Confucianism, Taoism, Buddhism, and animism are able to coexist and even sustain "mutual familiarity and regular interaction." Berling appreciates the Chinese ability to maintain multiple levels of faith and many streams of practice. Chinese towns, for example, have communitywide religious festivals. Individuals often incorporate elements of different traditions into their devotional lives. "All paths," she writes, "help the faithful in their spiritual progress."

VIDEOS

• *Antonia's Line* won the Academy Award for Best Foreign Language Film in 1996. On the last day of her life, an elderly Antonia recalls the time shortly after World War II when she returned with her daughter, Danielle, to the farm and village she had left as a girl. With great authority and generosity, she befriends a recluse, takes in the village simpleton, and provides a home for a retarded young woman who has been raped by a brother. Danielle, a painter, decides to have a baby without a husband and, years later, falls in love with daughter Therese's female tutor who also comes to live at the farm. Therese grows up to become a scholar, finds a maternal husband, and bears a daughter she names Sarah.

This film has been called a feminist fairy tale for its emphasis on the value of female friendships, independence, intuition, and solidarity. But its main theme crosses gender lines. Antonia is a great role model for the spiritual practice of hospitality. No wonder so many of the scenes in the movie take place around a very large dinner table.

• One of the best exemplars of spiritual hospitality in the twentieth century is Father Bede Griffiths. *A Human Search: The Life of Father Bede Griffiths* is a 60-minute profile of this Christian mystic filmed at the ashram he founded in southern India. The pathfinding Benedictine monk talks about his middle-class upbringing in England, his intellectual pursuits at Oxford, his experiment with communal living, and his 25 years as a monk. He relates how he was drawn to the Sacred Feminine after he had a heart attack.

For Father Bede, there are no boundaries, only new horizons on his spiritual journey. He is most interested in what the religions have in common, a respect evident in the ashram's rituals. The story of his life as a scholar, community leader, teacher, and mystic brings together the polarities of East and West, intuition and reason, heart and mind, female and male. His human search has much to teach us about the bounties and rewards of hospitality.

SPIRITUAL EXERCISES AND RITUALS

• Adopt a greeting gesture that conveys hospitality. In a Buddhist culture, you might be greeted by people putting their hands together, bowing, and saying "Namaste," which means "the god within me salutes the god within you." Some Arabs sprinkle salt, which cleanses and purifies, before strangers to signal goodwill toward them.

• Visit the religious service of a faith community other than your own. Jewish Lights has published two volumes on *How to Be a Perfect Stranger: A Guide to Etiquette in Other People's Religious Ceremonies.* They provide insights into the practices of 37 religious groups and denominations in the United States, including information on what happens during a worship service, what to wear, when to arrive and leave, who officiates, and what ritual objects and books are used.

• Host an interreligious festival at your congregation. Some activities you might consider: panel discussion among local religious leaders, an exhibit of art from different traditions, reading of sacred poetry and literature, demonstrations of religious dances and other activities.

PRAYER OR MANTRA

Mechtild of Magdeburg, a thirteenth-century mystic, once asked, "How shall we live?" This hospitality mantra is based on her answer.

Be welcoming to all.

IMAGERY EXERCISE

Rumi, in a poem included in *The Essential Rumi*, translated by Coleman Barks, gives us one of the images for this exercise: "This being human is a guest house. / Every morning is a new arrival. / A joy, a depression, a meanness, / some momentary awareness comes / as an unexpected visitor. / Welcome and entertain them all!" The Letter to the Hebrews (13:2) in the New Testament contains the same advice: "Do not neglect to show hospitality to strangers, for thereby some have entertained angels unawares." The intention of this exercise, "Welcoming," is to experience hospitality.

Close your eyes. Breathe out three long, slow exhalations.

Hearing a knock on the door of your house, see yourself going quickly to answer it and, without hesitating, opening the door and inviting whoever or whatever is there to come in. Who is your guest? What is your guest doing and saying? Sense and feel how you are welcoming your guest, even if he or she is not expected or acceptable to you.

Breathe out three times. See yourself sitting at your dinner table with all the seats being filled by strangers—people and other beings. Eating your meal, know that you are entertaining angels. What happens and how do you feel?

When you are ready, open your eyes.

JOURNAL EXERCISES

● Write a memory of a time when you were welcomed into somebody's home. What did your hosts do to make you feel at ease? Then reflect upon how you can be hospitable in other settings, such as at work or in your community.

● Write a memory of a time when a group to which you belonged excluded someone from membership because they were different. How do you feel about this action?

DISCUSSION QUESTIONS, STORYTELLING, SHARING

● As an ice-breaker at the next meeting, go quickly around the circle, each answering these questions: Are you a better guest or host? Which would you rather be?

● Asked to identify the most important question in life, Albert Einstein said, "Is the universe a friendly place or not?" On a scale of 1 to 10, rank the universe's friendliness. Then talk about how your assessment might influence your practice of hospitality.

● Tell a story about an encounter with another religion—a conversation with a believer, a visit to a sacred site, attendance at a ritual, or use of a practice—and what you learned from the experience.

HOUSEHOLD, GROUP, AND COMMUNITY PROJECTS

● Sharing a meal is a traditional way of extending hospitality. Make having people in for dinner a regular event in your household. Try to invite someone you don't know very well each time.

● Practice hospitality with the next video you rent. Set aside any tendency to criticize, any need to give a "thumbs up/thumbs down" response or to set standards for the acting and directing. Befriend the film, entrusting yourself to its images. Afterward, talk about what you have learned from this approach.

● Volunteer to be part of a welcome wagon project in your community. If none exists, work with your neighbors to produce an introduction to the community, illustrating it with pictures of special places.

● Find out what you can do to support the work of community organizations that are providing food, shelter, and legal and financial assistance to homeless people, immigrants, and refugees. Don't overlook the groups that are responding to international crises, such as the International Rescue Committee and Doctors Without Borders.

FICTION, POETRY, OR CHILDREN'S BOOK

The Holy Man by Susan Trott revolves around Joe, a 72-year-old teacher who resides in a "no-frills monastery." Pilgrims wait patiently in line outside his door to see him. His favorite bit of wisdom is: "If you look on everyone you meet as a holy person, you will be happy." Joe's Zen-like approach enables an angry man to befriend his temper; a grieving man, his possessiveness; and a persecuted woman, her dependence on an enemy. Joe is a world-class teacher of hospitality.

SPOKEN-WORD AUDIO

Huston Smith's *Religions of the World*, a 10-cassette audio retreat, is a substantive and completely accessible guide to the wisdom traditions of Hinduism, Buddhism, Confucianism, Taoism, Judaism, Christianity, Islam, and primal religions. The sagacious scholar, teacher, and author, who was born in China over 80 years ago to missionary parents, begins by relating how he came to practice hospitality toward different religions. Using stories, examples from sacred texts, and precise explanations, he discusses the six pillars of life that science cannot touch, the common aspects of the great traditions, four features of mystical experience, the remarkable similarities between Buddhism and Christianity, the allure of primal religions, and Confucianism's insightful perceptions of human relationships, among many other topics. Smith is a one-man interreligious dialogue.

ART

Louise Nevelson's environmental sculptures demonstrate hospitality in her choice of materials. She worked with found objects, what others might even call junk—furniture factory waste, chair legs, discarded duck decoys, lettuce crates, toilet seats, milk boxes. Her best-known pieces are large sculptural walls, such as the *Sky Cathedrals,* consisting of assemblages of boxes filled with wooden ornaments and these found objects.

MUSIC

John Cage was one of America's most influential composers. His merging of Western and Eastern traditions made him a pioneer of avant-garde music. He was very interested in chance, constructing his scores by using coin tosses and other indeterminate techniques. In other words, Cage was a master of hospitality—constantly opening his compositions and performances to what is, without trying to control them. For an example of this, check out his 1952 piece titled *4' 33"* which has no sound other than that of the environment in which it is performed. Music is going on all around us, but we won't notice it until we become more hospitable.

SEE ALSO:

Connections. Imagination. Openness. Nurturing. Unity.
X—The Mystery.

IMAGINATION

THE BASIC PRACTICE

In the spiritual life, imagination has two meanings. First, it is a human faculty—the part of us that traffics in images, symbols, myths, and stories. It is the capacity we all have for innovative thinking and creative expression. Second, the imagination is an inner reality, a boundless realm not defined by our senses or reason that we know from our dreams and can enter via certain exercises while awake. The practice of imagination encourages us to use this faculty and enables us to explore the realm.

Begin by learning the language of imagination. Keep track of the images that come to you spontaneously in association with your feelings and thoughts. Draw pictures of what you encounter in your dreams. Contemplate art and see yourself as part of the picture. Read myths and tell stories. Remember, through the ages spiritual pilgrims have found that it is possible to step into the inner realm of imagination. There you can find fuel for your journey and gifts of wisdom.

CATALYSTS, CONTRASTS, AND COMPANIONS

"You're just imagining that. It's not real." Unfortunately, many people associate imagination with "imaginary" and its connotation of "unreal." This is a difficult spiritual practice for those who think that everything has to be verified by sensory perception and empirical evidence. Reason also gets in the way of imagination, especially when it is codified into rationalism, which regards only logic and analytical thought as valid routes to truth.

When we discount the imagination, we cut ourselves off from the riches that can fuel our creativity. We limit the ways we can view the world and our own experience. There is much more to life than can be contained in a rational philosophy.

PERSPECTIVES

Imagination is more important than knowledge.
–ALBERT EINSTEIN

It is the imagination that gives shape to the universe.
–BARRY LOPEZ

Where the imagination is awake and alive, fact never hardens or closes but remains open, inviting you to new thresholds of possibility and creativity.
–JOHN O'DONOHUE

TEACHER

The soul, which thrives on images, is manifested in the imagination. This is the best practice, then, to consider contemporary discussions on the soul. The premier writer on this subject, and our teacher of imagination, is Thomas Moore. He has been a monk in a Catholic order and a therapist. In a trilogy of best-selling books, he has mapped out how we can care for our souls through the practice of imagination. "We tend to consider imagination too lightly," Moore writes, "forgetting that the life we make, for ourselves individually and for the world as a whole, is shaped and limited only by the perimeters of our imagination. Things are as we imagine them to be, as we imagine them into existence."

In *Care of the Soul: A Guide for Cultivating Depth and Sacredness in Everyday Life*, Moore presents an adventuresome meditation upon the sacred art of soulful living. One way of practicing imagination is reframing—seeing common experiences from a different perspective. Moore is a master at this, as he demonstrates by explaining what we can learn from our troubles, tragedies, follies, and feelings, including difficult ones such as jealousy and envy. He makes keen observations on the messages in mythology, psychology, philosophy, art, and the world's religions. He recommends paying attention to dreams, the "royal road to soul," and using storytelling to process the raw material of our lives.

In *Soul Mates: Honoring the Mysteries of Love and Relationship*, Moore assesses love, marriage, family, friendship, and community. He opens by stating "It's my conviction that slight shifts in imagination have more impact on living than major efforts at change." We can enrich our relationships by using imagination in our assessments of their different cycles, moods, transitions, and rhythms. For example, we can consider our personal mythology of love and acknowledge its sources in books, movies, art, and the experiences of our friends.

The Re-enchantment of Everyday Life is the most personal and practical of Moore's trilogy. He pinpoints imagination, magic, play, and mystery as wands that can renew and restore both our private and public lives. He offers us a passport to enchantment where nature is a teacher, our homes deliver sensuous pleasures, local spirits of neighborhood fuel our desire, and dreaming, music, and art take us beyond ourselves. Moore also revisions work and politics by rooting them in caring. In numerous small ways, he teaches us how to put imagination before information.

VIDEOS

● Two fruits of imagination are creativity and invention. In *Fly Away Home*, 13-year-old Amy comes to live with her estranged father, an artist/inventor, after her mother dies in an accident. At first distant and moody, Amy changes dramatically when she finds an abandoned nest of goose eggs and decides to raise the geese. She then realizes that they have to be taught to fly and how to migrate south for the winter. Amy and those who love her invent a way to carry out this daunting responsibility.

This story is based on actual experiments being conducted to change bird migration paths when their traditional routes and habitats have been destroyed. It is an example of using the imagination to create a better future for some of God's creatures.

● Two other movies are about journeys to the realm of imagination. *The Last Wave,* directed by Peter Weir, is about a lawyer in Sydney, Australia, who takes on a strange case involving the death of an Aborigine. Troubled by vivid dreams, this rational man soon finds himself attracted to the Aboriginal concept of the Dreamtime. This engrossing film demonstrates how the imaginal realm can affect waking life.

● In *House of Cards,* young Sally stops speaking after her father is killed while doing research at a Mexican ruin. A Mayan friend assures her: "People don't die. They go from one home to another." Upon returning with her family to the United States, Sally retreats to the imaginal world. One night her mother finds her sitting in the center of an elaborate house made of playing cards, pictures of the family, and Tarot cards. She recognizes that Sally is communicating through these images. Later, this concerned mother goes so far as to construct a model of the house of cards on their property, signaling her awareness that the realm where Sally has gone is as real as the empirical world of her brother and her doctor. Eventually, she even joins her daughter in a dream sequence. This extraordinary film shows deep respect for the imagination and spirituality of children.

SPIRITUAL EXERCISES AND RITUALS

● Devote an hour or two this week to gazing at clouds. Look for images in the formations—faces, animals, trails, buildings. Let your imagination roam! Also try cloud gazing with a companion. This exercise demonstrates the breath of the imagination, as two people rarely see the same things in the heavens.

● In ancient China, it was said that it takes two to create a masterpiece: an artist who imagines something beautiful and a person who appreciates it. Do your part in creating a masterpiece.

PRAYER OR MANTRA

This phrase from Bede Griffiths points to the boundlessness of the imagination.

Breathing in: You must . . .
Breathing out: go beyond.

IMAGERY EXERCISE

Several simple exercises can help you develop your ability to image and explore the inner realm of the imagination. Some people find that reporting to another person—a designated guide for the journey—helps them focus on images and ignore the rational thought intrusions that can disrupt the process. Here is a simple way to practice.

See yourself in a meadow, at the seashore, in a forest, or on a mountaintop ledge. Describe the view in front of you. Turn and continue describing until you have made a complete rotation. Notice where the sun is in the scene (if it is daytime). Describe what you are wearing and how you are feeling.

To expand the exercise, you might find yourself at the entrance to a cave, a garden, a chapel, or a temple. Go inside and describe what you find there.

JOURNAL EXERCISE

Keep a dream journal. People in all places and religious traditions have looked to dreams for spiritual insight and guidance. For good examples, see *Spiritual Dreaming: A Cross-Cultural and Historical Journey*, in which Kelly Bulkeley has gathered more than 200 dreams from Hinduism, Buddhism, Christianity, Islam, and Native American traditions. She covers a lot of thematic ground with dreams on snakes, flying, prophecy, conversions, creativity, and healing.

Use your regular journal or a special one reserved just for dreams. As you prepare for bed, date the page to signal your dreaming self that you welcome the images and insights from your imagination. You may also address a question or express a concern to your dream source by writing it on the page.

Record your night dreams as soon as possible after waking. On the left side of the page, write a narrative of what happens during the dream. On the right side, draw any images from the dream that strike you as significant. Over time, watch for recurring themes and images. Try to read what they are revealing about your life and the possibilities open to you. Look for answers to any special requests you have made.

DISCUSSION QUESTIONS, STORYTELLING, SHARING

• Go around the circle and have everyone name his or her favorite story or myth. How has this sample of the imagination enriched your life?

• Generations of people have grown up in environments hostile to the imagination. Share your personal experience, covering the role of imagination in your childhood, at home, in school, or in a religious community. What do you think can be done today to advance the cause of the imagination?

HOUSEHOLD, GROUP, AND COMMUNITY PROJECTS

• Creating a story in the home is one way to increase appreciation for imagination. Begin with "Once upon a time . . ." and see what comes next as you go around the dinner table or take turns at the computer. Make up tales about your ancestors as you look at old family photographs. Visit a historical site in your area; imagine what its people were like years ago. Go to an art or photography gallery; pick out a beautiful scene and imagine what it would be like to be there.

• The lives of artists revealed on video or in biographies, memoirs, and autobiographies show us the kind of determination and support needed to sustain our inner artist. Sponsor a film festival or a book reading about the creative life; invite artists in your community to serve on a panel afterward to answer questions from the audience.

• Volunteer to be a storyteller or reader at the local library, bookstore, hospital, senior center, church, synagogue, or other community center.

FICTION, POETRY, OR CHILDREN'S BOOK

The Famished Road won the prestigious 1991 Booker Prize for Nigerian poet and short-story writer Ben Okri. This novel is a spellbinding trip into the alternate reality of the imaginal realm. The main character, Azaro, is a "spirit child" living in an African village. He is subject to visions and hallucinations. Angels and demons buzz around him wherever he goes. He dreams and takes dangerous journeys on behalf of the suffering people in his village.

SPOKEN-WORD AUDIO

Living the Creative Life with M. C. Richards is an interview from New Dimensions Radio with a woman who knows a great deal about imagination. At age 80, she looks back on her experiences as a teacher at Black Mountain College, an innovator in higher education during the 1950s, and a resident at Camphill, a biodynamic farming community. Richards's creativity has infused everything she's done as a lifelong learner, a teacher, a potter, a painter, a poet, and a writer.

ART

Illustrated card decks are used by many people as a means of getting feedback from their inner world. These systems are also great ways to exercise the imagination. The 22 cards in the Major Arcana of the Tarot, for example, tell the story of the soul's journey to wholeness. To use cards to practice imagination, lay out all the cards in order and try telling the story they depict in your own words. Or choose just a few cards and allow their symbols to speak to you. After working with the images yourself, you may want to refer to books, usually packaged with the cards, that give their traditional meanings. Especially recommended card systems are *The Shining Woman Tarot* by Rachel Pollack, *The Haindl Tarot* by Hermann Haindl, *Motherpeace Round Tarot* by Karen Vogel, *The Celtic Book of the Dead* by Caitlin Matthews, and *Soul Cards* by Deborah Koff-Chapin.

MUSIC

"Imagine" is one of the most popular ballads John Lennon ever wrote. He asks us to see a world where people live in peace and share what they have with one another. The song connects us to all others who share this dream. Imagination, it asserts, is where our work for a better world begins.

SEE ALSO:
Beauty. Hope. Meaning. Vision. Wonder. X—The Mystery. Yearning.

 JOY

THE BASIC PRACTICE

Joy is an essential spiritual practice growing out of beauty, faith, grace, gratitude, hope, and love. It is the pure and simple delight in being alive. Joy is our elated response to feelings of happiness, experiences of pleasure, and awareness of abundance. It is also the deep satisfaction we know when we are able to serve others and be glad for their good fortune.

Invite joy into your life by staging celebrations. Host festivities to mark transitions and changes in your life. Toast moments of happiness you notice as you go through your day. Dance—jump for joy—as often as possible. Life is not meant to be endured; it is to be enjoyed.

CATALYSTS, CONTRASTS, AND COMPANIONS

We often talk about this spiritual practice in the same breath with its companions. We say joy and sorrow, happiness and sadness, smiles and tears, the ecstasy and the agony. The experience of one intensifies our awareness of the other. Sorrow, for example, may be the price we pay for joy; when we have known great happiness in a relationship, we feel its loss more deeply. Or think of those times when you laugh so hard you cry.

Joy usually will be part of a set of symptoms presenting in your life. The best protocol is to be thankful for the intensity of these feelings. When you are experiencing sorrow and sadness, when the tears are flowing, remember they can be stepping-stones to joy.

PERSPECTIVES

From joy I came,
For joy I live,
And in Thy sacred joy
I shall melt again.
–PARAMAHAMSA YOGĀNANDA

As you go through the day, become a spy in the kingdom of joy. Look for signs that strangers you meet are enjoying themselves, and actually or vicariously join them.
–SAM KEEN

Whatever joy there is in this world, all comes from wanting others to be happy.
–SANTIDEVA

TEACHERS

● The Jewish mystical tradition is our teacher of this spiritual practice. In *Finding Joy: A Practical Spiritual Guide to Happiness,* Dannel Schwartz, the spiritual leader of Temple Shir Shalom in Michigan, and Mark Hass, a journalist, apply the core concepts of Jewish mysticism to the modern quest for joy. The mystics understand a simple truth: "Happiness is to be treasured and welcomed into every life." Schwartz and Hass take that to mean that "making life more fulfilling and enjoyable is the basis of any spiritual formula for living." Using illustrative material from rabbinic teachers, Talmudic thinkers, proverbs, and contemporary celebrities, they show how happiness stems from using positive emotions, minimizing obstacles, expressing gratitude, following our dreams, setting goals, and waiting for opportunities. Joy is a deep-down satisfaction that comes from "collaborating with God in our destiny."

Schwartz and Hass emphasize again and again that joy is achievable, no matter what our problems may be, by taking specific steps. At the end of each chapter are "Exercises for the Soul" designed to help you come closer to happiness. For example: "Turn a negative into a positive. Place an audiotape that you especially like in your car, so that if you get stuck in traffic you can listen and enjoy it while you wait."

● Matthew Fox, a contemporary mystic, also emphasizes the primacy of joy in the spiritual life. *In the Beginning There Was Joy* is a jubilant book for children of all ages written by Fox and filled with gorgeous full-color illustrations by Jane Tattersfield. Wisdom and her maker—a.k.a. Mr. and Mrs. Joy—decide to create Boy Joy and Girl Joy in their own image but only after they have first created a universe of Light, a Temple of Joys (filled with everything from tiny atoms to galaxies), and a place to delight in (Earth). "Joy is your heritage," they tell the new humans, and with it comes beauty, creativity, grace, justice, diversity, play, and the arts. This bright and festive book is a unique tribute to the spiritual practice of joy.

● Dance is an expression of joy, according to Gabrielle Roth, an internationally acclaimed movement and theater artist. In *Sweat Your Prayers: Movement as Spiritual Practice,* she writes: "The more you dance, the more you sweat. The more you sweat, the more you pray. The more you pray, the closer you come to ecstasy." She identifies five major rhythms that draw out the dancer within all of us. Roth's stories, travels, and workshop experiences testify to the benefits of surrendering to "the wild, ecstatic embrace of dance."

VIDEOS

● At the heart of Shakespeare's comedies is a heightened vitality. That is certainly true in Kenneth Branaugh's lively screen version of *Much Ado About Nothing.* This movie exudes joy.

Don Pedro and his officers return from war and enter the governor's villa as if it were paradise on Earth. Love is in the air for two couples in particular. Young Claudio and Hero seem destined for each other but are pulled apart by treachery. Benedick and Beatrice bicker and argue against marriage until they are tricked into confessing their feelings for each other.

Some of the most joyous occasions in our lives are organized around occasions such as birthday parties and weddings. This movie concludes with just such a festive event—a marriage dance that goes on and on and on. Despite all the treachery and trickery, love triumphs in the end, and the joy evident on the screen is its strongest testimony.

● Joy is especially treasured following a period when one of its companions—deep sorrow, grief, or pain—has dominated our lives. In *Truly, Madly, Deeply,* Nina is an accomplished interpreter who lives alone in a dilapidated flat in London. She is distraught over the sudden death of her lover, Jamie, a cellist. She just can't get him out of her thoughts. Then one night he appears in her flat as a ghost with a body. She exuberantly accepts this miracle. But gradually he wears out his welcome by changing her living room furniture around and inviting his friends from the other world over for evenings watching videos of old movies. By the time Nina meets Mark, an art therapist, she's ready for a new lease on life. His mission accomplished, Jamie and his pals watch from the window as Nina ventures out again into the world.

This film shows how joy remains a wellspring underneath all the confusion, anxiety, and change in our lives. Watching the slow and surprising process whereby Nina is restored to the marvels of living is a delight to behold.

SPIRITUAL EXERCISES AND RITUALS

● Rejoice in the good fortune of someone else. By doing this you overcome the very human tendency to feel that there is a limited supply of happiness and someone else is getting your share. Express your happiness in a note or with call. Celebrate others' joys in your prayers by praying for all the people being married right now, all the people welcoming a new child into the family right now, all the people getting a promotion right now, all the people relaxing on vacation right now, and so on.

● Hildegard of Bingen has advised, "Be not lax. Be not lazy in the festive service of God." Create a ritual this week that grows out of a joy that takes you by surprise.

● Hasidic Jews, Sufi mystics, the early Christians, and the Shakers have expressed their delight in God through dance—oftentimes wild and ecstatic movement. Incorporate movement into your rituals: bending, swaying, clapping, pointing, turning around, jumping. Sweat your prayers through improvised dance.

● Rent one of those movies with a really happy ending. Enjoy the moment. Then watch a film that always moves you to tears. Cry freely, recognizing the connection between joy and sorrow.

PRAYER OR MANTRA

The rock group Three Dog Night took the phrase from the familiar hymn and put it on the Top-40 charts: "Joy to the world, all the boys and girls. Joy to the fishes in the deep blue sea. Joy to you and me." The beat is so infectious, it is more suitable as a mantra than as a meditative breath prayer. Repeat the mantra wherever you are.

Joy to the world.

IMAGERY EXERCISE

Colette Aboulker-Muscat is a world-renown teacher of imagination as a way for us to explore our inner reality and discover how to live in the depths of our experiences. She has created thousands of imagery exercises, sharing them with her students who come from many countries to her home in Jerusalem, Israel. In this exercise, you are encouraged to discover the benefits of "Dance."

Breathe out three times. Get in touch with your physical existence. Know that each breath has a purpose and a direction. Notice what is going on in your body.

Imagine that you are alone at the edge of a large, clear, quiet, and calm meadow with the sun above you and all the space to dance. Look at your meadow and be aware of your feelings. Then begin to dance freely.

Now see in this space another dancer dancing. He or she is offering to show you how to dance. You are free to accept, reject, or share this dance. See how the two of you dance together in the green, clear, quiet, large meadow. Then open your eyes.

JOURNAL EXERCISES

● Some of your most pleasurable times with your journal will be when you are rereading entries about joy. So don't let special events pass without recording what happened and how you felt. Every party deserves a journal entry, even if you capture only one happy moment.

● Occasionally, perhaps quarterly on the solstices and equinoxes, make a list of "What Brings Me Joy." Notice when the sources of your joy change, and add reflections on what this tells you.

DISCUSSION QUESTIONS, STORYTELLING, SHARING

● When in your life have you been filled with great joy? Were you alone or with others?

● Who has been the patron saint of joy in your life? Who has stifled or spoiled your joy?

● Share the story of a time when an act of service gave you great joy.

● What can be done to create a greater atmosphere of joy in your home and community? What will be your legacy of joy to the next generations?

HOUSEHOLD, GROUP, AND COMMUNITY PROJECTS

● Come up with a strategy that will help you "dance the day" rather than succumb to a "been there/done that" attitude. For example, play bouncy music while you scrub the bathroom floor.

● Go dancing with your partner and/or friends. Take classes. Rent any Fred Astaire movie or a film about ballet, disco, flamenco, or ballroom dancing. Act out the emotions the dance elicits in you.

● While visiting a hospital, day care center, nursing home, or other such facility, tell everyone you are collecting smiles today and see how many different ones you can gather.

● Add a happiness ritual to your celebration of one of the annual holidays. Have members of your group recall three of the most joyous moments you have experienced together during the past year. Write brief descriptions of some of them in a "Moments of Happiness" book that you review as part of this ritual next year.

FICTION, POETRY, OR CHILDREN'S BOOK

● *I'm in Charge of Celebrations* by Byrd Baylor with pictures by Peter Parnall will inspire you to create your own holidays. "Last year I gave myself one hundred and eight celebrations—besides the ones that they close school for," says the girl in this delightful children's book. She keeps a notebook where she records her celebrations: Dust Devil Day, Rainbow Celebration Day, Green Cloud Day, Coyote Day, and The Time of Falling Stars. Her very own New Year Celebration comes in the spring when her favorite cactus blooms and "makes me think I ought to bloom myself"; she spends a day "admiring things."

● This celebratory spirit is also characteristic of another book by the same creative duo, Baylor and Parnall's *The Way to Start a Day*. The narrator recommends greeting the sun each morning with a blessing, chant, or song—an act that joins you to people of all times and all cultures.

SPOKEN-WORD AUDIO

Mark Twain Tonight! is an entertaining two-cassette live performance by Hal Holbrook as the 70-year-old American writer who took great joy in the world around him, especially when he wasn't taking everything seriously. The witty novelist and social observer was able to sniff out the hokum in religion, patriotism, politics, and national developments at the turn of the century. "I was born modest but it wore off," Holbrook as Twain begins. He reminisces about his youth as a riverboat pilot, toys with an interviewer, pokes fun at temperance, reads from *Huckleberry Finn*, recounts a ghost story, and tells a few tall tales.

ART

Two images of abundant joy are Margaret Neve's *By Moonlight* and Henri Matisse's *Dance*. In the first, a girl leans backward, arms outstretched, as if to embrace the moonlight around her; her blissful look conveys her surrendering to joy. And in Matisse's famous painting, five nude figures dance in a circle on a green mound set into a rich blue sky. Hands joined and limbs fully stretched, they are exemplars of exuberant joy.

MUSIC

One of the best ways to feel in your heart and soul the spiritual dimensions of joy is to listen to the finale of Beethoven's masterful *Symphony No. 9, in D Minor, Op. 125*. This choral piece is based on Schiller's poem "Ode to Joy," which affirms the unity of all. The exalted movement pioneers the use of the human voice into the symphonic medium. It also celebrates freedom by incorporating different musical elements—fugue, march, choral, and recitative—to create an unconventional whole. To ride wave after wave of this surging sound is to experience the exhilaration of true spiritual joy and freedom!

SEE ALSO:
Beauty. Enthusiasm. Grace. Gratitude. Love. Play. Zeal.

JUSTICE

THE BASIC PRACTICE

Doing justice is a central imperative in Judaism, Christianity, and Islam. Buddhists are urged to be socially engaged. Hinduism, Taoism, Confucianism, and primal religions emphasize right relationships within communities as building blocks of justice.

This practice applies to the whole range of human interactions, and today it is also being extended to animals and the environment. It means that we deal fairly with others, recognizing the equality and dignity of all. It requires that we work to insure that all people, especially the poor and the weak, have access to opportunities. It assumes that none of us is free until all of us are.

Practice justice by demanding it. Words can be as forceful as deeds— the prophets of old proved that. Name injustices when you see them. Speak boldly and put your body and your money where your mouth is. Stand up and be counted.

CATALYSTS, CONTRASTS, AND COMPANIONS

Often we are propelled into the struggle for justice when we experience an injustice ourselves, when we are not treated fairly at work or our friendship is exploited by an associate. One day while reading the newspaper we may be shocked to learn of the oppression of certain groups in our society. Or we may step back and realize that we have been ignoring what are clearly injustices around us. Our very lack of concern can wake us up to the need for justice.

There is also a "shadow" side to this spiritual practice. Sometimes in our fervor for justice we decide that we can ignore the rights and dignity of those who oppose us. Instead of being justice seekers, then, we become fanatics.

PERSPECTIVES

Stands must be taken. If I am to respect myself I have to search myself for what I believe is right and take a stand on what I find. Otherwise, I have not gathered together what I have been given; I have not embraced what I have learned; I lack my own conviction.
–HUGH PRATHER

Justice is not an ideal state or theory but a matter of personal sensibility, a set of emotions that engage us with the world and make us care.
–ROBERT C. SOLOMON

We must not, in trying to think about how we can make a difference, ignore the small daily differences we can make, which, over time, add up to big differences we cannot foresee.
–MARIAN WRIGHT EDELMAN

TEACHERS

● Our first two teachers of the spiritual practice of justice both examine the political and social scene in the United States and draw conclusions about what is needed to bring about a more just society. *Tikkun* magazine editor Michael Lerner focuses on structural change in his book *The Politics of Meaning.* He presents a full-scale attack on the selfishness, materialism, and cynicism afoot in the culture. Envisioning a future where "the uniqueness and preciousness of every human being" is taken seriously, Lerner outlines nonpartisan proposals for the economy (ethical impact reports), education (study of the world's religions), the workplace (job rotation), family (family support networks), and health care (more volunteerism in hospitals). Lerner is very good at naming the tendencies that undermine justice in the world today.

● Marianne Williamson, our second teacher, is good at identifying concrete steps in justice-making. "The fabric of American society must be rewoven one loving stitch at a time: one child read to, one sick person prayed for, one elder given respect and made to feel needed, one prisoner rehabilitated, one mourner given comfort," she writes in her call to spiritual politics *The Healing of America.* A Unity Church minister, Williamson salutes the rich philosophical and political resources of democracy but laments our current era of passive citizenship. The solution is to convert spiritual conviction into a political force. Some of her ideas for doing this include citizen salons to discuss issues, prayer vigils, and soldiers for peace.

● Latin American theologian Leonardo Boff covers another aspect of justice in *Cry of the Earth, Cry of the Poor.* Justice seekers must not only attack inequality and poverty, they must work for the healing of the environment. According to this Christian author, we are called to be guardian angels of the Earth and "sons and daughters of the rainbow." The challenge is to see ourselves "as alongside things, as members of a larger planetary and cosmic community."

VIDEOS

● Documentary filmmaker Michael Moore is a crusader for justice. He attacks systemic injustices in the American economy in his two clever and feisty satiric films, *Roger and Me* and *The Big One.* In the former, released at the end of the 1980s economic boom, he tries to confront the chairman of General Motors about the effects of plant shutdowns on the people of his hometown of Flint, Michigan. In *The*

Big One, he's still trying to get some answers from corporate executives: Why in the mid-1990s are they laying off workers and sending jobs overseas when their companies are making staggering profits and receiving tax breaks from the government? Moore is making one basic point: The rich are busy widening the gap between the haves and the have-nots with a vengeance.

• The need for economic and racial justice is the theme of *The Long Walk Home*. Set in Montgomery, Alabama, during the 1955 bus boycott by the African-American community, the film's insights into the dynamics and costs of racism transcend the specifics of time and place. Miriam Thompson, the suburban wife of a prosperous businessman, and Odessa, her housekeeper, break down the racial barriers that are designed to keep them apart and act in solidarity with other justice seekers in their community. Both characters are moral mentors who teach us about the rigors of change and commitment.

• Finally, the religious traditions offer many examples of men and women who have risked their lives, and sometimes given them, for justice. Many Christians see a direct line from the moral outrage of the Hebrew prophets to the righteous indignation of Jesus Christ. French Canadian filmmaker Denys Arcand shares this view. *Jesus of Montreal* is the compelling story of an actor who, while directing a Passion play on the grounds of a hillside shrine overlooking the city of Montreal, gets caught up in the role of Jesus.

Using modern equivalents to the life of Jesus of Nazareth, Arcand delivers a telling critique of institutionalized Christianity and a savage assault on the hallowed idols of secular society, including conspicuous consumption, advertising, sexism, and the media. In this film, the spiritual practice of justice involves passion, compassion, and living for others.

SPIRITUAL EXERCISES AND RITUALS

• In the Kabbalah, violet is one of the seven frequencies of light. It stands for justice as an attribute of God's consciousness. Wear something violet today as a reminder to do justice in the world.

• The next time you find yourself facing a difficult ethical situation, repeat the following Native American prayer: "May we be helped to do whatever is most right."

• Hold a Council of All Beings. Each participant in the circle speaks for another life-form—an animal, plant, tree, body of water—expressing that being's concerns. You might talk about threats to the being's habitat or freedom, the effects of pollution, natural disasters, and wars. After all the beings have spoken, talk as humans about your responsibilities to correct some of the environmental and cultural injustices you have identified. For a detailed description of this ritual, see *Coming Back to Life: Practices to Reconnect Our Lives, Our World* by Joanna Macy and Molly Young Brown.

PRAYER OR MANTRA

Here is a simple mantra that has been chanted on picket lines and marches.

> Breathing in: Justice Here . . .
> Breathing out: Justice Now.

IMAGERY EXERCISE

The intention of this exercise, "Making a Stand," is to discover how justice grows from our daily actions.

Breathe out three times. Imagine yourself going about your daily activities in a very rhythmic manner . . . getting up at the same time . . . eating regularly . . . having an established balance between times of work and times of recreation . . . finding a pace that feels right to you personally . . . not allowing anyone or anything to interfere with your rhythm. Know that you are doing all that you want and need to do when you are keeping to this rhythmic lifestyle. Open your eyes.

Close your eyes. Breathe out one time. See yourself standing in one place. You are standing there even when you have urges to go off and do something else. You are standing there when someone comes along and tries to push you off your place. Sense how you can resist any distractions and any forces or shocks that are coming at you. Know that by standing firm, you are being free. Then open your eyes.

JOURNAL EXERCISES

● According to Dr. Martin Luther King, Jr., life's most persistent question is "What are you doing for others?" Search your soul and then write an honest answer in your journal.

● Think about the various banners you have carried in your lifetime. Draw a page of them—the slogans you've worn on buttons and T-shirts, the signs you've carried, the bumper stickers on your car. What kinds of causes do you tend to support? Which have you abandoned? Which do you still support enthusiastically? How do you account for any shifts in your allegiances? On the opposite page from your slogans, write a reflection on what they say about you.

DISCUSSION QUESTIONS, STORYTELLING, SHARING

● Identity an injustice that troubles you. What emotion first made you aware of it? Then talk about one action you can take to combat it.

● Do you think that all people are born with a yearning for justice, or does it have to be taught? Think back to your childhood and recall your most vivid experience of justice or injustice. Share your story.

● What criteria do you use in choosing which organizations or causes you will give money?

HOUSEHOLD, GROUP, AND COMMUNITY PROJECTS

● Devote one of your meals together, or an hour after dinner, to a "Week in Review." Talk about what is happening in the world, especially politically and economically. Share news items that you think the others might not have seen. Consider the facts and also share your feelings. Decide together on one action you can take in response to the state of the world—prayers, letters to newspapers and magazines, letters to your elected representatives, petitions, contributions, etc.

● The equitable distribution of the world's resources is a justice issue. Keep track of the consumption patterns in your home. Try to consume less so that there will be more available for others.

● Another way to combat economic injustice is to revive the ancient practice of bartering in your community. Experiment with this. For example, baby-sit for your neighbor's children in exchange for tutoring or cooking lessons. Offer to drop off a friend's dry cleaning on your way to work in exchange for her programming your VCR.

● Identify the agencies and commissions in your community with responsibilities to combat racism and poverty, both fundamental problems underlying many justice issues. Inform yourself about pending legislation and judicial rulings. Find out how you can make your opinions known.

FICTION, POETRY, OR CHILDREN'S BOOK

At the core of the spiritual practice of justice is the recognition of the dignity of all people. In *A Lesson Before Dying* by Ernest Gaines, Jefferson, a slow-witted black man, is sentenced to death for his participation in a robbery in which three men were killed. His godmother calls upon Grant Wiggins, a black schoolteacher, to convince Jefferson to walk tall to his execution. Wiggins has troubles of his own, but he does reach out to the alienated prisoner. Although both men feel deprived and devalued, they are able to bring out the best in each other. By doing so, they practice justice in the fullest sense of the term.

Spoken-Word Audio

● One of the ways to do justice is to give generously to causes you believe in. *The Soul of Money with Lynn Twist* is an interview by Michael Toms of New Dimensions with the founding executive of the Hunger Project. She believes that money can be the voice of your commitment and a vehicle for the expression of your highest ideals. She advises listeners to see themselves as philanthropists using their wealth to build a better world.

● *The Micro-Lending Revolution with Alex Counts and Muhammad Yunus,* another New Dimensions interview, is an astonishing account of the Grameen Bank of Bangladesh, which has, over the past 21 years, loaned more than $2 billion to 3 million people who have no money or collateral to put up to secure the loans. Muhammad Yunus explains this microlending program that has helped many families pass over the poverty line. Here is a vision of justice to stir the soul.

Art

In *Mexican Muralists: Orozco, Rivera, and Siqueiros*, Desmond Rochfort describes the revolutionary creations of three artists who were fervently interested in justice for the poor and the weak. The spectacular color reproductions of their public art in this large-format book covers a period from the 1920s through the early 1970s. David Alfaro Siqueiros's mural *From the Dictatorship of Porfirio Diaz to the Revolution* contrasts the plebian heroes of the 1910 Mexican Revolution with the jaded leader and his morally bankrupt political stooges and courtesans. Here justice comes through a strike that sets the stage for real political change.

Music

If there is any one person in the twentieth century whose music is synonymous with the spiritual practice of justice, it is Pete Seeger. "Songs won't save the planet," he once said, "but then neither will books or speeches. Songs are sneaky things; they can slip across borders." And into hearts. They can set the conscience on fire and spur individuals to stand up for what is right.

Where Have All the Flowers Gone: The Songs of Pete Seeger features the best of his folk ballads performed by such artists as Bruce Springsteen, Bonnie Raitt, Jackson Browne, Judy Collins, Tom Paxton, Donovan, and many others. Practice justice by listening to "We Shall Overcome," "If I Had a Hammer," "Where Have All the Flowers Gone," "One Grain of Sand," and "Turn Turn Turn."

SEE ALSO:

Compassion. Faith. Kindness. Hope. Openness. Peace.

KINDNESS

THE BASIC PRACTICE

Kindness is the first of the three great treasures advocated by Lao
Tzu. The Buddha taught that generosity is a primary quality of an awak-
ened mind. Muhammad regarded kindness as an essential sign of faith.
Jewish and Christian ethics are built upon deeds of kindness, as are the
daily interactions of people of primal traditions.

The spiritual practice of kindness encompasses a range of small acts
and habits that we know as old-fashioned good manners—saying "please"
and "thank you," waiting your turn, lending a helping hand, or cheering

someone up with a smile. It applies not just to your relationships with other people; etiquette in the spiritual life extends to things, animals, plants, and the Earth.

This practice also means being generous with your presence, your time, and your money. Give freely without expecting anything in return. Just do it. Kindness is not a quid pro quo endeavor.

CATALYSTS, CONTRASTS, AND COMPANIONS

Few of us would describe ourselves as unkind, cruel, or nasty, yet we would have to admit that we often miss the mark on this spiritual practice. Just remember the many times you have been hurt by someone not doing something—the call that didn't come when you were feeling low, the thank-you note that never appeared, the missed appointment—and then consider how often you have neglected to act in similar circumstances. Kindness is very susceptible to the sin of omission.

Still, acknowledging that we have missed another's kindness can make us want to be kind more consistently ourselves. This is one of those situations when a negative experience has a positive outcome.

Of course, sometimes we are simply too self-involved to notice that we are not being kind. Selfishness quickly undermines manners. And generosity is difficult for both the miser and the glutton.

PERSPECTIVES

Be kind for everyone is carrying a heavy burden.
–IAN MACLAREN

Our work-a-day lives are filled with opportunities to bless others. The power of a single glance or an encouraging smile must never be underestimated.
–G. RICHARD RIEGER

There is no need for temples; no need for complicated philosophy. Our own brain, our own heart is our temple; my philosophy is kindness.
–THE DALAI LAMA

TEACHERS

● Our first teacher of kindness is Wayne Muller. He has been a therapist and spiritual counselor for more than 20 years and is the founder of

Bread for the Journey, a nationwide organization that supports the efforts of local people serving the poor, hungry, and others in need. Through his work, he has gathered many examples of the little acts that are characteristic of this spiritual practice.

In *How, Then, Shall We Live?* Muller focuses on four questions at the center of the human journey: Who am I? What do I love? How shall I live, knowing I will die? What is my gift to the family of the Earth? The author skillfully balances inner growth with outward service, illustrating his points with wonderful stories from the spiritual traditions, poetry, and his own experiences.

Muller discusses acts of kindness in the section on gifts, emphasizing that they need not be showy or dramatic. "Some of us stop our natural impulse to be generous," he writes, "because we are afraid our offering will not be large enough, not impressive enough. But the most beautiful gifts are the small, lovely things." Kindness could be cooking for a friend, apologizing for a hurt, telling stories to children, tending a garden, or speaking an encouraging word. "A gift is like a seed; it is not an impressive thing. It is what can grow from the seed that is impressive."

• Kindness and generosity are two of the spiritual disciplines recommended by Rabbi Rami M. Shapiro in his book *Minyan: Ten Principles for Living a Life of Integrity.* Although the path of daily practice he recommends has been informed by the eighteenth-century Hasidic tradition of the Baal Shem Tov, it is one that will appeal to seekers of other backgrounds as well.

The author, who is rabbi of Temple Beth Or in Miami, Florida, emphasizes that spirituality is a "conscious practice of living out the highest ethical ideals in the concreteness of your everyday life." For example, generosity (*tzedakah*) means setting aside a percentage of your income for charity and regularly giving spontaneously to people requesting your help on the street. Kindness (*gemilut chesed*) includes lending money without interest, visiting the sick, washing the dishes, and hanging up your clothes, thus showing respect even to the things in your house.

VIDEOS

• The spiritual practice of kindness frees us from the isolation and the alienation that seems to be so rampant today. When we reach out to others, we open our hearts and theirs as well. *Grand Canyon* perfectly illustrates this process. Set in contemporary Los Angeles, the film deals with the serendipitous interactions of six people whose days are set on edge by the fear and uncertainty accompanying urban violence, racial conflicts, and the constant frustrations of modern life.

Yet despite the palpable tensions all around them, these individuals ask themselves the right questions: Am I giving enough? Are my eyes open? How do I say thank you? Can I make a difference in the lives of others? As the characters connect, interact, and influence each other, new possibilities grow out of their deeds of kindness. In fact, we could even say that the gifts they exchange are modern-day miracles.

● *Babe* is a delightful Australian film that celebrates the dignity and variety of animals—the whole story is told from their perspective. A taciturn farmer guesses the correct weight of a piglet at a fair and takes the animal home convinced that there is something special about him. And there is: He's the embodiment of kindness.

Babe befriends Ferdinand, a duck who upsets the hierarchical social order of the farm by acting like a rooster. Then, through a series of dramatic turns, Babe learns the trade of sheepherding and overcomes the stigma of being a stupid pig or, worse, Christmas dinner. Instead of intimidation, he uses affirmation to keep the sheep moving. His spiritual practice of kindness works wonders in the end.

SPIRITUAL EXERCISES AND RITUALS

● The Sufis speak of "secret charity" where a person benefits from your anonymous actions and doesn't have any chance to respond. Try to make an anonymous gift at least once a week. Buy a ticket for someone at the end of the museum line. Leave a dollar bill next to a tree in the park.

● Be on time. Being late wastes people's valuable time; being early intrudes upon their time for other activities, including private time. Call ahead if you are running late; postpone your entrance if you are early.

● The Buddha taught the virtue of making the "seven offerings that cost nothing." They are a compassionate eye, a smiling face, loving words, physical service, a warm heart, a seat, and lodging. Increase the number and frequency of your kindness offerings.

PRAYER OR MANTRA

This breath prayer is a reminder that kindness is an active virtue.

> Breathing in: May I reach out . . .
> Breathing out: with kindness.

Imagery Exercise

Most of the religions recommend a daily review of your behavior. One part, often called "The Examen of Consciousness," identifies those times when you have become aware of the presence of God. The other part, "The Examen of Conscience," looks at your behavior and whether your actions have moved you closer to or farther from God and others. Deeds of kindness, of course, are part of this movement.

A variation of the examen includes the correcting of behavior. When you see something that you want to change, you enter into it imaginally and change it, thus signaling your inner self of your desire to act differently. The following exercise, which is to be done at the end of the day, enables you to move closer to God and others through such acts of correction. It is based on the "Nighttime Reversing" exercise created by Colette Aboulker-Muscat that appears in books on imagery by her student Gerald Epstein.

Just before going to sleep, lying in bed with your eyes closed, review your day, moment by moment, moving backward in time. Start with the last event of the day and relive it in imagery. Continue in reverse order, reliving again your activities and conversations. Notice how you responded at times when you felt God's closeness. Watch for moments when you were kind to others in thought, word, or deed. Feel again what you felt when others were kind to you. See yourself showing gratitude for any experiences of kindness.

Also notice the times when you failed to be kind to people, animals, things, and the Earth. Recall each event slowly and carefully, correcting your attitudes and behavior in those situations where you had difficulty. Continue this reversing and correcting process until you are back at the moment when you woke up.

When you have finished giving thanks and making corrections, you can go to sleep. If you find that you fall asleep before finishing, do not be discouraged. Repeat the exercise every night until you are able to finish it.

Journal Exercise

Write a portrait of "The Kindest Person I Know," including specific examples of this person's kind deeds. Tristine Rainer in *The New Diary* makes an interesting observation about the value of writing portraits, especially of someone you admire: "By writing diary portraits of people who intrigue you, you enter their qualities in your book, in your space, and begin the process of recognizing and taking posession of those qualities."

DISCUSSION QUESTIONS, STORYTELLING, SHARING

● Giving to others is one part of the spiritual practice of kindness. Another is being able to receive graciously the gifts of others. Which are you better at? Why?

● Kindness is contagious. Share the story of a time when you "caught" an impulse to be kind from another person. When have you influenced others to be kind?

● Do you think kindness is valued in contemporary society? Some argue that young people grow up thinking that they cannot afford to be kind, that there is nothing to be gained from it. Do you agree or disagree with this assessment of our culture's attitude toward kindness? Explain your opinion with specific examples from your experiences.

HOUSEHOLD, GROUP, AND COMMUNITY PROJECTS

● Reframe household responsibilities as acts of kindness. For example, dusting is being kind to the table. Emptying the litter box is being kind to the cat. Hanging up your clothes is being kind to them. Draw up a list of etiquette practices toward members of your household, pets, the place where you reside, the natural world, and neighbors.

● Keep a bank or box in your home and deposit loose change in it. Every time you go out to dinner, you might put money to pay for another meal in the box. Hold a household council to decide how to distribute your generosity fund.

● Rabbi David Cooper points out that in the Jewish tradition, it is considered a high level of charity to help people become more self-sufficient by enabling them to educate and train themselves or to start their own business. As a group, begin a Scholarship or an Entrepreneur's Fund.

● One of the best ways to combat incivility in our society is for small groups to periodically brainstorm lists of basic courtesies that they affirm and agree to extend for the maintenance and strengthening of the community. Little things do count. Consider these commitments: not to interrupt when someone else is talking, not to talk in theaters during the movie, to cover your nose and mouth when you sneeze, to pick up litter, to let someone in a hurry ahead of you in line.

● Donate blood through local hospitals and other programs. Help organize a blood drive at your place of work or worship.

FICTION, POETRY, OR CHILDREN'S BOOK

The "children's book" that best reflects this practice is not the usual kind of book written for children. Rather, it is a book of stories about and by children called *The Kindness of Children* by Vivian Gussin Paley. The author, a former kindergarten teacher, describes what happens when young children are given the chance to make up stories and act them out with their classmates. The kids produce moments of happiness and hopefulness for each other: "These spontaneous storytellers create little homes for one another where everyone can imagine playing a role and no one is left out."

Using the children's stories as examples, Paley demonstrates the ripple effect of kindness. She tells one group of children how a kindergarten class found a way for a severely disabled boy named Teddy to be in their play. This story reminds a girl of a time when she was on a bus and someone read a newspaper story about how a gorilla saved a little boy; seeing everyone so happy that day made her want to do something good, so she gave up her seat to an old lady. Another true incident about two troublemaking boys helps the children see their potential for friendship. Through hearing and telling stories, the children are witnesses to acts of kindness.

SPOKEN-WORD AUDIO

On *All I Really Need to Know I Learned in Kindergarten*, Unitarian minister and best-selling essayist Robert Fulghum remembers what he learned in school about kindness: "Share everything. Play fair. Clean up your own mess. Say you're sorry when you hurt somebody." On this popular audio he also talks about looking for love in strange places and paying attention to nature's small miracles.

ART

The oppression and the nobility of the poor are accentuated in the paintings of Mexican artist Diego Rivera. In *The Flower Carrier*, a kneeling man is burdened by a large basket of flowers on his back. A woman lends support, adjusting the balance of the load. It is a small act but a helpful and kind one.

Music

The song "Get Together" by Chet Powers, made famous by The Youngbloods, gives us the key to kindness—smiling on our brothers and trying to love one another right now. In "Bridge Over Troubled Water" by Simon & Garfunkel, the singer goes even further. He promises to always be there, like a bridge over troubled water, when you are weary, feeling small, down and out, on the street, and even when your time has come to shine. Here kindness is easing the mind.

See also:

Connections. Hospitality. Justice. Love. Nurturing. Openness.

LISTENING

THE BASIC PRACTICE

As is true so many times in this Alphabet, one spiritual practice is associated with others. Listening involves attention, being present, and hospitality, and it is a component of devotion, nurturing, and wonder.

Listening is our bridge to the wisdom of sacred texts and spiritual teachers. It is an essential part of the discernment process whereby we identify God's messages for us. Listening enables us to tune in to others and our inner voices of intuition and conscience. It is how we know we are part of the natural, technological, and media worlds all around us.

But it takes practice to be a really good listener. Start by listening like a baby does upon encountering a sound for the first time. Then listen like a child, noticing music, rhythm, and the variety of noises. Next, tune in to the messages coming to you from all directions and multiple levels of experience. And remember the advice of Native American seers: Speak only half as much as you listen.

CATALYSTS, CONTRASTS, AND COMPANIONS

There is perhaps no greater way to show our regard for our friends, family, and associates than to truly listen to them. The "listening heart," as this attitude is called, leads to a deepening of relationships and a greater sense of self for all parties. And this kind of communication isn't limited to human interactions. Listen to an animal, the waves on the beach, or the roar of a city neighborhood, and you will come to a greater appreciation of your place in the world.

Conversely, an inability or unwillingness to listen is a symptom of self-centeredness. It signals that we are shut up in ourselves, not interested in participating in what is going on around us. It can also indicate an obliviousness to our own best interests that may be trying to make themselves known through our inner voices. In a universe where so many things are speaking to us on so many levels, it is not wise to ignore the voices.

PERSPECTIVES

You wish to see: listen. Hearing is a step toward vision.
–SAINT BERNARD OF CLAIRVAUX

The universe is composed of subjects to be communed with, not objects to be exploited. Everything has its own voice. Somehow we have become autistic. We don't hear voices.
–THOMAS BERRY

The true human is someone who is aware, someone who is, moment by moment, totally and completely merged with life. He is a listener. She is a listener. Out of that capacity of inner and outer listening comes the quality of humility. The true listener is no longer defined by desires or attachments. Instead, he or she is sensitized to consciousness.
–JOSEPH RAEL

TEACHERS

● Our primary teacher of the spiritual practice of listening is W. A. Mathieu, a composer and musician at a center for Sufi dancing. In *The Musical Life: Reflections on What It Is and How to Live It,* he recommends that you train yourself "to be open to vibration at every level, to appreciate it wherever you find it." The hum of traffic, the samba in brushing your teeth, the thumping of your blood, the falsetto produced with a yawn, the pitch of a tapped object—life is full of such enchantments for the ears. "Every sound," according to the author, "is like the first Word, a creation story in itself. Sound is the audible form of vital energy that passes through your life."

Mathieu uses this broad understanding of music as the entry point to a heightened sensitivity to the universe. Music is within us; music is all around us. That is why a certain song can spark a memory and we are transported to the past. That is why the phrase "we make sweet music together" describes a good thing. And that is why we can refer to a mystical experience as something akin to the music of the spheres.

● In the monastic traditions and most spiritual growth programs, listening to scripture and inspiring texts is an essential discipline. Two excellent books by members of Catholic orders are tutorials on this process. *The Song of the Seed: The Monastic Way of Tending the Soul* by Macrina Wiederkehr is structured as a 30-day retreat on Jesus' parable of the seed and the sower in the Gospel of Luke; she encourages listening through such activities as reflective reading, meditation on the text, and journaling. *The Cup of Your Life* by Joyce Rupp is a six-week program built around the metaphors associated with a common drinking cup. Listening to God and your deeper self is practiced through prayers, reflections using a cup, scripture reading, journaling, and a simple activity to be done throughout the day.

● *Intuition: The Path to Inner Wisdom* by Patricia Einstein, an intuitive counselor and workshop leader, is filled with tips and exercises designed to help you gain access to the guidance of the "small voice within." This kind of listening yields great dividends as intuition is related to creativity, empathy, synchronicity, experiences of déjà vu, clairvoyant reality, and the collective consciousness.

VIDEOS

• Two movies starring Jodie Foster offer different perspectives on the importance of listening. In *Contact*, she plays Ellie Arroway, a driven American astronomer who is using highly sophisticated radio telescopes to listen for signs of extraterrestrial intelligence in space. When she picks up a message from Vega, a star 26 light-years away, scientists from around the world join her in an effort to decipher the continuing communications. Eventually they discover instructions for building a machine for intergalactic travel, a trip Ellie desperately wants to make. For her the ultimate adventure in the universe is listening, and she practices with great focus and intensity.

• Those who have mastered the art of listening can hear more than the rest of us do. They are highly sensitive to their surroundings and alert to the many sides of every story. In *Nell*, Jodie Foster plays a woman raised in an isolated cabin in the deep woods by her mother whose speech was distorted as the result of several strokes. After her mother dies, Nell is discovered by Dr. Jerome Lovell, a country physician, who is mystified by her strange speech patterns. Dr. Paula Olson, a psychologist, wants to take her to a university to study her behavior in order to learn more about the interplay between nature and nurture in human development.

While these two scientists try to figure out what to do about her, Nell is carefully listening to the yearnings behind their words. Eventually through her they get in touch with their feelings and the simple joys of the natural world.

SPIRITUAL EXERCISES AND RITUALS

• Make an appointment with a spiritual director and meet with him or her regularly. These guides have been trained to recommend resources and practices to help you improve your ability to listen to what the world and God have to say to you about your spiritual life.

• *Lectio divina* (divine reading) is a way of deep listening to a scriptural text. Here's how it is generally done in the Christian tradition. Pick up a sacred text or holy scripture and call upon God to be present with you. Then read for 10 or 15 minutes from the text slowly, reflectively, pausing with any phrase or word that catches your attention, noting any new understandings you receive, especially regarding its meaning to your life. Some people find it valuable to read the text aloud. Listen to it with the ear of your heart and be receptive to God speaking to you through this vehicle. When you feel that you have heard a message, thank God and take the "Word" with you into the day.

• In Christianity, a vigil is a time that has been set aside for patient, quiet, and reverent listening. Vigils may be held in a holy place to focus on the meaning of an event in the life of Christ or a saint, or to engage in self-examination in preparation for a ceremony. Often they are done with a community and for a purpose, such as a vigil for peace or to protest capital punishment. Organize a vigil with your spiritual community. You will need to decide on a purpose, location, style (silence, singing, candlelight, etc.), and length.

PRAYER OR MANTRA

This breath prayer comes from an image used by W. A. Mathieu.

Breathing in: Make an altar . . .
Breathing out: of my ears.

IMAGERY EXERCISE

Jesuit priest Anthony de Mello has an exercise where you invite God to pay attention to the sounds of the natural world through you. It uses an "Altered Point of Ear."

Close your eyes. Begin by listening to the rhythm and the sound of your own breath. Then allow the sounds in the room around you to fall gently on your ears. Do not think about them, simply hear them as sounds. . . . Now see yourself as a cat wandering through your house and hearing with the cat's ears. . . . See yourself becoming a bird flying through the air and hearing with the bird's ears. . . . See yourself as a tree standing in your backyard and hearing with the tree's ears. . . . Feel yourself becoming part of the earth and hearing what the earth is hearing. . . . Now hear what God is hearing from the world right now. Rest in the sensation that God is listening through your ears. . . . When you are ready, open your eyes.

JOURNAL EXERCISES

• In *Who Cares? Simple Ways You Can Reach Out*, Marcy Heidish, who has served as a hospital chaplain, describes a useful tool from her training—the "listener's log." She wrote verbatim records of her visits with patients in order to learn how much she actually heard and how helpful her responses were. Log some of your conversations in your journal. Then ask yourself these questions, suggested by Heidish: Did you create a receptive atmosphere? Did you take over or grow distant? When were the moments of breakthrough, connection, and insight?

● Make lists to assess how you listen: I always listen to . . . ; I rarely listen to . . . ; I could improve how well I listen to. . . .

DISCUSSION QUESTIONS, STORYTELLING, SHARING

● Go around the circle and have everyone either describe or make a favorite sound. What do you associate with it?

● Share an example of a time when you listened to your body. This could be feedback about an illness, an intuitive hit, or another type of sensation. Did you heed the message?

● Read a story aloud. Notice how your experience of the tale is affected by hearing it.

HOUSEHOLD, GROUP, AND COMMUNITY PROJECTS

● Make tape recordings of household sounds. Speed them up or slow them down. Listen for rhythm, meter, pauses. Describe each other's laughs. Talk about your needs for different kinds of sounds and/or silence.

● Put on a lecture series for your community on improving listening skills. Counseling and therapy organizations should be able to provide speaker suggestions. Topics might include: listening to your children/parents; developing your intuition; hearing the hidden messages in the media; identifying animal calls.

● Sometimes the sounds we want to hear are drowned out by a cacophony of noises coming out of our radios, cars, machines, and tools. Do a survey of your neighborhood to determine what sounds people appreciate and which are bothersome. Learn what the sound pollution guidelines are for your community, and report any offenders.

FICTION, POETRY, OR CHILDREN'S BOOK

John Fox presents workshops on the interface between meaning-making and writing poetry. In *Poetic Medicine: The Healing Art of Poem-Making*, he challenges us to listen to what is happening around us and use it as a source of poems. He has gathered poems by ordinary people that explore the pain and love between parent and child; reflections on intimacy, marriage, and longing; and attitudes about loss, illness, and death.

Poetry emerges from listening to our deepest emotions, and listening to poetry enables us to hear others on the deepest levels.

SPOKEN-WORD AUDIO

Musical Midwifery for the Dying with Therese Schroeder-Sheker, an interview by Michael Toms of New Dimensions Radio, shines a spotlight on the extraordinary listening ministry of a gifted harpist, singer, and founder of the Chalice of Repose Project in Missoula, Montana. Taking a cue from medieval monks who used music and beauty to usher people into the next world, she and her associates have created healing deathbed vigils that are designed to attend to the physical and spiritual needs of dying patients. Therese Schroeder-Sheker talks about the importance of hearing the patients' desires for their deaths as well as coordinating the music at their bedsides to the rhythms of their bodies.

ART

Michelangelo Merisi da Caravaggio's *Calling of Saint Matthew* depicts the spiritual practice of listening. Levi, the tax collector who will be named Matthew, is seated at a table with four assistants when Jesus appears in the room and summons him with a simple gesture of his hand. Levi's face is illuminated with light from the doorway, but it is a different kind of attention that he responds to. Calls and messages, some of them nonverbal, are always coming to us from all directions. The challenge is to recognize the important ones, which may be possible only when we have learned how to listen.

MUSIC

Paul Winter and his associates create music to combat what eco-philosopher Thomas Berry calls human autism—our inability to listen to any voices other than those of our own kind. On *Earth: Voices of a Planet* and *Wolf Eyes: A Retrospective,* Winter on soprano sax is joined by Paul Halley on keyboards, David Darling and Eugene Friesen on cellos, and other musicians in tributes to the old growth forests, rain forests, oceans, and other remaining natural habitats of the planet. But the most important collaborators on these song poems are the recorded wildlife: spotted owl, elephant, Weddell seal, musican wren from the Amazon, Australian lyrebird, European blackbird, bottlenose dolphin, orca whale, and timber wolf. The message here is urgent. We can't allow these voices to be silenced.

SEE ALSO:
Attention. Being Present. Hospitality. Love. Openness.
Silence. Teachers.

LOVE

DAILY CUE, REMINDER, VOW, BLESSING

Seeing a heart shape—in a card, a shadow, or the clouds—
is my cue to practice love.

•

Hearing a love song on the radio, I am reminded of the importance
of vocalizing about my loves.

•

When I am embraced by my lover, I vow to banish fear
from our midst.

•

Blessed is the Heart of the Universe whose love makes
us into lovers.

THE BASIC PRACTICE

Love of self, love of neighbors, and love of God are the foundational stones of the world's religions. Spiraling out from the core of our being, our other loves are also cobblestones on the spiritual path: love of family, of partner, of friends, of community, of animals, of nature, of country, of things, of hobbies, of work. Love is not something that you just fall into, as the romantic songs suggest. Love is a spiritual practice. You can get better at it over time.

Begin by recognizing that you can't love others until you truly love yourself—body, mind, and soul. As you move through a day, be aware of love's expressions emerging from you or coming toward you—attraction, focus, absorption, desire, adoration, security, trust, empathy, caring, harmony, contentment, communion. Practice extending the reach of these feelings. It is through loving that we experience the love of God.

CATALYSTS, CONTRASTS, AND COMPANIONS

Fear always trips us up on the spiritual path, and it surfaces most often around the practice of love. We are afraid to love and worry that nobody will love us back. We are apprehensive about the quality of our love relationships: Are they strong enough, good enough, durable enough? Whereas we don't usually question the quality of our acts of kindness, say, we put performance measurements on our loving.

Love and intimacy go together, but if we have been disappointed by love, we worry that intimacy is beyond our reach. We fear that we have lost the ability to feel love, or that we are just not lovable, or that we will be hurt again. Sometimes we even fear that love will change us.

Hearing all this fretful thinking, God the Beloved writes one prescription over and over: Fear not! I love you.

PERSPECTIVES

When you understand how to love one thing, then you also understand how to love everything.
–NOVALIS

Love was meant to be also a sign, a symbol, a messenger, a telltale of the Divine. . . . Love is a messenger from God saying that every human affection and every ecstasy of love are sparks from the great flame of love that is God.
–FULTON J. SHEEN

The things that matter most in our lives are not fantastic or grand. They are moments when we touch one another, when we are there in the most attentive or caring way. This simple and profound intimacy is the love that we all long for.
–JACK KORNFIELD

TEACHERS

• According to our first teacher, Sam Keen, the most important question in life is "How can I become a more loving human being?" As an elder and a philosopher, he brings a breadth of experience and wisdom to bear on this subject in *To Love and Be Loved.* One of his discoveries: Love is "both a pathway to and a revelation of what is most real." Another is that love has many more varieties than the familiar one of coupling. Indeed, "When we focus obsessively on romance, the single most irrational, volatile, and often illusory form of love, we fail to consider that love may be an art involving skills that need to be developed and practiced throughout a lifetime."

Using stories, poems, and reflective exercises, Keen explores 16 elements of the practice of love: attention, desire, knowledge, sensuality, empathy, compassion, enjoyment, care, storytelling, repenting, self-love, commitment, co-creation, adoration, sexuality, and enchantment. In the final section, "Meditation on Faith, Hope, and Love," he muses on the cosmic context of our evolution as loving beings.

• Another teacher of love is Daphne Rose Kingma. In *A Lifetime of Love,* a collection of brief and enchanting essays, she focuses on the spiritual dimensions of interpersonal relationships. She defines them as depth, something that has the capacity to move us emotionally; meaning, what has significance; and intimacy, the experience of closeness that brings pleasure to life. Couples need to cherish each other's souls and champion each other's inner growth. This means, to give a few examples, sharing transcendental moments, being extravagant with praise, expressing fears, acknowledging ambivalence, learning lessons from conflicts, and integrating the divine erotic.

• A third teacher of love is Mother Teresa of Calcutta, this century's most visible saint. The religious order she founded cares for destitute, orphaned, and dying people in 100 countries. Several collections of her words are available. *Mother Teresa: No Greater Love,* edited by Becky Benenate and Joseph Durepos, is an especially nice one. Two examples: "Spread love everywhere you go. Let no one ever come to you without leaving better and happier." "Love each other as God loves each one of you, with an intense and particular love."

VIDEOS

• Most spiritual traditions proclaim that fear prevents us from being able to love. In *Defending Your Life,* Daniel, a divorced ad executive, dies in an automobile accident on his fortieth birthday. He wakes up in a place called Judgment City and learns that after a review of his life, a decision will be made about whether he goes on to a higher adventure in the universe or returns to Earth again. During the examination, as a series of episodes from his life are projected on a screen, Daniel sees how constant anxiety has ruled his behavior and choices. When he meets Julia, a radiant woman who laughs at his jokes and appears headed for glory, he gets another chance to move from fear to love.

• *Tender Mercies* is a poignant movie about the healing power of love. When Mac Sledge, a burned-out country-and-western singer-songwriter, marries Rosa Lee, a widow whose husband was killed in Vietnam, they are both trying to drive away the shadows of their past. Her boy, Sonny, wants to accept Mac but first he must come to terms with the father he never knew. This deeply spiritual film shows how these three people are reborn through the power of love, gaining strength even in the most broken places of their lives.

• Someone once asked the psychic Edgar Cayce, "Am I growing spiritually?" Cayce's reply was "Ask your family." Love in the family context must be renewed again and again. This is the theme of *What's Eating Gilbert Grape*. Gilbert Grape is a diligent young man who works at a grocery store in a small Midwest town but spends most of his time looking after his hyperactive and mentally retarded 17-year-old brother. His 500-pound mother hasn't left the house for seven years, since the suicide of his father. When Gilbert falls in love with Becky, who is traveling through the area with her grandmother, she helps him to see his mother and brother in fresh ways.

• The hardest thing of all is to love the unlovable—individuals who seem to be beyond respect or understanding. In *Dead Man Walking*, Sister Helen Prejean, a Catholic nun, agrees to be the spiritual adviser for Matthew Poncelet, who has been sentenced to death for the brutal murders of two teenage lovers. Regularly visiting him in prison, she demonstrates the power of love as a seedbed for compassion and forgiveness. Even as he is put to death, she never wavers in her role as the emissary of God's love for Matthew.

SPIRITUAL EXERCISES AND RITUALS

• In the morning, ask yourself: "Who and what am I going to let aboard the ark of my heart today?" In the evening, review your day, warmly greeting your loves.

● Whenever you feel that fear is blocking out the expression of love, go wash your hands, saying "I am washing away my fears so I can love."

● Try the Quaker practice of "holding someone in the light" by visualizing that person in the circle of God's love and presence.

PRAYER OR MANTRA

In *Teachings on Love,* Thich Nhat Hanh writes: "To love is to be there for him, for her, and for them." He offers four mantras that are especially valuable for those in intimate relationships.

1. Darling, I am here for you.
2. I know you are there, and I am very happy.
3. Darling, I know you are suffering. That is why I am here for you.
4. Darling, I am suffering. Please help.

IMAGERY EXERCISE

"Rainbow," an exercise created by Colette Aboulker-Muscat, and her exercise "Meeting of the Minds Through Love," adapted and added here, reveal the range and impact of your love.

Breathe out three times. See a rainbow coming out of your abdomen. See the colors of the rays of the rainbow going to all the people you love. See the color of the ray going to the one you love the most.

Breathe out one time. See yourself going in the direction of the one you love and know that he or she is sensing your love. Stop and recognize yourself as a lover. Then, see and sense his or her love melding with your love.

Breathe out three times. Sense that you and the one you love are one mind. Send this one mind you have connected with to other minds.

Breathe out one time. Send all the minds that you have met to the only One Mind. Then open your eyes.

JOURNAL EXERCISES

● Write or draw a tribute to a love of your life. What do you love about him or her?

● According to Rabbi David Cooper, "Kabbalists say that love is based on a desire for completion—to be whole, to be in harmony, to be connected, and to be free." Write about what completes you. It does not have to be a person; it could be your work, an experience in nature, a hobby, or something else.

DISCUSSION QUESTIONS, STORYTELLING, SHARING

● If you have a partner, share the story of how you met and fell in love. Or tell how you discovered one of your other loves.

● Dr. Dean Ornish, a cardiologist, believes that love and intimacy have a positive effect on healing all kinds of diseases and maladies. Have you found this to be true? Share a story from your experience.

● Children's book author Madeleine L'Engle says that *The Secret Garden* is one of her favorite books because it shows how love breaks through selfishness and triumphs in the end. What book or movie contains your favorite depiction of the power of love?

HOUSEHOLD, GROUP, AND COMMUNITY PROJECTS

● English poet Rupert Brooke once cataloged all the things he loved most in life. Among those on his list: "white plates and cups, clean-gleaming, ringed with blue lines; . . . wet roofs beneath the lamplight; . . . and hair that is shiny and free." Have members of your family or group make a list of 10 things they love most. Give some of them a place of honor in a "Celebration of Life and Love."

● "In a world so torn apart by rivalry, anger, and hatred, we have the privileged vocation to be living signs of a love that can bridge all divisions and heal all wounds," Henri J. M. Nouwen wrote of the Christian church. With your spiritual community, create a project that enables you to be signs of love in the world.

FICTION, POETRY, OR CHILDREN'S BOOK

● Two children's books testify to a mother's unconditional love for her child. In *The Runaway Bunny* by Margaret Wise Brown with pictures by Clement Hurd, a little bunny threatens to run away and become a fish, and his mother vows to be a fisherman; he will become a rock, and she a mountain climber; he a flying trapeze artist, and she a tightrope walker crossing the air to him.

● In *Mama, Do You Love Me?* by Barbara M. Joosse and illustrated by Barbara Lavallee, set in the Arctic, a little girl learns that her mother loves her "more than the whale loves his spout" and will love her "till the stars turn to fish in the sky," even if she stayed away to sing with the wolves or turned into a walrus. These stories are analogies of God's unreserved love for the Creation, no matter what we do.

SPOKEN-WORD AUDIO

Love relationships give us a chance to develop our capacities for understanding, commitment, honesty, and patience. On *Journey of the Heart: Intimate Relationship and the Path of Love,* clinical psychologist John Welwood explores ways in which spiritual growth is engendered in a couple's love for one another. He sees relationship as an opportunity to get to know ourselves more deeply and to expand our connections with others and the world around us.

ART

Marc Chagall is the artist who best demonstrates this spiritual practice in all of its richness and dramatic variety. He once stated, "Everything can and will be transformed in life and art if we speak the word love without shame . . . in it lies the art."

Check out the deliriousness of romantic love in *The Birthday,* where a man floats in the room after greeting his future bride with a kiss and a bouquet of flowers. The love for community shows through the half-remembered and half-imagined images in *I and the Village.* And there is Chagall's deep love for God revealed in a series of awesome paintings on biblical characters: *Abraham and the Three Angels, Noah and the Rainbow,* and *Moses Receiving the Tablets of the Law.*

MUSIC

Pop music has provided us with a smorgasbord of songs about love as a touchstone emotion in our lives. There are so many to choose from! Here are our Top 10, listed by the artist (not necessarily the writer) whose rendition we particularly enjoy: "The Air That I Breathe" by the Hollies, "The Power of Love" by Celine Dion, "When I Need You" by Leo Sayer, "Loving Her Was Easier Than Anything I'll Ever Do Again" by Willie Nelson, "All You Need Is Love" by the Beatles, "If Not for You" by Bob Dylan, "Let It Be Me" by the Everly Brothers, "You Send Me" by Sam

Cooke, "I Honestly Love You" by Olivia Newton-John, and "You're the Inspiration" by Chicago.

SEE ALSO:

Compassion. Enthusiasm. Forgiveness. Nurturing. Teachers. Yearning. You.

MEANING

THE BASIC PRACTICE

Meaning is one of those overview terms that seems to sum up the spiritual life. Many people, in fact, define spirituality as the search for meaning and purpose. But this is also a specific practice that can be learned, developed, and applied. It involves both seeking and making.

Seek meaning by looking for the big picture encompassing your experiences. Watch for patterns in the world and in your own behavior. Make meanings by attaching analogies, metaphors, symbols, and stories to things and events. See what messages come to you when you regard them in this way. Expose yourself to the various values assigned to everyday life by popular culture, philosophy, and the world's religions. Learn more about how you can understand things. Take a course. Go to a lecture. Listen to a tape.

CATALYSTS, CONTRASTS, AND COMPANIONS

Everything in the world has meaning. Nothing happens by chance. To everything there is a purpose. If you find yourself hesitating upon reading these statements, you are not unusual. We live in a time of rampant cynicism. This is a major block to spiritual literacy and the practice of meaning.

If we think nothing deserves to be taken seriously, then it is easy to regard what happens to us as insignificant, capricious, and pointless. After all, what really matters if the universe is characterized by random occurrences? On a personal level, this translates to the feeling that there is no direction to our lives.

If what you are doing doesn't seem important, it's time to work with the practice of meaning. Your place in the larger picture may not become apparent immediately, but you will increase your ability to discern the possibilities available to you. Eventually the regular practice of meaning yields understanding, not only of who you are but why you and everything else are here.

PERSPECTIVES

Meaning does not come to us in finished form, ready-made; it must be found, created, received, and constructed. We grow our way toward it.
–ANN BEDFORD ULANOV

The work of religion is to open our eyes to see a world where everything swirls with meaning.
–RICHARD ROHR

Existence will remain meaningless for you if you yourself do not penetrate into it with active love, and if you do not in this way discover its meaning for yourself. Everything is waiting to be hallowed by you.
–MARTIN BUBER

TEACHERS

• For Jacob Needleman, professor of philosophy at San Francisco State University, meaning is the manna of human existence. In three important books, he examines how people tend to deal with money, love, and time and how the desire for more of each of these intersects with the search for meaning. He taps into the "teachings of wisdom" that underlie the world's religions and spiritual philosophies to support his insights.

In *Money and the Meaning of Life*, Needleman observes that money has become for many of us "the key to understanding the great purpose of human life." Through the soul searching of two students, he shows the way to escape from the tyranny of money and to realize that the only true wealth is self-understanding.

In *A Little Book on Love*, Needleman argues that "we are born for meaning, not pleasure unless it is pleasure that is steeped in meaning." To sustain a love relationship, couples need to nourish each other's inner life and search for truth. Those who do so can handle problems of communication and trust as well as the rigors of a constantly changing world.

In *Time and the Soul*, Needleman ponders where all the meaningful time has gone and suggests ways to get it back. Key to this search for meaning is the understanding that time rushes by when we are not engaged enough in life. We can use our time to connect with the deeper Self and hence discover what we are meant to be in the universal scheme of things.

• Dr. Larry Dossey is another teacher of this spiritual practice. In *Meaning and Medicine*, he explores how meaning can set forces in motion to effect both illness and wellness. Using illustrative material from his patients and those of other scientists and physicians, he demonstrates that "what we think about an event—the meaning we attribute to it, the interpretations we make—translates into actual physical manifestations." Dossey makes a strong case for doctors and patients to honor the mind/body connection while also acknowledging that different individuals will derive unique and often idiosyncratic meanings from their symptoms.

VIDEOS

• The search for meaning is often propelled by our need to discover whether our life really matters. John Sayles's movie *Men with Guns* revolves around a wealthy physician in an unnamed Latin American country. Nearing retirement and concerned about his legacy, he decides to go visit the medical students he has trained to serve poor villagers in the countryside. After an isolated life in the city where he was indifferent to the political struggles of his times, the doctor is now exposed to the harsh exigencies of civil war. Hundreds of men, women, and children have been slaughtered by the army or the guerillas. This powerful film challenges us to confront those meanings that hold the key to life and death.

• Another film about the attempt to extract meaning from tragic circumstances is *The Sweet Hereafter*, based on Russell Banks's 1991 novel. When a school bus in a small town in British Columbia swerves off the highway and plunges into a lake, fourteen children die. The story circles around the difficult themes of public and private loss and the very human impulse to take something positive away from an inexplicable event.

• In *Educating Rita*, the protagonist is a hairdresser who decides that the purpose of life is not to acquire but to inquire, so she enrolls in an independent studies program in English literature. She has a conviction that learning will bring meaning into her life. Both Rita and her tutor, a rumpled alcoholic professor, undergo changes as a result of their close encounter with self-knowledge.

• The main character in the comic film *Alice* also changes directions after a quick course in self-knowledge. Despite an abundance of material possessions, she has lost touch with her feelings. She goes to see a Chinese therapist, who gives her a series of herbal treatments ostensibly to help her with back problems. After several sessions with some unexpected results, she has a better idea of who she is, who her friends and family are, what her needs are, and what her gifts are. In sum, she discovers a new and genuine meaning for her life.

SPIRITUAL EXERCISES AND RITUALS

• Before you pick up a new book or magazine, or as you sit down to watch a video or listen to some music, pause and ask Spirit to open your heart, mind, and soul through the spiritual practice of meaning. Call in wisdom. Later, before leaving this learning experience, say a blessing for the author or the artist to convey your thanks for his or her contribution to your life.

• Fight the pollution of cynicism by plumbing the depths of your experiences. Get in the habit of regularly doing spiritual readings of your relationships, work, body, hobbies, and other activities. The examples in *Spiritual Literacy* will be particularly helpful training sessions for this exercise in making meanings.

• Make up an "Ethical Will." Written in the form of a personal letter to be read after your death, this is a statement of the values you hold dear, the wisdom and lessons you have found to be most useful in living your life, and the meanings you want to pass on to your heirs. Reviewing and revising your Ethical Will regularly encourages you to shape your legacy.

PRAYER OR MANTRA

Many of our most heartfelt prayers take the form of questions. Here is one to be used as a mantra.

> Breathing in: Old Wise One, . . .
> Breathing out: what shall we make of this?

IMAGERY EXERCISE

Another exercise from Colette Aboulker-Muscat is designed to help you identify the meaning of a symptom, such as a sore knee or a tightness in your throat. She believes a symptom is always an indication of a need for a change.

Breathe out three times. Be aware of some physical symptom you are experiencing. Try to increase the symptom by focusing on it. Then eliminate this symptom by gradually feeling the reduction of the symptom— by letting go of it, by forgetting it, by fighting it, by explaining in what way it has to change. Feel the reduction of the symptom in the way that is best for you until it disappears.

Breathe out one time. Be open to being aware of the message this symptom is sending to you. Be aware of what message it is sending to others. Be honest about whether you are willing to make the change that the message is giving you. When you feel you have received the message, open your eyes.

JOURNAL EXERCISES

● At one time or another, we all have to ask whether spiritual meaning is found in security or risk, certainty or doubt. In your journal, make a list of the places where you have looked for meaning. Make a second list of the places where you haven't looked. Write the reasons why you have looked where you have and not looked elsewhere.

● An epiphany is a sudden and often surprising realization of the meaning of something—a "lightbulb" or "aha!" experience. It might be a new understanding of yourself or a perception of reality that you never considered before. Many of the passages in *Spiritual Literacy* were chosen because they had an "aha!" quality for us. Make your own collection of epiphanies and copy them into your journal.

DISCUSSION QUESTIONS, STORYTELLING, SHARING
- Describe a recent situation where you consciously asked yourself: What is the meaning of this? What did you learn?
- Talk about a book, movie, lecture, or retreat experience that gave you a fresh understanding of the spiritual meanings in the ordinary.
- What elements of contemporary culture serve as blocks or obstacles to your interest in the spiritual practice of meaning? How do you deal with them?

HOUSEHOLD, GROUP, AND COMMUNITY PROJECTS
- Create a mural of proverbs in your home. These brief sayings carry wisdom from the past and different cultures. Many also contain spiritual advice, such as "Silence is golden." Check the library for collections of proverbs.
- Make a household commitment to each learn at least one new thing every week. Consider these sources of meanings: lectures at libraries, conference centers, bookstores; encyclopedias and other reference books; television documentaries. Report on the most interesting things you are learning during one of your meals together.
- Sharing meanings within a group context is also a rewarding activity. Here are some "meaning" discussion starters: What ritual, holiday, or possession means the most to you? What landscape or place has special meaning for you? Recall a meaningful moment from childhood, adolescence, young adulthood, middle age, elderhood. When have you found meaning in suffering? Have you ever felt deprived of meaning?

FICTION, POETRY, OR CHILDREN'S BOOK
The Cunning Man by Robertson Davies is an entertaining and enlightening novel set in Toronto about the life and work of Jonathan Hullah, an unorthodox physician known for his unusual diagnostic skills. He wins many patients with a practice informed by the wisdom of perennial philosophy. This physician invests his work with spiritual meaning and savors all his experiences.

SPOKEN-WORD AUDIO

The Seven Storey Mountain by Thomas Merton is a classic in the spiritual journey genre. Here the Trappist monk recounts familial influences on his character, the many travels of his youth, and his years of study at Cambridge and Columbia. Merton's hunger for meaning and his prophetic critique of a life without sacred dimensions is as relevant today as it was in 1948.

ART

George Segal's white plaster sculptures are composed of figures of human beings involved in mundane activities. "People have attitudes locked up in their bodies and you have to catch them," the artist wrote. This is his quest for meaning and our chance to make a spiritual reading of his art. Look at *Bus Riders*, in which Segal presents four figures caught in a moment of time. What does their body language reveal about their personalities and characters? And what does the sculpture as a whole say about our times?

MUSIC

Austrian composer Gustav Mahler wrote *Das Lied von der Erde (The Song of the Earth)* in 1908–1909, shortly after the death of his favorite daughter from scarlet fever and after he was diagnosed with a debilitating heart condition. Consisting of six movements, the composition is based on Chinese poems about loneliness, youth, beauty, renewal, and death. This powerful yet supremely poignant music covers a wide range of emotions as the composer reaches for meaning in the face of death. In the final section, "The Farewell," words added by Mahler reveal that he has found it: "The dear earth everywhere blossoms in spring and grows green again. Everywhere and eternally the distance shines bright and blue. Eternally."

SEE ALSO:

Connections. Imagination. Teachers. Transformation. Vision. You.

NURTURING

DAILY CUE, REMINDER, VOW, BLESSING

A warm and reviving bath is a cue for me to find ways
to nurture myself.

•

A supportive letter from a friend is a reminder of my duty
to nurture others.

•

Whenever I feel burned-out, I vow to take some time
for self-care.

•

Blessed is the Divine Mother who calls us to nurture ourselves
so we can nurture others.

THE BASIC PRACTICE

A spiritual journey is usually considered to be a movement toward community and Spirit, but an essential loop of our route must pass through the realm of self. We have to find out who we are before we can make commitments to others. We have to care for our own souls in order to have the energy and strength to care for our families, our neighbors, and the Earth.

There are many ways to practice nurturing, and everyone will find his or her own best ways to receive and give nourishment. The spiritual traditions emphasize two in particular. The first is study. Be a lifelong learner; read and contemplate sacred texts and other sources of inspiration that take you deeper into yourself and out into the wider world. Second, keep the Sabbath. Dedicate some of your time to leisure and reflection.

CATALYSTS, CONTRASTS, AND COMPANIONS

A regular regimen of nurturing helps you achieve a balance in your life between inner exploration and outer involvement, time alone and time with others, work and play. Feeling imbalanced—that things are out of whack in your life—is a sure sign that you need to step back and engage in self-care to regain your equilibrium.

Actually, we usually recognize our need for nurturing by its contrasts—feeling deprived, ignored, and neglected. If you are starved for attention, most likely you lack spiritual sustenance in other areas of your life as well.

There are also shadow elements associated with nurturing. We can be so involved in nurturing ourselves that we become totally self-absorbed. We can go too far under the guise of nurturing others, so that our caring becomes a way of controlling them. Or we can sacrifice ourselves and our best interests in our concern for others, mistaking codependency for nurturing. Again, a lack of balance is the key symptom.

PERSPECTIVES

Self-care is not selfish or self-indulgent. We cannot nurture others from a dry well. We need to take care of our own needs first, then we can give from our surplus, our abundance.
–JENNIFER LOUDEN

Looking deeply at any one thing, we see the whole cosmos. The one is made of the many. To take care of ourselves, we take care of those around us.
–THICH NHAT HANH

To care for another (person, animal, forest, river) appropriately one must learn what *they* need to flourish. Care means "planning with care," giving serious attention and thought; it means "handling with care," avoiding

damage and loss; it means "leaving in the care of," protecting and guarding; it means "feeling care for," being concerned about.
–SALLIE McFAGUE

TEACHERS

• The Goddess spirituality movement is one place to look for teachers of this practice. Carol P. Christ is a religious scholar who lives in Greece and is the director of the Ariadne Institute for the Study of Myth and Ritual. Nurturing life is one of the touchstones she identifies as a way of making the mythos of the Goddess into an ethos, or way of life. In *Rebirth of the Goddess: Finding Meaning in Feminist Spirituality*, she writes: "To nurture life is to manifest the power of the Goddess as the nurturer of life. To honor, respect, and support mothers and children. To recognize all people and all beings as connected in the web of life. To embody the intelligent love that is the ground of all being."

Growing numbers of women and men, Christ observes, are tapping into the nourishing vitalities of the Goddess. Grounded in the body, the Earth, and nature, speaking to the interconnectedness of all life, the Goddess balances the patriarchal, disembodied, dualistic, and transcendent image of the Divine common in Western religions. For women, the Goddess represents female strength and counters cultural prejudices. For men and women alike, the Goddess is a reminder of our participation in the cyclical rhythms of life, death, and rebirth in nature.

• We also nurture ourselves when we create a rhythm of sacred times in our lives. Donna Schaper in *Sabbath Sense: A Spiritual Antidote for the Overworked* describes innovative ways to "take back our time and take care of our souls—one moment at a time." Although Schaper, a United Church of Christ minister, affirms the value of a traditional Sabbath— one day a week for rest, leisure, and worship services—she recommends that we also regularly pause to honor Spirit during our everyday rounds. Activities such as walking, gardening, homemaking, or just plain loafing take us away from our chaotic existence and give us a different perspective on time. Rituals help us unify our fragmented schedules. The Sabbath is nurturing because it encourages us to *be* more and to *do* less.

VIDEOS

• The spiritual practice of nurturing recognizes that everyone has the need to bring something to life. In many societies, men are denied this experience. *City Slickers* is about three friends from New York City who experience a journey of self-discovery on a two-week vacation at a dude ranch out West. It is the ultimate fantasy trip for these men who were raised on films and television shows about cowboys.

The story touches upon many of the issues facing men today, including aging, sexuality, relationships with friends and father figures, and finding out what is truly important to them. In the most touching scene, one of them helps deliver a calf, revealing the nurturing side of himself he has kept hidden.

● To maintain a friendship over time we need to practice nurturing. That's the message of *Fried Green Tomatoes.* An unhappily married middle-aged woman and an octogenarian living in a retirement home strike up a friendship. The older woman lifts the younger one's spirits by recalling the story of two Depression-era women whose close relationship gave their lives grounding and meaning. This movie highlights those moments when individuals find fulfillment in sharing, giving, and supporting each other from the bottom of their hearts.

● *Searching for Bobby Fischer* is one of those true-to-life films where nothing much seems to happen in the way of character development, yet lives are changed, values are tested, and a soul is forged. At seven years of age, Josh is a natural chess whiz. His father wants him to excel in the competitive chess world, and his teacher pressures him to become a winner with a killer instinct. However, much to the delight of his mother, Josh also learns to express the caring side of his personality at a national championship meet. The inner practice of nurturing his soul provides the balance he needs for the outer world of competition.

SPIRITUAL EXERCISES AND RITUALS

● Get up one hour earlier every day, or start your regular activities one hour later. Devote the hour to study, which in both Judaism and Islam is regarded as a sacred activity.

● Take time every night for self-nurturing. Dr. Christiane Northrup, author of *Women's Bodies, Women's Wisdom,* suggests that at bedtime, you look back over your day and see where you have invested your energy. Give yourself credit for all the things you have accomplished, focusing on what you have completed rather than on what you still have to do. Also notice if you are troubled by something that happened or if you are irritated with anyone. Strong feelings indicate that part of your energy still remains with the situation. Before you go to sleep, call your energy home so it will be available to renew and heal your body during the night.

● Rabbi Abraham Joshua Heschel called the Sabbath "God's sanctuary in time." Set aside one day a week for rest, recreation, and special
devotional activities. The Sabbath is a perfect occasion to savor the pleasures of friends and family, to delight in the beauty of the natural world,
to listen to music, to contemplate art, or to engage in unhurried sex with
your partner. This is also a time to give up some of the things you regularly
do, such as shopping, watching television, working, doing chores, even
talking.

PRAYER OR MANTRA

This breath prayer reminds us that the basic rhythm of the spiritual
life reflects nurturing.

> Breathing in: Receiving . . .
> Breathing out: Giving.

IMAGERY EXERCISE

The movie *The Bear* follows a bear cub, orphaned when its mother is
killed in an avalanche, that meets a wounded male grizzly bear. As they
both recover from their losses, they have numerous adventures. The intention of this exercise is to experience being nurtured and nurturing.

Breathe out three times. See yourself as a bear cub enjoying a summer
day with your mother. You are eating honey from a hive found in the
rocks on the mountain. You and your mother are licking the excess off of
each other's mouths.

Breathe out one time. You are the cub scampering down the moun-
tainside looking for company. You see a very large grizzly bear. Coming
closer, you see that he is injured. While he rests, you are cleaning out his
wound with your tongue.

Breathe out one time. Hear the splash splash of water as the big bear
catches fish in a stream. Sense the fish he tosses to you.

Breathe out one time. Traveling with your mentor, know what it
means to be a bear.

Breathe out one time. With your friend, find a quiet place to rest.
When you have become silent, open your eyes.

JOURNAL EXERCISE

The most common word association with nurturing is mothering. All of us, male and female, single or married, old or young, have the potential to give birth and raise something in the world. In a prayer written for Mother's Day, Pamela Spence Bakker used the following images. Choose those you most identify with and reflect upon them in your journal.

Some of us give birth to: children, ideas, art, music. Some of us raise: animals, flowers or vegetables, our friends, our parents, our brothers and sisters, interest in a cause, money for charity, concerns, our voices against injustice, our eyebrows, Cain.

DISCUSSION QUESTIONS, STORYTELLING, SHARING

● Talk about what you learned about this spiritual practice when you were growing up. You might share a story about taking care of a pet or younger brothers and sisters. Were you encouraged to nurture yourself?

● What are some of the blocks and hindrances that keep you from taking time to care for your soul and your spirit?

● Who has been most influential in helping you develop an ethic of caring and tenderness?

HOUSEHOLD, GROUP, AND COMMUNITY PROJECTS

● A garden is an ideal household project to practice nurturing. Learning about the plants' needs, planting, watering, weeding, pruning, and dealing with pests teaches worthwhile lessons about patience, discipline, obstacles, hope, vision, and transformation.

● Set up a study club. The idea is to meet regularly with others—preferably 8 to 10 people—to talk about something you have researched. Rotate responsibility for making an original presentation and answering questions afterward. Study clubs encourage us to grow together in community and to continue our search for depth and meaning.

FICTION, POETRY, OR CHILDREN'S BOOK

Leo Lionni's picture book *Frederick* reveals that nurturing can come from many sources. A group of field mice are busily collecting food for the winter—all except Frederick. He is gathering other kinds of supplies. Months later, when it is dark and gray outside, Frederick comforts his friends with his poetic descriptions of the warmth of the sun and the vivid colors of the flowers.

Spoken-Word Audio

True self-care includes attention to our physical bodies and our emotional needs. *Health Journeys*, a remarkable series of guided imagery tapes created by Belleruth Naparstek, encourages this kind of nurturing. The tapes use a combination of verbal directions and meditative music to focus and direct the listener's imagination, while fully engaging the senses and the emotions. The tapes have been endorsed by physicians and therapists and are currently essential components of the health and healing programs of hospitals, support groups, and thousands of individuals worldwide.

One side of each tape is a guided journey, carefully scripted for a specific intention; the other side contains affirmations, short statements for reflection. The "General Wellness" tape, for example, is designed to uplift and relax, to help the body eliminate unhealthy cells and tissue and to replace them with strong new growth, to encourage psychological healing and growth, and to invoke a sense of connection with the universe. Other tapes in the series—more than 30 are available—address such conditions as asthma, cancer, depression, grief, stress, surgery, weight loss, and trauma (PTSD). At Naparstek's web site, www.healthjourneys.com, she explains how and why guided imagery works, offers tips and encouragement, and presents the latest research findings on its effectiveness.

Art

Impressionist painter Mary Cassatt gives us many examples of individuals looking after themselves and others. In *On the Balcony*, a woman has chosen a beautiful place where she can lose herself in her reading. In *The Garden*, an older woman sits outside doing needlework; her sad yet clearly focused eyes convey that this hobby is a source of solace to her. *The Bath* shows a woman washing herself from a basin of water; the simple elegance of the room, conveyed through pastel colors on a cream laid paper, creates the impression of a private and sacred space. In *The Child's Bath*, a nanny washes a little girl's feet, a gesture of service and nurturing recognized in many spiritual traditions.

Music

The sung lullaby is associated in all cultures with nurturing. *Globalullabies* by Freyda is an impressive sampling of traditional lullabies from Czechoslovakia, Nigeria, the Isle of Man, Japan, Germany, Russia, Mexico, and France, as well as Shaker and Yiddish songs. *Dedicated to the One*

I Love by Linda Ronstadt features superb performances by the folk-rock artist of popular lullabies and some pop tunes sung in the slow, soothing style of a good-night blessing.

SEE ALSO:
Compassion. Connections. Love. Meaning. Play. You.

OPENNESS

DAILY CUE, REMINDER, VOW, BLESSING

Opening a window is a cue to open my mind to new ideas
and experiences.

•

When I hold an empty cup, I am reminded to remain open
and receptive.

•

Seeing a sign, a book, or a film in another language, I vow to be
open to the messages coming to me from other cultures.

•

Blessed is the Holy One whose openness to us is a model for how
we should be open to the world.

THE BASIC PRACTICE

It is important in the spiritual life to keep an open mind, open to ideas,
experiences, people, the world, and the Sacred. Openness is an ability to
go with the flow, as Taoism puts it, without expecting predetermined
outcomes. It means being receptive to new possibilities without prejudging
them. It is an ability to make yourself available to out-of-the-ordinary
opportunities. Indeed, openness to the unknown, the exotic, and the bi-
zarre is usually seen as the mark of a free spirit.

You can increase your openness by practicing empathy. Move outside yourself into another's situation. Try to access the other's feelings and ideas. For the purposes of practice, the more eccentric your choice, the better.

CATALYSTS, CONTRASTS, AND COMPANIONS

The contrast to openness is closed-mindedness. Pessimistic people who have armored themselves against preconceived disappointments are not open. Dogmatic and stubborn people are basically unapproachable.

How available are you to others? How interested are you in others, especially those quite different from you? How flexible are you? Do you usually think you already know how things are going to come out? Are you willing to try something new? These are the questions to ask to assess your openness and to determine the benefits you might derive from this practice.

PERSPECTIVES

By being receptive, we can avail ourselves of the spiritual wealth available to us.

By being open, we can receive things beyond what we ourselves might imagine.
–DENG MING-DAO

Openness is a receptivity to everyone and everything. It is quite fundamentally an other-centeredness, a disposition of availability to others.
–WAYNE TEASDALE

Heartful practice is about keeping the heart open to the world around us— to people, places, ourselves, and the Divine. It means coming from a place of empathic attunement. It's about seeing the connections, the interlocking webs of energy among people and things, and residing as much as possible in that place of no separation.
–BELLERUTH NAPARSTEK

TEACHERS

● In our multicultural and pluralistic world, openness to other cultures is especially important. Anthropologist Mary Catherine Bateson is our teacher of this practice. *Peripheral Visions: Learning Along the Way* presents many examples from her involvement with other cultures—in Iran, Israel, and the Philippines—to demonstrate what can be gained from encounters with other ways of life. No single model is sufficient for understanding;

many stories have more than one meaning. We must broaden our focus and delight in a diversity of experiences, even those that are peripheral, marginal, or distant. She affirms the values of allowing both continuity and discontinuity in our way of life and being flexible as we improvise new paths to self and communal fulfillment.

Openness, for Bateson, is a way of learning, and it is a sacred path. "Curiosity is a good place to start if one is going to encounter the sacred," she observes. Another useful approach is empathy: "Insight, I believe, refers to the depth of understanding that comes by setting experiences, yours and mine, familiar and exotic, new and old, side by side, learning by letting them speak to one another."

• Madonna Kolbenschlag, a social philosopher, identifies Mary Catherine Bateson, along with Pierre Teilhard de Chardin, Thomas Merton, Audre Lorde, and Joanna Macy, as mentors of openness. In *Eastward Toward Eve: A Geography of Soul*, she uses a 1994 lecture trip to Japan as an opportunity to explore what can be learned by a "journey into difference"—between male and female, East and West, God and self, yin and yang. She looks to the "the subjugated knowledge" of women, indigenous people, gays and lesbians, people of color, refugees, artists, people who are differently abled, and other groups for fresh avenues to personal and cultural transformation. Openness, here, is the ability to see clearly, without preference or prejudice, and with empathy.

VIDEOS

• *Dances with Wolves* is a shining parable about the spiritual practice of openness. This Academy Award–winning film is set on the Dakota Plains during the 1860s. Lt. John S. Dunbar, a cavalry officer in the U.S. Army, sets up camp at a deserted outpost deep in territory inhabited by the Lakota. When these Native Americans learn that he is peaceful and even friendly, they welcome him in a series of intricate rituals. Dunbar's openness enables him to find a new community whose values enrich and expand his kinship with the land, its elements, and its animals.

• We don't have to enter into a strange culture or travel to distant lands to be challenged to practice openness. It can happen when strangers come into our communities. *House of Angels*, a Swedish film, addresses this issue. A beautiful blond cabaret performer inherits an estate from her grandfather and moves with her leather-jacketed boyfriend to a small conservative town in current-day Sweden. The presence of these two bohemian outsiders, who dress and act bizarrely, immediately throws the tranquil community into turmoil. But the outgoing local minister takes it upon himself to set up a series of encounters between the townsfolk and the strangers. The spiritual practice of openness by one person can positively affect a whole community.

● The impact of an individual is also a theme in *The Spitfire Grill.* Percy Talbot arrives in the small town of Gilead after serving five years in prison. She begins working for Hannah, the owner of a local eatery, and makes friends with Shelby, an insecure young mother. She also draws out a mysterious recluse living in the nearby woods. Because she has known pain herself, she is able to transmute it for others, creating new possibilities for the people around her.

Her openness, however, is shadowed by the narrow-mindedness of Shelby's husband, Nahum. He's a dogmatic, authoritarian type who has suffered many disappointments in life. He projects his anger on Percy, the outsider, with tragic results. Still, the process of openness has begun in Gilead and its citizens will never view strangers in the same way again.

SPIRITUAL EXERCISES AND RITUALS

● Open your mind today to some author, philosophy, or religious perspective that you have always regarded as weird or alien. Read an article or go to a lecture.

● Attend an ethnic celebration—a parade, folk dance, or music festival—in your community and talk with participants about their heritages. Or eat at an ethnic restaurant and ask about the food and the people serving it.

● Expand your repertoire of seasonal rituals by observing some from other cultures. Mythologist Joseph Campbell once noted, "The celebrations of the world are a reverent part of the human heritage." *Celebrations Around the World: A Multicultural Handbook* by Carol S. Angell outlines more than 300 festivals and religious holidays from Angola to Zimbabwe. Here are three examples.

January 11–13 is Makra Sankrant (Winter Festival) in India. Small silk bags containing sesame seeds mixed with sugar are offered to friends with the greeting "Eat this sweet sesame and speak sweetly to me," an expression intended to assure there will be no quarreling in the year.

In Iran, No-Ruz, or the New Year, is celebrated on March 21–22. The family gathers in new clothes bought for the occasion around a table, which is decorated with a candle for each family member, fresh greens grown from wheat or lentil seeds, and a goldfish in a bowl. It's believed that the goldfish will turn over in its bowl at the moment when the new year begins. The touching Iranian film *The White Balloon* centers around a little girl's efforts to get a special goldfish for the holiday.

September 12 is Respect for the Aged Day in Japan, a day to honor older relatives and family friends. It's a good time to write letters to elders and visit them in their homes.

PRAYER OR MANTRA

This prayer is from William Penn, an English Quaker who founded the colony of Pennsylvania in America, which he envisioned as a place of religious and personal freedom.

O God, help us not to despise or oppose
what we do not understand.

IMAGERY EXERCISE

The ability to empathize with other people, to identify with and understand their situations, is an important part of the spiritual practice of openness. This exercise is adapted from a longer version in *Staying Well with Guided Imagery* by Belleruth Naparstek.

Position yourself as comfortably as you can and take a couple of deep, full, cleansing breaths. . . . Now, imagining and sensing a place where you feel safe and peaceful . . . you look out in front of you and see a screen . . . and you become aware of a human form beginning to appear on it . . . someone you want to understand better. . . . And you see that, undetected by him or her, you can softly and easily enter the screen to walk around this person and have a closer look. . . . And now for the sake of your own learning, for just a short while . . . sliding past the boundaries and slipping into the body of this other person, feeling what it is like to be in their body, looking down and seeing their clothing, seeing out from their eyes what the world looks like . . . sounds like . . . feels like . . . as you breathe their breath . . . feel their feelings.

And now, very gently wishing this body good-bye and moving back into your own body, feeling grateful for your ability to move so easily here and there, you step out of the screen, back to your peaceful place . . . and coming back into the room whenever you are ready . . . knowing that you are better for this . . . and so you are.

JOURNAL EXERCISES

● Review the questions under "Catalysts, Contrasts, and Companions" at the beginning of this chapter, then write an assessment of your own openness. Be candid about both your strengths and your weaknesses in this practice.

● Make a list of out-of-the-ordinary things you would like to do. Brainstorm the wildest new experiences you could have to open your mind. Choose one to follow up on this year.

DISCUSSION QUESTIONS, STORYTELLING, SHARING

● Have an international story festival. Each member of the group shares a short folk tale from another culture that gives you a fresh insight on life. It might be something heard while traveling or found in a book at the library.

● What values do you think are most useful in breaking down the barriers of suspicion and fear of strangers? What does your religious tradition say about the treatment of outsiders?

HOUSEHOLD, GROUP, AND COMMUNITY PROJECTS

● Rent a foreign film or watch a travel documentary to learn more about a culture different from your own. Talk afterward about what you found most interesting about the people and their way of life.

● Support an exchange student from another country. If it is not possible to have someone live in your home, contribute money to sponsoring organizations and attend events where you can meet foreign students.

● Have a potluck dinner at your church, synagogue, or club, sharing dishes from other countries. Come prepared to talk about your dish or, if you have traveled to the country, to show pictures.

FICTION, POETRY, OR CHILDREN'S BOOK

Solar Storms is a novel by Linda Hogan about an encounter with both one's roots and the unknown. After years in foster homes, 17-year-old Angel returns to her Native American family. Together with three of her women elders, she journeys through the wilderness to her ancestral homeland. Angel's unique coming-of-age is achieved through the practice of openness on many levels.

Spoken-Word Audio

On *Walking the Four-Fold Way,* anthropologist Angeles Arrien is interviewed by New Dimensions Radio host Michael Toms. She reveals what her studies of indigenous people have shown her about the four archetypal paths of the warrior, healer, visionary, and teacher. Arrien, whose practice of openness is evident here, makes it clear that all of us can learn from the wisdom of other cultures.

Art

One way to gain access to another culture is through its distinctive art. A good example of this is provided in *Wisdom from the Earth: The Living Legacy of the Aboriginal Dreamtime.* Anna Voight and Neville Drury examine the history, ceremonies, and cosmology of these indigenous people, illustrating many of their points with color photographs of ancient and contemporary Aboriginal art. Here are paintings of the Rainbow Serpent, the Creator of Life; representations of Dreamtime ancestors; and story paintings about the cycles of life.

Music

The international flavor of music today is unmistakable. The spiritual practice of openness challenges us to sample albums from around the world. Here are three with which to begin your cross-cultural experiences. The Girls of Angeli come from a Sámi (Lapp) village in northern Finland, where their indigenous culture is still respected. On *The New Voice of the North,* they sing about village life through traditional "yoiks," a form of chanting that to the Sámi is both a way of talking and of purifying oneself. The members of Yothu Yindi are among the traditional owners of a region of Australia's Northern Territory. *Tribal Voice* mixes Aboriginal concerns with more contemporary rock music. *Journey to the Amazon,* featuring Sharon Isbin on guitar, Paul Winter on saxophone, and Thiago de Mello on percussion, celebrates the sounds and rhythms of the rain forest and its inhabitants.

See Also:

Compassion. Connections. Hospitality. Justice. Kindness. Listening. Unity.

PEACE

THE BASIC PRACTICE

Peace is built on the foundations of other spiritual practices: connections, compassion, justice, unity. It is a goal of all spiritual people. Peace is
an inner state of well-being and calm. It is also an outer project of promoting
nonviolence, conflict resolution, and cooperation in the world. The root of
the Hebrew word for peace, *shalom*, means "whole" and points to this
twofold meaning: peace within oneself and peace among people.

Practice peace by refusing to participate in violence either through
language or behavior, either directly or indirectly. Try to stay composed
no matter how agitated those around you become. Meet conflict with

equanimity. Disarm yourself—lower your guard—as a first step in disarming the world.

CATALYSTS, CONTRASTS, AND COMPANIONS

The inner mirrors the outer. Those conditions that upset the equilibrium of the world—anger, aggression, discord—upset our inner peace as well. You need to deal with them on both levels. Encounters with violence—a contrast to peace—invariably demonstrate the importance of this practice.

Feeling worried, upset, or "crazed" can also get you started doing peace. These states often signify that your emotions have gotten the better of you, and a practice to restore your equanimity is needed. Being even-tempered creates a feeling of serenity. Whereas being agitated can drain your energy, inner calm increases your stamina so that you can sustain your efforts to make the world a more peaceful place. This time the inner supports the outer.

PERSPECTIVES

When you are proclaiming peace with your lips, be careful to have it even more fully in your heart.
–SAINT FRANCIS OF ASSISI

Active nonviolence flows from a disarmed heart with the truth that the unity already realized inside us is also present in all humanity.
–JOHN DEAR

Welcoming a person with a greeting of peace and harmony is akin to welcoming God, for God is peace.
–THE ZOHAR

TEACHERS

● Our first teacher of peace is Bernie Glassman, cofounder of the Zen Peacemaker Order, a community of social activists from around the world. His book *Bearing Witness: A Zen Master's Lessons in Making Peace* is one of the most important works ever written on peacemaking. He believes that this spiritual practice involves letting go of preconceived ideas and answers, seeing places of great agony as places of great healing, ending all dualistic thinking, and steering one's life by the lights of empathy, compassion, openness, and zeal.

Peacemaking is a function of bearing witness. Glassman writes: "When we bear witness, when we become the situation—homelessness, poverty, illness, violence, death—the right action arises by itself. We don't have to worry about what to do." By identifying with all parts of a situation—actually going to the streets to beg for food or checking into a hospital as a patient—we thoroughly engage all aspects of ourselves, thus creating the milieu for wholeness, healing, and peace.

● Paul Fleischman, a psychiatrist, also teaches that peace, both inner and outer, is a way of life. "All of your thoughts and actions can facilitate your growth in peace. . . . Starting from many different courtyards and doorsteps, it always converges on purity of heart, horizonless perspective, and service to the common cause."

In order to delineate the multiple meanings of inner peace, Fleischman looks at the lives of people who have pursued it with dedication, creativity, imagination, discipline, and devotion. He finds hints of peace as a dynamic force in the simple lifestyle of the Shakers and in the organic farming of Helen and Scott Nearing. Walt Whitman's ecstatic poetry and Mahatma Gandhi's nonviolence are two more examples. John Muir and Henry David Thoreau are heralded for their discoveries of peace in the natural world. Father Daniel Berrigan shows us the prophetic dimensions of peace, and Indian poet Rabindranath Tagore demonstrates a life of peace in action. Fleishman enables us to see this spiritual practice as "a natural phenomenon, a sweet memory, and a provocative force."

● Henri J. M. Nouwen, a Catholic priest and prolific writer on social ministry, is another significant teacher of the practice of peace. Editor John Dear surveyed Nouwen's 40 books and assembled nearly all of his writings on peace, disarmament, and social justice in *The Road to Peace: Writings on Peace and Justice.* Nouwen talks about seeking peace through the civil rights movement, while serving the poor in Latin America, through his work with handicapped members of the L'Arche community, and in his service of people with AIDS.

"Nothing is more important in peacemaking than that it flow from a deep and undeniable experience of love," Nouwen observes. "Only those who know deeply that they are loved and rejoice in that love can be true peacemakers." The danger for peace activists is that they will make all war-makers into enemies. Again and again, Nouwen comes back to the insights of Oscar Romero and Thomas Merton who grounded their nonviolence in prayer and community solidarity.

VIDEOS

• As a visionary of peace and a practitioner of nonviolence, Mohandas K. Gandhi (1869–1948) left an indelible mark on India and on the world. Richard Attenborough's film *Gandhi* begins in 1893 as the young English-trained lawyer arrives in South Africa and ends in 1948 with his assassination and funeral in the newly independent nation.

Dr. Martin Luther King, Jr., who adapted Gandhi's *Satyagraha* (nonviolence) techniques in America, once said: "Gandhi was inevitable. If humanity is to progress, Gandhi is inescapable. He lived, thought and acted, inspired by the vision of humanity evolving toward a world of peace and harmony." We find in Gandhi's exemplary life insights into the interplay of religion and politics, the significance of spiritual discipline, reverence for life, solidarity with the poor, voluntary simplicity, and moral leadership—all things that make for peace.

• The Dalai Lama is another true hero of peace. Martin Scorsese's film *Kundun* presents a sober and reverent portrait of the fourteenth spiritual leader of Tibet from his discovery in a small village in 1937 through his escape to India in 1959.

When the boy his teachers call Kundun reaches the age of 15, his homeland is invaded by the Chinese Army of Chairman Mao Zedong. The crisis leads officials in the Tibetan government to vest the Dalai Lama with temporal power to quell the fears of the populace. In a brief encounter with Mao, the young Tibetan leader recognizes that his society of spirit and nonviolence clashes with China's culture of materialism and militarism. This presentation of the childhood and adolescence of the fourteenth Dalai Lama vividly depicts the courage it takes to adhere to the principle of nonviolence in the face of suffering and injustice.

SPIRITUAL EXERCISES AND RITUALS

• Thich Nhat Hanh points out that we need to be careful not to ingest all the violence we see in movies, TV shows, games, and books, lest we water the seeds of violence that we all carry inside us. Go on a violence fast. Give up all violent entertainment.

• Equanimity is the quality of being even-tempered and unaffected by outside influences. It does not mean that you are indifferent to what is happening around you; you just don't allow it to upset your inner peace. Here's a basic equanimity practice. Whenever you feel a strong emotion coming on—a response to pain or pleasure, success or failure, extreme stress or thorough relief—say to yourself, "This, too, will pass."

• This ritual for peace is suggested by James Conlon in *Ponderings from the Precipice*. Try it with some concerned friends. "Go to a place where destruction and violence have taken place. You may find yourself in the inner city, where people are mistreated or abused, or in a place where pollution abounds, in a toxic dump where poison and aggression against Earth is painfully present. In silence, be present to this locus of violence. Allow this place of human pain or ecological devastation to speak to you. Observe what is here; what do you see, hear, touch, smell? What do you think? After ten minutes, focus your attention specifically on the pain of the people or the place where violence has occurred."

PRAYER OR MANTRA

This mantra comes from the lyrics of John Lennon's song.

> Breathing in: Give peace . . .
> Breathing out: a chance.

IMAGERY EXERCISE

Fran Peavey's experience, which is related on page 353 of *Spiritual Literacy,* is the inspiration for this exercise, "Hugging the World."

Breathe out three times. See and sense the round globe of the Earth in your arms. With your fingers, trace the shape of the continents, dip into the waters of the oceans, walk up the sides of the mountains. Reach out to any beings you encounter as you travel around the globe. Feel what they are feeling. Hear what they are saying.

Breathe out one time. Sense and know that you are comforting the beings and comforting the Earth. Then open your eyes.

JOURNAL EXERCISES

• Maha Ghosananda, a Cambodian Buddhist teacher, says, "When you make peace with yourself, you make peace with the world." In your journal, make peace with yourself about something that has upset your internal equilibrium or your harmony with others.

• The next time you are tempted to rip someone apart or give them a piece of your mind, write a letter in your journal that you never send.

• Collect pictures that have a calming, peaceful effect on you. Paste a few of them at the back of your journal to contemplate during those times when you feel ill at ease with yourself and the world.

DISCUSSION QUESTIONS, STORYTELLING, SHARING

• What does the idea and the ideal of the peaceable kingdom where the lion lies down with the lamb mean to you? What steps have you taken this week to make the world a more peaceful place?

• Mahatma Gandhi said that "noncooperation with evil is as much a duty as is cooperation with good." Give an example of a situation when you have found that noncooperation, nondoing, or not taking sides has supported peace.

• Who is the most forceful and impressive peacemaker you have ever encountered? What did you learn from that person?

• What institutions in society should be teaching people the arts of peaceful resolution of conflict?

HOUSEHOLD, GROUP, AND COMMUNITY PROJECTS

• Be instruments of God's peace in your home. Refrain from the use of sarcasm, ridicule, or teasing as weapons against each other.

• Make your household a witness for peace in the world. Sign "The Family Pledge of Nonviolence" available from the Families Against Violence Advocacy Network (Institute for Peace and Justice, 4144 Lindell Boulevard, #408, Saint Louis, MO 63108). Commitments in this pledge include: respect self and others, communicate better, listen carefully, forgive, respect nature, play creatively, and be courageous. Periodically review how you are all doing with the pledge.

• Identify "conflict resolution" projects in your community. Sometimes they are called "anger management" programs. Bring one of them to your church, synagogue, school, library, workplace, or other community center.

FICTION, POETRY, OR CHILDREN'S BOOK

Jesuit priest Daniel Berrigan is a disturber of the peace. Always has been. That, of course, is part of what it means to be a peacemaker. The status quo must be challenged. Berrigan's quest for peace and justice has taken him around the world and has resulted in years spent in prison. *And the Risen Bread: Selected Poems, 1957–1997* brings together the best of his work from 14 volumes of poetry. "Peacemaking Is Hard" sums up Berrigan's ministry as an antiwar protester and a follower of "a man [who] stood on nails."

SPOKEN-WORD AUDIO

One of the most significant aspects of the practice of peace is equanimity—being calm, centered, and serene. An image often used to illustrate this state of being is the mountain. It is unwavering whether the sun is shining on it, rain is falling on it, or it is being covered with snow. On *Your Buddha Nature: Teachings on the Ten Perfections,* therapist, author, and meditation instructor Jack Kornfield explores the path of mindful living in Buddhism. One of the ten perfections is equanimity, a virtue that untangles and purifies. Kornfield uses a relaxed and gracious teaching style, which in itself is a grand illustration of this practice.

ART

Artists have given us many different images of peace to comfort our souls. John Constable's *The Cornfield* soothes us with its unspoiled countryside vista. Camille Pissarro's *Landscape at Chaponval* also displays the tranquility of a rural scene, this one of field and village under a blue sky flecked with fluffy clouds. The becalming wonders of nature are presented in Washington Allston's *Landscape with a Lake.* True serenity is evident in Peter Severin Kröyer's *Summer Evening on the Southern Beach,* where two ladies stroll down a deserted beach.

MUSIC

Musicians through the centuries have expressed the yearning for two kinds of peace—inner serenity and a world without war. On *Rhythms of Peace,* Tibetan Nawang Khechog plays the bamboo flute, inviting listeners to experience a profound inner calm. His music, created spontaneously while he is playing, is intended to inspire peace within our hearts.

Three classic pop songs capture the other kind of peace: "Give Peace a Chance" by John Lennon, "Peace Will Come" by Melanie, and "Peace Train" by Cat Stevens.

SEE ALSO:

Compassion. Connections. Forgiveness. Justice. Unity. You.

 PLAY

DAILY CUE, REMINDER, VOW, BLESSING

Hearing someone laugh is my cue to practice play.

•

A swing set reminds me that all ground is playground.

•

Whenever I participate in a game, I vow to make my play
more cooperative and less competitive.

•

Blessed is the Giver of Life who welcomes our play in celebration
of the lightness of our being.

THE BASIC PRACTICE

Coyote. Nasrudin. Saint Francis and his order of Jesters of the Lord. Zen masters. Taoist sages. Hasidic storytellers. Clowns and performance artists. Such prophets—and all spiritual traditions have them—encourage us not to take ourselves too seriously. They say that what we know is not worth knowing, and what's worth knowing cannot be known through our ways. To our sensible selves, their actions seem silly, shameless, even shocking. But they have an important role in the spiritual life. They carry the banner for the spiritual practice of play.

Play is the exuberant expression of our being. It is at the heart of our creativity, our sexuality, and our most carefree moments of devotion. It helps us live with absurdity, paradox, and mystery. It feeds our joy and wonder. It keeps our search for meaning down to earth.

Practice play by doing things on the spur of the moment. Take time out to experiment, to try on different parts, to relax. Laugh heartily at jokes, situations, and yourself. Remember, laughter heals body, mind, and soul, and, by extension, communities.

CATALYSTS, CONTRASTS, AND COMPANIONS

Most of us don't play enough. We're either too "busy," a code word for workaholism, or we're too serious, mistaking earnestness for accomplishment. We're predictable, too, equating free-spiritedness with irresponsibility. The best treatment for these conditions is play. We need to lighten up.

But there is also a shadow side of play. Sometimes we get so involved in role playing and just having a good time that we never reveal our true selves. Then we need the company of other fools to point out the folly of our foolishness.

PERSPECTIVES

The comic spirit masquerades in all things we say and do. We are each a clown and do not need to put on a white face.
–JAMES HILLMAN

Shut your mouth, close your lips, and say something!
–ZEN MASTER PAICHANG

Laughter is a holy thing. It is as sacred as music and silence and solemnity, maybe more sacred. Laughter is like a prayer, like a bridge over which creatures tiptoe to meet each other. Laughter is like mercy; it heals. When you can laugh at yourself, you are free.
–TED LODER

TEACHERS

• Dean Sluyter, who has taught nonsectarian approaches to meditation for 25 years, understands the importance of play. His *Why the Chicken*

Crossed the Road & Other Hidden Enlightenment Teachers from the Buddha to Bebop to Mother Goose is an imaginative guide through the crazy wisdom of contemporary pop culture. There are chapters on cosmic jokes ("What—Me Worry?"; "Take My Wife . . . Please!"), sacred nursery rhymes ("Mary Had a Little Lamb"; "She Loves Me, She Loves Me Not"), exploding proverbs ("Easy Does It"; "Now Is the Time for All Good Men"), and accidental hymns ("I Can't Get No Satisfaction"; "Happy Trails").

He dazzles us with epiphanies growing out of these cultural artifacts. "Knock, Knock" jokes ask "Who's there?" and challenge our limited concepts of self, just like the teachings of the world's religions. The nursery rhyme "I'm a Little Teapot" reminds us that our lives must be upset ("tip me over") before we can be free of confining walls ("pour me out"). And why did the chicken cross the road? When we are playing, we don't have to ask "why" at every juncture of the journey. Besides, the answer is: to get to the other side.

• Shaun McNiff, our second teacher of this spiritual practice, celebrates play's part in creativity. In *Trust the Process: An Artist's Guide to Letting Go,* he draws on personal experience and his work with creative art therapies to reveal how experimentation, improvisation, and constant reframing—elements usually present in play—can be antidotes to creative blocks such as fear of self-disclosure, low self-confidence, and anxiety over what others will think. He shows how by gathering and arranging things in collages, framed constructions, altars, or special shelves, we can playfully express our feelings toward our possessions.

In a chapter entitled "Play and Ornamentation," McNiff recommends experimenting with art materials, shapes, patterns, and colors. "Start by ridding yourself of the idea that play is subjective and egocentric," he advises. "It is actually the opposite. Play requires immersion in 'otherness.' I get out of myself when I play and I enter an imaginative realm that is a distinctly different stage of being."

VIDEOS

• *Forrest Gump* is an enchanting and creative parable about a contemporary holy fool. He is part of a long line of such characters in spiritual stories. These individuals follow the dictates of their hearts and pay little heed to the pursuit of worldly power, status, or financial success. Their brand of selflessness is free of reason's madness and the ego's grandeur. That is why they are so often deemed crazy and live as outsiders.

Forrest, who has an I.Q. just below normal, is raised by a single mother who lavishes love on him. Because he is able to focus on the present moment and not worry about results, he becomes an incredibly fast runner and a champion Ping-Pong player. He manages to maintain his optimism and good-heartedness all through the political, social, and cultural turmoil of the 1960s. But what is really surprising about him is his loyalty to his friends and his unswerving love for one woman. "I'm not a smart man," he says at one point, "but I know what love is." Like many a holy fool before him, Forrest knows what is worth knowing.

• Roy in the movie *Tin Cup* is another holy fool. His stage is the professional golf circuit. At the beginning of the film, he is quite happy running a seedy driving range in Texas and hanging out with his caddy and their beer-guzzling friends. Although he has plenty of natural talent as a golfer, his love for spectacular and difficult shots has limited his competitive prospects.

Roy has a mystical and poetic appreciation of the game, a bent that comes to the fore when Dr. Molly Griswold, a therapist, shows up for a lesson. He immediately falls in love with her. Soon he is vying for her affections with another golfer, even going so far as to compete in the U.S. Open. But at the crucial point when he needs to make a decision based on what is reasonable, Roy confounds everyone. He knows that in love and in sports, playing it safe can't hold a candle to taking risks and acting from the heart.

SPIRITUAL EXERCISES AND RITUALS

• Do something completely outrageous at least once a week. Call it your "play date."

• Find small ways of making your work more playful. For example, post cartoons on your door or keep stuffed animals on your desk.

• Take a five-minute laugh break every day. Keep a collection of jokes or pictures that always set you off. Cultivate friendships with people who can make you laugh.

• Shaun McNiff thinks anyone can be playful with art. For example, try writing graffiti: "There is a sense of expressive delight and a shattering of convention when we magnify and exaggerate our habitual repertoire of handwriting gestures." Scribble words, phrases, and random marks all over the surface of a large sheet of paper. Experiment with words that hold positive and negative energies for you. Let your marks be bigger and bolder every time you do this exercise.

PRAYER OR MANTRA

Dean Sluyter suggests that Bugs Bunny's classic line is a mantra. The first part evokes "the pause before formless awareness concretizes into words and thoughts: the wisdom of uncertainty, omnidirectional openness to all possibilities, the child-mind that is required to enter the kingdom of heaven." The second phase presents the challenge for our meditation: "What's the story? What's reality?"

> Breathing in: Eh, . . .
> Breathing out: what's up, Doc?

IMAGERY EXERCISE

Movement is how the body expresses its playful nature. This exercise, "Spontaneity," was created by Colette Aboulker-Muscat of Jerusalem, Israel.

Close your eyes and breathe out three times. Focus your attention on your body and let go, so your body can do whatever it wants to do without planning or direction. You are becoming aware of parts of your body that want to move. Let these parts of your body move in any way. Be graceful, awkward, flowing, whatever feels right.

Breathe out three times. Sense these moving parts bringing other parts into movement. Sense some movement changing and developing into other sorts of movements. See and feel how when some movements stop, others may emerge. Continue to focus your attention on your body, and let it be free.

Breathe out one time. See how you limit and inhibit yourself and what parts of your body are tense and held in. When you do, clean out the parts in any way you wish and let them be free.

When you are ready, open your eyes.

JOURNAL EXERCISES

● Write about your favorite hobby and the delight it has given you over the years. How does it express your playfulness?

● Often a key to increasing the play in our lives is identifying what comes naturally to us—what does not seem like work. Use your journal to develop a plan to give more time to activities that are effortless for you.

● Have play pages in your journal—every few days. Doodle. Draw silly faces. Experiment with finger-paints, crayons, colored pencils. Paint with a toothpick or an old toothbrush.

DISCUSSION QUESTIONS, STORYTELLING, SHARING

● When was the last time you truly let yourself go and abandoned yourself fully to play? What did it feel like?

● The greatest criticism of religious and spiritual people is that they take themselves too seriously. What role does humor play in your faith, and why is it important to you?

● Tell jokes and share funny stories at one of your group meetings. Impersonate your favorite humorists. Show scenes from comedies. Pass around cartoons. Play group games you remember from your childhood birthday parties. Puzzle over riddles. Act out charades. Stop anyone from being serious, even for a moment.

HOUSEHOLD, GROUP, AND COMMUNITY PROJECTS

● In *Feasting with God: Adventures in Table Spirituality*, Holly W. Whitcomb provides plans for "An Outrageous Feast" designed to help us get in touch with our most flamboyant selves. Guests wear outrageous costumes and bring an outrageous food that speaks of excess—the creamiest cheesecake, the pizza with the most toppings. Everyone shares an outrageous fantasy and commits to doing one outrageous deed for the common good.

● Spend an afternoon at the local playground. Get to know your neighborhood better by trying out its toys.

● Create a "Fools Festival" for a group in your community, perhaps a ward at the hospital or a nursery school. Wear humorous outfits and take the makings for more. Paint each other's faces. Put on silly skits. You might plan all this merry-making for April Fool's Day.

FICTION, POETRY, OR CHILDREN'S BOOK

Browse through the humor sections of your local bookstore or library for the makings of an evening of play. Check out books of jokes, bloopers, and cartoons by such masters of jest as Gary Larson, Jules Feiffer, George Carlin, Scott Adams, Tracey Ullman, and Steve Martin. A good book to bring home is *Play with Your Food* by Joost Elffers. Here you will find ideas for carving pumpkins and creating delightful little animals out of fruits and vegetables. Play with your brussels sprout pig, mushroom man, squash goose, pear bear, leek freaks, banana octopus, mouse yam, orange cat, and all the rest of the menagerie.

SPOKEN-WORD AUDIO

Down through the ages, saints, fools, poets, and comedians have challenged conventional wisdom and tried to get us to see the value of what we too often reject—mystery, paradox, and the unity of all things. *Crazy Wisdom* by Wes "Scoop" Nisker presents the humorous and insightful epiphanies of Socrates, Zen masters, Hasidic storytellers, Beat writers, and contemporary humorists.

ART

There is something about the art of Paul Klee that is positively ingratiating. We find ourselves smiling at an image, laughing at the accompanying title, giddy with the overall effect. *A Child's Game* conveys the delight of a young girl running through a garden with a goose. *Genie Serving a Light Breakfast* is a humorous ditty revealing Klee's idiosyncratic world of fantasy. *Dance, You Monster, to My Soft Song!* conveys the absurdity of a tiny pianist trying to direct an enormous floating balloon man. And in *The Creator*, the artist's playfulness even extends to how he imagines the Godhead—hovering in the pink cosmos with arms spread and garments flowing as if in a dance.

MUSIC

In music, playing around comes out as jazz. Stan Kenton was the leader of several progressive jazz bands in the 1940s and 1950s. Emotional, radical, unpredictable, and original are adjectives frequently used to describe his records. *Kenton in Hi-Fi*, recorded in 1956, is a good sampling of this sound with Kenton on piano and members of his various bands on saxophones, trombones, trumpets, guitars, and percussion.

Included are two of Kenton's theme songs, "Artistry in Rhythm" and "Eager Beaver."

 QUESTING

DAILY CUE, REMINDER, VOW, BLESSING

The sight of an airplane or a train is a cue for me to practice questing.

•

Whenever I travel from one time zone into another, I am reminded of the need to keep my questing spirit alive.

•

When I encounter someone who believes he or she has all the answers, I vow to honor all the questions.

•

Blessed is the Great Host who fills our lives with the adventure of questing.

THE BASIC PRACTICE

Questers venture into the unknown, confront difficulties and dangers, and return home with new understandings of themselves and the world. A pilgrimage, part trip and part ritual, is prescribed in all the religious traditions for those seeking healing and renewal. The impetus for the journey could be an urge to explore one's spiritual roots, a desire for absolution, a wish to pay homage, or a question that needs answering.

To practice questing, you have to leave home, both literally and figuratively. Travel to a sacred place where something has happened before

---

and see what happens to you now. Don't stop, even if you stumble, until you have found a gift or an insight to bring back with you. If you can't go far, make an inner journey. Ask questions. Look for replies in areas where you have never thought to go before.

CATALYSTS, CONTRASTS, AND COMPANIONS

Questing is a companion of adventure. We thrill to the quest! This kind of travel broadens your horizons and gives you practice dealing with new situations. It increases your capacity to take risks. It helps you overcome any timidity or fear of the unknown that may be holding you back.

Questing also serves as an antidote to certitude, thinking that you know all the answers. It encourages you to be a seeker, to keep searching for different strategies to meet the challenges of our times.

PERSPECTIVES

All of the larger-than-life questions about our presence here on Earth and what gifts we have to offer are spiritual questions. To seek answers to these questions is to seek a sacred path.
–LAUREN ARTRESS

We are summoned, we feel, because something in the universe says, "You have hero material in you." A summons, we believe, asks us to go on a quest. It places us in a mythical context.
–DAVID SPANGLER

Each well-considered question can lead to a whole universe of wisdom, because one insight leads to another as the answers come.
–EVAN PRITCHARD

TEACHERS

• Paulo Coelho is a Brazilian author whose quest literature has captured the hearts and minds of people around the world. In *The Alchemist: A Fable About Following Your Dream*, Santiago, an Andalusian shepherd boy, has a dream about finding a treasure near the pyramids in Egypt. On the advice of a gypsy woman and with gifts from a mysterious king, the boy summons his courage, sells his sheep, and travels to Africa. When a thief steals his money, he has to take a job in Tangier before joining a caravan crossing the desert.

Santiago's story is an archetypal quest. The boy answers a call, is equipped for the journey, is tested along the way, and at the end finds what he needs to return home and realize his destiny. The experience is life-changing. He learns to trust his heart, to read the world for signs of God, and to accept the ways of love.

• Jean Shinoda Bolen, a Jungian analyst, was also invited to undertake a quest; her call came in 1986 from an admirer of her best-selling book *Goddesses in Everywoman*, who offered her an all-expenses-paid pilgrimage to sacred sites in Europe including Chartres, Glastonbury, Avalon, Findhorn, and Iona. *Crossing to Avalon: A Woman's Midlife Pilgrimage* is Bolen's account of this journey of self-discovery and personal renewal. Throughout the book, she moves fluidly between outer events and inner reflections. On the road, she meets sister pilgrims who share the stories of their lives and encourage Bolen to get in touch with the feminine mysteries.

At one point, Bolen notes that pilgrims go to sacred places in order to "quicken the divinity within themselves, to experience spiritual awakening, or receive a blessing or become healed." The trip has all these effects on the author, and by bearing witness to them, Bolen helps her readers recognize similar moments of quickening in their own lives.

• Another teacher of questing is Sue Bender, an artist and family therapist who finds herself mysteriously drawn to the quilts and faceless dolls made by Amish women. She intuits in these creations a clarity and a calm that is definitely missing from her cluttered and frantic existence in Berkeley, California. "Is there another way to lead my life?" she wonders. This question animates her quest.

She asks two Amish families, one in Iowa and one in Ohio, to allow her to stay with them. They help her see the value of humility, austerity, simplicity, pleasure in hard work, and community. However, the real challenge comes when she returns home and tries to incorporate these values into her "crazy quilt life." Her meditations on these experiences are included in *Plain and Simple: A Woman's Journey to the Amish*. It captures the struggle many seekers face when they try to turn their lives around.

VIDEOS

• The quest for the new and the undiscovered has led explorers to the highest mountains, the deepest oceans, the most impenetrable jungles, the most forbidding deserts, and the far reaches of outer space. Some of these travelers seek fame and fortune. Others are driven by curiosity or a desire to know about other cultures. All of these impulses are presented in *Mountains of the Moon*. It is the story of two expeditions during the middle of the nineteenth century to discover the source of the Nile in Africa.

This is an old-fashioned adventure movie filled with colorful characters, perilous events, exotic native practices, and breathtaking cinematography. The central character, Richard Burton—a historical figure who was a widely traveled explorer, scientist, poet, and linguist with a yen for cross-cultural experiences—is a quester par excellence.

• *Joe Versus the Volcano* is a wild, weird, and wonderful adult fairy tale about a man who travels halfway around the world to discover why his life is still worth living. In the beginning, Joe is a very unhappy young man working at a dreadful job who is told he has an incurable "brain cloud." When an eccentric millionaire then offers him unlimited expense money if he will go to the South Pacific and jump in a volcano, Joe agrees.

On the journey, Joe comes alive. He does some soul searching and wakes up to the beauty all around him. His quest shows him the importance of taking risks, especially for the one he loves.

• Another video, *Wide Awake*, illustrates the importance of questions in the spiritual life. Joshua Beal is about to enter fifth grade at a Catholic school for boys. Deeply troubled about the death of his beloved grandfather, he decides to go on a quest to find God and ask, "Is my grandfather all right?"

Joshua tries to find answers through prayer, fasting, and meditation. He seeks counsel from a nun at school, the priest he sees for confession, and a cardinal visiting from Rome. His quest eventually compels him to respond to a bully who threatens him, an unpopular boy who yearns for attention, and an emergency involving his best friend.

SPIRITUAL EXERCISES AND RITUALS

• Make a pilgrimage to a sacred site. Almost every community has places that have been honored for their spiritual significance, so if you cannot afford to go far, you can still engage in this type of questing. However, a cross-cultural experience is highly recommended.

Some spiritual exercises will make your pilgrimage more meaningful. Choose an intention for your journey: what you hope to discover, learn, or receive. Research the history of the site and the rituals performed by pilgrims there. Write letters or keep a journal to record your impressions. Take photographs, make sketches, and save postcards and mementos to use to spark memories of your experiences in years to come. Be prepared to tell the story of your journey upon returning home. Mark the dates on your calendar and create an annual ritual to commemorate your pilgrimage experience. More ideas for meaningful pilgrimages, as well as descriptions of sacred sites, can be found in *The Art of Pilgrimage: The Seeker's Guide to Making Travel Sacred* by Phil Cousineau; *Sacred Journeys: An Illustrated Guide to Pilgrimage Around the World* by Jennifer Westwood; and *The Atlas of Holy Places and Sacred Sites* by Colin Wilson.

• Walk a labyrinth. During the Crusades in the Middle Ages, when it was too dangerous for most Christians to make the pilgrimage to Jerusalem, pilgrimage cathedrals were established throughout Europe. The last stage of the pilgrimage was walking a labyrinth laid out in the tile floor of the cathedral.

This way of questing is being rediscovered in our time. Labyrinths are available in many churches and community centers; to find one near you, check the Labyrinth Locator at the website at www.gracecom.org or contact Veriditas, the worldwide labyrinth project headquartered at Grace Cathedral in San Francisco, which is directed by Dr. Lauren Artress. Her book *Walking a Sacred Path* includes many comments from individuals who have been transformed by their walking meditations. Artress believes the labyrinth is a "tool to guide healing, deepen self-knowledge, and empower creativity."

PRAYER OR MANTRA

This breath prayer is suggested by the death song of the Yokut Indians.

Breathing in: All my life, I am . . .
Breathing out: seeking, seeking, seeking.

IMAGERY EXERCISE

The quest is one of the most common experiences in the realm of imagination. This exercise was created by Gerald Epstein of New York, New York.

Breathe out three times. See yourself turning a globe in your hand and putting your finger on one spot. This is the place where you need to go on your quest. Know what your intention is for undertaking this journey.

Breathe out three times. See yourself as a knight finding your way to this place. Arriving at your destination, discover what gift is there for you.

If it is a meeting with a being, ask for the lesson you are to bring back from this journey. If the gift is an object, examine it carefully and decide whether you will put it back or take it with you, knowing its significance to you.

Breathe out one time. See yourself returning triumphantly to your home. How do you look and feel?

Breathe out again and open your eyes.

JOURNAL EXERCISES

• Any time you go on a journey, whether an imagination as in the last exercise or by traveling, write an account of your experiences, illustrating it with sketches. The format suggested for a dream journal (see the chapter on "Imagination") is especially useful for this kind of journal entry. What significant lessons and images stand out as you recall this journey? Reflect upon your intention for the quest and whether you fulfilled it.

• Keep a list in your journal of the key questions you are living with. You might put it on the first page, thus signaling that you want to work with the questions in this journal. Or after rereading a journal, compile a list of the questions you considered during this period of your life.

DISCUSSION QUESTIONS, STORYTELLING, SHARING

• Share the story of a quest—exterior or interior—you have undertaken that changed your life.

• Discuss the importance of questions on a spiritual journey. If you are part of a religious tradition, what is its attitude toward questions?

HOUSEHOLD, GROUP, OR COMMUNITY PROJECTS

• After your next vacation with family or friends, set aside an evening to put together a photograph album and scrapbook. As you recall your experiences, identify the "quest" qualities in your travel.

• Go as a group to a sacred site in your area. If necessary, volunteer to be "keepers" of the site and to guide others to deeper experiences there.

FICTION, POETRY, OR CHILDREN'S BOOK

Some of the best-loved children's literature is about questing—Lewis Carroll's *Alice's Adventures in Wonderland,* C. S. Lewis's seven-volume *The Chronicles of Narnia,* and J. R. R. Tolkien's *The Hobbit* and *The Lord of the Rings* trilogy. A recent addition to this genre is *Crow and Weasel* by Barry Lopez. Two adventurers travel far from their village, encountering places and people they never previously imagined, including Eskimos in the Far North. They gain important knowledge from animal allies— Mouse, Badger, and Grizzly Bear. On the journey, they learn about friendship, respect for others, and the sacredness of relationships. They also realize one of the most important aspects of questing—the need to share the story of their experience with the larger community.

SPOKEN-WORD AUDIO

Beryl Markham's 1942 autobiography *West with the Night* is an up-close and personal account of the life of an extraordinary woman who epitomizes the spirit of adventure. Julie Harris gives a very dramatic reading on an audio abridgement that covers Markham's childhood in British East Africa on her father's farm, her legendary airplane flight across the Atlantic, and her exploits as a bush pilot.

ART

Frederic Remington is the preeminent painter of the rugged frontier of the American West. In 1905–1906 he created 10 portraits of explorers, including the Spaniards De Soto and De Vaca and the Americans Lewis and Clark, for *Collier's Weekly* magazine. In one, called *The Unknown Explorers,* two men are depicted astride their horses on a narrow mountain pass. Clearly, they have no idea what might lie around the next bend.

MUSIC

The Missing Peace is a one-woman musical quest written by Ron Melrose and sung by Judy Malloy. It is the engrossing story of Brianna, a young woman from a barren land who goes on a quest to find her missing mother, who also represents the feminine face of God. The maiden receives gifts for the journey from a crone, is tested on a passage across the water, encounters and heals a dragon, and returns home to bring greening to her land and a message of balance and hope to her patriarchal society. "Open your soul larger than your fear," she is advised, and she does by asking questions and embracing opposites.

SEE ALSO:

Devotion. Meaning. Openness. Reverence. Vision. Yearning.

REVERENCE

DAILY CUE, REMINDER, VOW, BLESSING

Passing by a grand tree is my cue to practice reverence.

•

Seeing the respect given to great spiritual leaders reminds me to
reverence the holiness of all human beings.

•

When I meet people who don't care about animals and nature,
I vow to balance their indifference with my commitment.

•

Blessed is the Friend of the World who is pleased when we
practice reverence toward people, places, animals, and things.

THE BASIC PRACTICE

Reverence is the way of radical respect. It recognizes and honors the
presence of the sacred in everything—our bodies, other people, animals,
plants, rocks, the ground, and the waters. It is even an appropriate attitude
to bring to our things, since they are the co-creations of humans and the
Creator.

Nothing is too trivial or second class for reverence. But it has to be
demonstrated with concrete actions. Don't abuse your body—eat right,
exercise, get enough rest. Don't abuse the Earth by being wasteful of its

gifts. Protect the environment for your neighbors and future generations.

Reverence is also a kind of radical amazement, a deep feeling tinged with both mystery and wonder. Approaching the world with reverence, we are likely to experience its sister—awe. Allow yourself to be moved beyond words.

CATALYSTS, CONTRASTS, AND COMPANIONS

There is one unmistakable message in the spiritual practice of reverence: Because everything is touched by the sacred, everything has worth. This practice, then, builds self-esteem.

Its opposite is irreverence, the "dissing" of the Creation. Examples aren't hard to come by: pollution, wasteful consumption, cruelty to animals, exploitation of forests, overuse of the land. On a personal level, irreverence may manifest as ennui, a kind of world-weariness. Or it may take the form of a defiant disregard for the feelings of others and a reckless, devil-may-care use of resources.

PERSPECTIVES

Be full of care with everything entrusted to you. Everything you touch or see, everyone for whom you have responsibility, is to be viewed as something cherished by God, and thus to be cherished by you.
–NORVENE VEST

I cannot but have reverence for all that is called life. I cannot avoid compassion for everything that is called life. That is the beginning and foundation of morality.
–ALBERT SCHWEITZER

When one is aware of God's greatness and strength one is overcome with a feeling of awe. Rather than being a frightening experience, it is a sweet and beautiful awe, the awe that comes from standing in the presence of the infinite.
–ARYEH KAPLAN

TEACHERS

● To walk the path of reverence, we must have a deep respect for all of life, for the lessons of change and death, and for the marvels of the

natural world. Terry Tempest Williams, author of *Pieces of White Shell,*
Coyote's Canyon, Refuge, An Unspoken Hunger, and *Desert Quartet,* is an
ideal teacher of this spiritual practice.

Refuge: An Unnatural History of Family and Place is her masterwork.
Williams, a Mormon, serves as naturalist-in-residence at the Utah
Museum of Natural History. She grew up knowing that the natural world
has spiritual value and that "God can be found wherever you are, especially outside." She writes about a seven-year period during which she is
besieged by death and destruction. The Great Salt Lake floods the fragile
wetlands in northern Utah and threatens one of her favorite spots, the
Bear River Migratory Bird Refuge. Then her mother is afflicted with ovar-
ian cancer, and her grandmother succumbs to old age.

Williams confronts and reflects on these experiences through a lens
of reverence. She is entranced by birds that can bridge continents. She is
brought to her knees by the beauty of the desert. As her mother lies dying,
she finds herself breathing the word "awe." She alternates exquisite
observations about the many species of birds she is studying with revealing
testimonies about the solace and renewal she experiences from a sense of
place. This combination is a veritable tutorial on reverence.

• Barry Lopez is another writer whose practice of reverence enables
him to feel a kinship with all creatures. *About This Life: Journeys on the*
Threshold of Memory is a collection of autobiographical essays by the
National Book Award winner who is best known for *Of Wolves and Men*
and *Arctic Dreams.* Lopez pays his respects to the varieties of life he encounters on his travels, whether diving the coral reefs off Bonaire, exploring the difficult terrain in Antartica, or flying around the world with
air freight. In one essay, he honors his own body; examining his hands,
he remembers his history through what they have touched.

Lopez also acts with reverence. On a cross-country trip, he stops to
move the bodies of animals killed on the highway. A man asks him, Why
bother? " 'You never know,' I said. 'The ones you give some semblance
of burial, to whom you offer an apology, may have been like seers in a
parallel culture. It is an act of respect, a technique of awareness.' "

• Linda Hogan, Deena Metzger, and Brenda Petersen, frequent writers of essays on nature and the spiritual life, are the editors of *Intimate*
Nature: The Bond Between Women and Animals. They have assembled the
works of well-known writers, indigenous women, field scientists, journalists, poets, and wildlife workers who share a common interest in "the
reconciliation between the human family and our sister creatures." Not

only will this book give you many examples of reverential relationships, it will introduce you to other fine teachers of this spiritual practice.

VIDEOS

• The complexity and diversity of life can bring us to a feeling of reverence. *Microcosmos* is an innovative documentary directed by French biologists Claude Nuridsany and Marie Perennou. During one day in a French countryside meadow, we zoom with the cameras down into the grass and witness a caterpillar transforming into a butterfly. Insects on stems of flowers look like high-wire artists. We witness snails copulating, ants scurrying to escape being eaten by a pheasant, a spider capturing grasshoppers in its web, and the birth of a mosquito.

Nature as a backdrop for these happenings is sometimes peaceful and sometimes terrifying. A thunderstorm during which rain violently pelts our new circle of friends is especially scary. *Microcosmos* is a fascinating film with extraordinary camera work that takes us into the complex world of little creatures and leaves us smiling with amazement.

• In Tibet, it is not uncommon to see Buddhist monks buying live fish at the market and taking them to a lake or river to be set free with a blessing. The video movie *Turtle Diary* is about a similar act of reverence. A lonely clerk in a bookstore and a best-selling author of children's books share an interest in the sea turtles at the London aquarium. A keeper at the zoo helps them when they decide to liberate the turtles by taking them to the ocean. Reverence comes from the soul and can change lives.

• After four centuries of seclusion, the Kogi, descendants of a pre-Columbian civilization, asked BBC filmmaker Alan Ereira to visit their homeland in the Sierra Nevada mountains of northern Colombia. *From the Heart of the World: The Elder Brothers' Warning* is the message they asked him to carry back. Seeing themselves as guardians of life on Earth, the Kogi demonstrate what it is like to live with reverence. They have seen signs of an ecological crisis in changing bird migrations and the lack of snow in the high mountainous regions. They urge the industrial world to change its ways.

SPIRITUAL EXERCISES AND RITUALS

• Bowing is a traditional act of reverence. Show your reverence for a person by making a physical bow—or an inner bow—to his or her living spirit.

• Adopt a tree, a park, a beach, or a highway, and look out for its welfare. In its honor, include in your daily prayers petitions to alleviate the sufferings of dying plants and trees, polluted waterways, and toxic lands.

● Do something to show your respect for animals and your desire to see them not suffer. For example, avoid products tested on animals. Eat a vegetarian diet, even if only for one day a week.

● Create rituals to mark the changes of the seasons around the time of the solstices and equinoxes. Conduct your rituals in nature or bring some piece of nature into your ritual space.

PRAYER OR MANTRA

This mantra reminds us that reverence leads to amazement.

> Breathing in: I stand in awe . . .
> Breathing out: of all Creation.

IMAGERY EXERCISE

The inspiration for this exercise is the series of excerpts in *Spiritual Literacy* in which people express their reverence for trees (pages 144–147). Part of it is adapted from "The Garden of Eden" exercise in *Healing Visualizations: Creating Health Through Imagery* by Gerald Epstein.

Close your eyes. Breathe out three times, and imagine yourself sitting with your back against a tree that has branches hanging down with green leaves. Breathe in the pure oxygen that the leaves emit in the form of a blue-golden light. Breathe out carbon dioxide in the form of gray smoke, which the leaves then take up and convert into oxygen. Sit there making a cycle of breathing with the tree.

Breathe out one time. Feel and sense how you are connecting with the tree with your body. Sense the energy coming up from the Earth, through the tree's trunk and branches, and into your body. Feel how this energy moves through your whole body and how some of it goes out your feet and legs back into the Earth again. Sit there becoming one with the tree. What are you sensing from the tree now? How do you feel?

When you are finished, see yourself making a gesture to thank the tree and open your eyes.

JOURNAL EXERCISES

• Decide upon a "Rule of Respect." Write resolutions on how you intend to show respect to your body, animals, plants, things, and other people. Make them very concrete. For example: I will go for at least a 15-minute walk each day. I will oil the tools that need it once a month. I will not tease my dog.

• Keep a "Trash Journal" either singly or as a household. For one month, measure and weigh the garbage you create. Don't overlook the food waste that goes into the garbage disposal. Note what other kinds of trash you tend to produce. See which items can be recycled or reused and determine what else you can do to reduce your garbage load.

DISCUSSION QUESTIONS, STORYTELLING, SHARING

• Describe the most awesome experience you have had in nature. Or describe your most vivid encounter with a wild animal.

• Who has helped you cultivate a sense of reverence for life and for the natural world?

HOUSEHOLD, GROUP, AND COMMUNITY PROJECTS

• In your household, try not to have any leftover food or to let any extra portions go to waste. Hint: This will require careful shopping. In your community, support food banks and programs that collect safe but unservable food from restaurants for distribution to hungry people.

• Find out which animals from your part of the world are currently on the "Endangered Species" list. Ask animal rights and wildlife conservation groups what you can do to help these and other creatures survive in their natural habitats. Also, do your part to help other local animals through volunteering at an animal shelter, helping with educational programs for animal care, and the like.

• Obtain field guides to the plants, trees, birds, and small animals indigenous to your area. Learn the names of these neighbors. Read up on behavior patterns, territory, diet, and other qualities that distinguish one from another. Knowing names and characteristics is a way of honoring the diversity of the Creation.

• Using inclusive language is another mark of reverence. Review the language you use in worship, prayers, songs, and other community activities, and, if necessary, revise it.

FICTION, POETRY, OR CHILDREN'S BOOK

A Timbered Choir: The Sabbath Poems 1978–1997 by Wendell Berry is filled with demonstrations of his reverence for life and the natural world. The author, who lives and farms in Port Royal, Kentucky, has over the years used the Sabbath for long looking and listening. In these poems, he muses on the changing rhythms of the seasons and the cycles of death and rebirth. Berry sings his praises of trees, animals, and the beauty of a place he deeply respects.

SPOKEN-WORD AUDIO

Stephen Mitchell's *Bestiary: An Anthology of Poems About Animals* takes us on a wide and fascinating journey through the animal kingdom with portraits of a snail, a hawk, a panther, and a sparrow. The selections range from the familiar (Gerard Manley Hopkins's "The Windhover" and William Blake's "The Tyger") to the exotic (haiku by the Japanese poet Issa). Pablo Neruda writes lovingly about a cat, a bee, a hummingbird, and a rabbit. One of the most dramatic poems revolves around D. H. Lawrence's close encounter with a snake at a water trough. His feelings range from fear to awe.

ART

Albrecht Dürer's attention to the glories of the natural world make him a worthy practitioner of reverence. His respect for animals is evident in *Young Hare* and *The Little Owl*—two paintings, rich with telling details, that reveal the distinctive stances and moods of these small creatures. You can almost hear them breathing. The same sensory impact comes through in *Three Linden Trees*, where Dürer conveys his admiration for the beauty, dignity, and vibrancy of the trees.

MUSIC

Awe, according to the dictionary, is "a mixed emotion of reverence, respect, dread, and wonder inspired by authority, genius, great beauty, sublimity, or might." That is a perfect description of the impact of Samuel Barber's *Adagio for Strings, Op. 11.* The piece begins quietly, then builds in intensity and complexity to an almost overwhelming feeling of sublime involvement, only to subside and build again. This awe-inducing effect is maximized upon multiple listenings to different arrangements. One CD includes eight different versions, including performances by the Strings of the Boston Symphony Orchestra, James Galway on flute, the Canadian Brass, and the Choir of Trinity College, Cambridge.

SEE ALSO:
Connections. Compassion. Devotion. Kindness. Meaning. Unity. Wonder.

SHADOW

THE BASIC PRACTICE

The spiritual practice of shadow encourages us to make peace with
those parts of ourselves that we find to be despicable, unworthy, and
embarrassing—our anger, jealousy, pride, selfishness, violence, and other
"evil deeds." In Christianity, shadow aspects show up as the seven deadly
sins. Muslims talk about *nafs* as our lower selves, and Buddhists refer to
negative emanations of mind. Societies and cultures also have dark sides.

This practice aims at wholeness by unifying the dark and the light inside and around us. Start by looking closely at yourself, especially your flaws. Take responsibility for your actions, particularly those that have had unfortunate outcomes. By owning your shadow, you embrace your full humanity.

CATALYSTS, CONTRASTS, AND COMPANIONS

Shadow is a corrective to any tendency to make spirituality into simplistic feelings of sweetness and light; it balances Pollyanna thinking. People do terrible things to each other, sometimes because of their beliefs and in the name of their religion. Individuals, even those who are deeply spiritual, go through dark nights of the soul when depression and not-knowing take on terrifying dimensions. Nature, the source of so much inspiration, also has its shadow elements—hurricanes, earthquakes, droughts. By honestly acknowledging these aspects of life, we move toward a more rounded view of reality and build the foundation for personal wholeness.

The spiritual practice of shadow is also called for when we discover that we are projecting aspects of ourselves onto others—both our negative qualities and our untapped talents and powers. The latter are "golden shadows," our nobler aspects that we tend to attribute to teachers, celebrities, sports superstars, and national heroes we admire. Practicing shadow means you reclaim all your flaws and gifts, accepting yourself in all your complexity.

PERSPECTIVES

"Yea, though I walk through the valley of the shadow of death" can be understood as the walk through our own dark side.
–TIAN DAYTON

We must not despise the rough, the dark, the empty, the cowardly, the flawed or the crooked. It is a package deal.
–JOHN R. MABRY

When we watch the news at night, most of what we are seeing is a reflection of what is inside ourselves.
–RONALD ROLHEISER

TEACHERS

• Our teachers of this spiritual practice cover shadow issues in individuals and the society as a whole. Debbie Ford is a consultant, teacher, and faculty member of the Chopra Center for Well Being in California. In *The Dark Side of the Light Chasers: Reclaiming Your Creativity, Brilliance and Dreams,* she unpacks the gifts of our shadow aspects. She writes: "You must go into the dark in order to bring forth your light. When we suppress any feeling or impulse, we are also suppressing its polar opposite. If we deny our ugliness, we lessen our beauty. If we deny our fear, we minimize our courage. If we deny our greed, we also reduce our generosity. Our full magnitude is more than most of us can ever imagine."

Ford examines the process of projection whereby we attribute our sense of inferiority to others. She demonstrates concrete ways we can own our dark qualities and use them in the pursuit of wholeness. She explains why we keep meeting the same people and situations that push our buttons over and over again. She challenges us to accept the God-given gifts that make us special instead of giving this gold away to others. Her book is an incisive reframing of the value of the dark side of life.

• Societies have shadows, too. America's idealism, for example, has served as a force field for good in the world, but our self-righteousness and refusal to acknowledge evil has resulted in great suffering and pain. In *The Shadow in America: Reclaiming the Soul of a Nation,* editor Jeremiah Adams has brought together a group of poignant essays on some of the most troubling and unsavory aspects of American culture. They are racial hatred, violence, addiction, warped ideas regarding sexuality, and destruction of the environment.

Adams notes: "The American ethos, our endearing yet naive tendency to deny one's own share of human imperfection, has finally become a collective burden, embedded in our institutions, our nation's policies, and even in what we'd like to believe is our 'individualistic' national character." The essayists in this helpful volume suggest ways we can reclaim the soul of the nation by coming to terms with shadow issues.

VIDEOS

• It is a sad thing to watch a beloved family member or friend brought low by his or her shadow. Robert Redford's screen adaptation of Norman MacLean's 1976 autobiographical novel *A River Runs Through It* is a riveting study of this kind of self-destructiveness. The narrator of the story looks back over his early life in Missoula, Montana, where he grew up with his younger brother, Paul. Their father, a Presbyterian minister, teaches him one of his spiritual practices—fly-fishing. Over the years, this sport brings out the best in the three men, giving them an opportunity to commune with nature while testing their wits and agility.

But as a young man, Paul, a newspaper reporter, plunges into compulsive drinking and gambling. In a conspiracy of silence, the family avoids talking to him about his addictions. *A River Runs Through It* reveals that we can't run or hide from our demons. To heal, we must face them, and often to do so, we need the help of those who love us.

● The films of writer and director John Sayles often focus on the collective shadow. In *City of Hope,* he takes a long, hard look at the rhythms of anger, frustration, idealism, and hope that pulse through a contemporary working-class city. Through the activities of over three dozen characters, we see some of the results of shadow repression in urban life—crime, violence, political chicanery, racial polarization, rapacious capitalism, the demise of the work ethic, the breakdown of the family, and the devaluation of civic activism. This complex and ethically profound film also shows how the collective shadow is acknowledged or resisted through the choices we make every day. Indeed, these decisions are what determine the quality of urban life.

SPIRITUAL EXERCISES AND RITUALS

● D. Patrick Miller suggests that we view our most grievous flaws and failures as a string of menacing hitchhikers whom we cannot afford not to pick up on our journey to a full and rich life. Make a list of your shabbiest inner characters. Then open your car door and make friends.

● The next time you see a sensitive film or a serious television movie, square off with the character who is most unlike you, who is the "other." Step into that character's part and see how you might behave in his or her shoes. Learn what you can from this character.

● This exercise is from Debbie Ford. Monitor your conversations to see what kind of advice you tend to give other people. What are you telling them they need to do to make their lives better? Reflect on whether the advice you give to others is actually advice to yourself.

PRAYER OR MANTRA

This breath prayer is a variation on Jesus' admonition that we love our enemies.

Breathing in: I love . . .
Breathing out: my inner enemies.

IMAGERY EXERCISE

This exercise, "Toward Away," was created by Colette Aboulker-Muscat of Jerusalem, Israel. It enables you to work with ambivalent feelings, one area where shadow tends to manifest.

Breathe out three times. Imagine something that attracts you so much that you would like to move toward it. See it clearly and be aware of how you feel and how your body feels, particularly your face. Now let your feelings flow into your slow movements toward the thing that attracts you. Now move slowly away from this thing and let your movements express how you are still drawn back to it, even as you are moving away.

Breathe out three times. Imagine that very close to you is something specific that repels you strongly, something that you want to move away from. See it clearly and recognize all your feelings toward this thing, especially in your face. Let your feelings express how you are flying away from this thing. Now move again toward this thing that repels you and discover what it is that repels you. Then discover something that you can appreciate, something that actually attracts you toward it. Now move slowly away, being aware of how you are moving and feeling.

When you are finished, breathe out and open your eyes.

JOURNAL EXERCISES

• Make a list of people you cannot stand. Identify the qualities in them that you dislike the most. Now recognize that those same qualities are part of your character makeup. Work with these shadow qualities. Have them tell you their stories, why they have shown up in your life, and what they would like you to do about them.

• Identify your golden shadows, those unused talents and gifts that for some reason you are more comfortable admiring in others than claiming in yourself. Who have you projected yours onto? Call these aspects of yourself home and have a dialogue with them in your journal.

DISCUSSION QUESTIONS, STORYTELLING, SHARING

• Share a story about how you came to recognize one of your shadow qualities. Perhaps you were informed of it by someone whose opinion you respect. Or perhaps you saw this trait in someone else and realized that the spotlight belonged on you.

- Discuss the idea that when we reject others, we are really rejecting our own shortcomings. Give examples to support your opinions.
- Have you ever experienced a "dark night of the soul"? What did you learn about yourself during this period?

HOUSEHOLD, GROUP, AND COMMUNITY PROJECTS

- Make a list of the shadow aspects of your household (i.e., selfish, greedy, proud), group (exclusive, self-satisfied), or community (tendency to demonize enemies, oppressive). Figure out some ways to bring the shadow into the light. For example, in the community, letter-writing campaigns are a start.
- Practice recognizing the shadow in the news reported on television or in your newspaper. Keep a Shadow Scrapbook and use it to remind you of prayer needs.

FICTION, POETRY, OR CHILDREN'S BOOK

Madeleine L'Engle's trilogy of award-winning children's books, *A Wrinkle in Time, A Wind in the Door,* and *A Swiftly Tilting Planet,* are profound and imaginative meditations on the best strategies for dealing with the shadow presences in our lives. In all three novels, Meg Murry and her younger brother, Charles Wallace, aided by a number of heavenly beings, must outwit and disarm the agents of darkness. In *A Wrinkle in Time,* Meg practices love in order to save Charles Wallace from being taken in by the stifling powers of "IT." In *A Swiftly Tilting Planet,* Charles Wallace literally goes inside people from other times to face down the shadow tendencies that are affecting history.

In our favorite of the three, *A Wind in the Door,* fallen angels called "Echthroi" are destroying—Xing—large chunks of the Creation. Meg learns that only by recognizing, naming, and loving these beings, who are both inside and outside of us, can she prevent them from doing more harm. Here is Meg engaged in the spiritual practice of shadow: "I Name you, Echthroi. . . . My arms surround you. You are no longer nothing. You are. You are filled. You are me."

SPOKEN-WORD AUDIO

On *Romancing the Shadow: Illuminating the Dark Side of the Soul,* Connie Zweig and Steve Wolf make a convincing case for befriending our unappealing thoughts, hidden fantasies, and ignoble feelings. To romance the shadow is to hold opposites together, to confront our self-sabotaging behavior, and to read messages in everyday events. Throughout this audio presentation, the two psychotherapists use case histories and mythic tales to illustrate the dark side of the soul.

ART

Critics have talked about the contemplative and mystical undertow of Mark Rothko's large abstract expressionist paintings, and the artist affirmed his intention to convey metaphoric and spiritual meanings through them. We see in Rothko's later works an illustration of the practice of shadow—the duality of light and dark and the meeting of these opposites. In *Untitled* from 1968, an acrylic on paper, a pool with shades of black is surrounded and intersected by a textured gray border, a metaphoric embrace of the darkness. In *Untitled (Black and Gray),* done in 1969–1970, Rothko gives us two fields of color meeting each other without recoiling. The viewer is drawn into something that looks simple on the surface yet is actually very weighty and deep. Like the spiritual practice of shadow, this painting takes us into the realm of paradox and mystery.

MUSIC

On the Rolling Stones' album *Beggars Banquet,* the song "Sympathy for the Devil" by Mick Jagger and Keith Richards describes a world where everything is in turmoil. Cops are criminals, and all the saints are sinners. The Devil is not a monster but "a man of wealth and taste." The nature of his game is puzzling, unless we see it in terms of the spiritual practice of shadow. Then it all becomes a bit clearer, especially the suggestion that we are all accomplices in the deaths of the Kennedys and other acts of violence. "If you meet me," says the Devil, "have some courtesy, have some sympathy and some taste." Or else.

SEE ALSO:

Attention. Compassion. Openness. Teachers. X—The Mystery. You.

 SILENCE

THE BASIC PRACTICE

Silence is often referred to in terms of space: the immensity inside, the cave of the heart, the oasis of quiet, the inner sanctuary, the interior castle, the sacred center where God dwells. For centuries, people have used this practice as a rest and renewal stop on the spiritual journey. It provides a way to periodically withdraw from the world. You may go into silence as a prelude to prayer, or you may seek it as the place where through meditation you can contact your deeper self and Spirit.

How can you find this inner quietude and tranquility? You must make room for it—literally. Find a space of physical silence where you can sit quietly, away from distracting demands, voices, and sounds. Go there every day. It is the gateway to your interior silence.

CATALYSTS, CONTRASTS, AND COMPANIONS

Our world contrasts sharply with the inner world of silence. We are bombarded daily with the noise of crowded residences, workplaces, and entertainment sites. The clamorous voices of the media are always trying to get our attention. We live amid the seemingly relentless roar of our machines, our tools, and our toys.

Very few places today are soundproof. The norm is noisy verging on chaotic. The Tower of Babel still stands in our midst, a grim reminder that our various expressions can divide and even conquer us.

When this world feels overwhelming and chaos seems to be getting the better of us, silence is a powerful antidote. This practice increases our capacity for contemplation. It enables us to focus our attention on deep matters of the heart. It is where we can commune with things greater than the cacophony all around us.

PERSPECTIVES

Within each of us there is a silence—a silence as vast as the universe.
–GUNILLA NORRIS

Silence is the shaft we descend to the depths of contemplation. Silence is the vehicle that takes us to the innermost centre of our being which is the place for all authentic practice.
–ELAINE MACINNES

The silence is there within us. What we have to do is to enter into it, to become silent, to become the silence. The purpose of meditation and the challenge of meditation is to allow ourselves to become silent enough to allow this interior silence to emerge. Silence is the language of the spirit.
–JOHN MAINS

TEACHERS

• Barbara Erakko Taylor, a columnist for *Catholic Review,* has written a memoir about silence that is a good introduction for anyone exploring this spiritual practice. *Silence: Making the Journey to Inner Quiet* is a profound and practical book on the fears, questions, and responses that emerge around what she calls her "sixth sense."

Silence woos Taylor in different places and periods of her life—in a shopping mall, a hotel room, and a sequoia forest, while she is rocking her children, building a stone wall, and making soup. She writes: "In my possessive stalking of silence, I had sought to capture it, ripping it from its source of holiness. But it refused to be entombed by me. It withdrew so completely I had no way to follow it. When I gave up hope, then it illumined itself." Taylor eventually builds silence into her daily routine of prayer, reading, writing, and work. Silence unfurls itself in her life as a sacramental presence.

● Silence as the gateway to experiences of the sacred is discussed by two other teachers. Protestant clergyman Morton Kelsey brings more than 50 years of parish life, college teaching, and lecturing all over the world to his examination of this practice in *The Other Side of Silence: Meditation for the Twenty-First Century*. He defines it as "the art of letting down the barrier that separates our rational consciousness from the depth of our souls."

Since so many people today are unfamiliar with silence, Kelsey presents several aids to achieving it, including attention to breathing, practicing the presence of God, Zen, and yoga. "Silence unbinds a person from ordinary perceptions and attitudes and offers a fresh look at life and reality," he continues. It provides access to the inner universe—the other side of silence—that can be explored using the imagination. Kelsey is particularly persuasive in his discussion of the importance of spontaneous images that arise during a period of silence and provide keys to the inner life.

● Anthony de Mello, a Catholic priest and retreat leader, also advocates silence as the starting point for discoveries of the Divine. *Sadhana: A Way to God: Christian Exercises in Eastern Form* presents awareness exercises, fantasy or imagination exercises, including some based on the spiritual exercises of Saint Ignatius of Loyola, and devotional prayer. Most of them begin with a quieting-down period. De Mello explains: "It is this minimal silence that you have within you that we shall build on. . . . As it grows, it will reveal to you more and more about yourself. . . . And in and through this revelation you will attain . . . things like wisdom and serenity and joy and God."

VIDEOS

There is a shadow side of silence. Sometimes we use it as a weapon to punish those who have hurt or ignored us. We armor ourselves with silence so that we don't have to communicate or deal with our problems. This is the theme of *The Quiet Room*, a flawlessly acted and perfectly realized Australian film about a seven-year-old girl's emotional response to the complicated small world she lives in. As a protest against the disintegration of her parents' marriage, this unnamed little girl quits talking. However, we hear her thoughts in response to the actions of her concerned mother and father. For example, overhearing an argument in the next room, she thinks, "You're hurting my heart."

Although her parents still play with her and read to her, the little girl yearns for the closeness she observed between them when she was three years old—a noisy time of family hugs. She doesn't like where they live either. She wants to move to the country and get a dog. The little girl resists all her parents' efforts to pull her out of silence until she is ready. And when she finally speaks, there is love and truth in what she says.

SPIRITUAL EXERCISES AND RITUALS

● Incorporate minutes of silence into your daily routine: Observe one silent minute at your desk before beginning work, while sitting at a park bench during lunch, in your car before starting the drive home, or after watching the evening news.

● Psychotherapist Gunilla Norris writes, "When we make room for silence, we make room for ourselves." Create a space for silence in your house or some other place where you know that you will not be disturbed. Spend a regular period of time there—10 minutes a day is a good starting period. Good techniques to get to silence include meditating on a sacred word or mantra, concentrating on the breath, or gazing at a candle.

● Go on a silent retreat for a weekend or, if possible, a week. Many monastic communities offer rooms and will honor your desire not to speak for a period of days. You can also do a silent retreat at home with the cooperation of others in your household. In addition to your not speaking, consider cutting off all communications coming to you from outside, including telephones, television, and e-mail.

PRAYER OR MANTRA

This prayer is best said with a rhythmic chanting of the words and a pause for contemplation after each line. The phrase is from Psalm 46:10.

Be still and know that I am God.
Be still and know that I am.
Be still and know.
Be still.
Be.

IMAGERY EXERCISE

This exercise, "Entering the Silence," is based on a practice of the Seneca (Native American) nation. The imagery is adapted from the words of Twylah Nitsch:

Close your eyes. Breathe out three times.
Listen and hear the Silence. . . . Listen and see the Silence. . . .
Listen and taste the Silence. . . . Listen and smell the Silence.
Breathe out one time. Listen and embrace the Silence.
When you are finished, open your eyes.

JOURNAL EXERCISES

● Write a response to this thought by Hermann Hesse: "Within you there is a stillness and a sanctuary to which you can retreat at any time and be yourself." Sit quietly with your journal. Go to that quiet place. If you want, draw a picture or describe the qualities of your inner silence.

● Write about an experience of silence. Where were you? Was it during a particular period of your life? Did you enjoy being silent? Did you find any part of the experience difficult? What did you learn? In other words, assess your aptitude for silence.

DISCUSSION QUESTIONS, STORYTELLING, SHARING

● Share a story about some time when you were able to tap into the potential of silence as a seedbed for creativity or inspiration.

● Have you ever found it was necessary to go away just to escape the noise of the modern world? Where did you go and what kind of silence did you encounter?

● What role has silence played in your spiritual development? If you were raised in a religious tradition, how was silence regarded?

HOUSEHOLD, GROUP, AND COMMUNITY PROJECTS

● Eat a meal this week together in silence. Afterward, discuss your experiences and decide whether to make this a regular part of your household routine.

● Sharing silence in a group context is a worthwhile discipline. Join a group or form one of your own. It could be organized around mindfulness practice, centering prayer, or just sitting in silence without any structure.

● Many communities, surprisingly, have few places where people can go to be quiet, safely, alone. Church sanctuaries used to provide this service, but many of them are locked during nonworship hours. Parks usually have areas designated for children or dog runs but no places where someone seeking silence can go. Survey your community to identify places of peace and quiet. Then organize a group to develop other sanctuaries of silence.

FICTION, POETRY, OR CHILDREN'S BOOK

Joseph Bruchac's *The Arrow Over the Door,* a book for young readers, is set in 1777 and based on a historical meeting of Quakers and Native Americans just before the battles of Saratoga, New York, crucial events in the Revolutionary War. The narrative alternates between two teenage boys—Samuel Russell, a member of a Quaker community, and Stands Straight, an Abenaki Indian on a mission to scout for King George. Their paths converge at a Quaker meeting hall. Stands Straight and those with him realize that they share a respect for silence with the people sitting inside. And because of that common ground, they can pursue peace together.

SPOKEN-WORD AUDIO

Jon Kabat-Zinn reads his best-seller *Wherever You Go, There You Are* and makes a fine case for mindfulness meditation as good training for "being," rather than constantly "doing," in our daily lives. It emphasizes living in the moment, which turns out to be good for the health of body, mind, and spirit. It can reduce our levels of stress and induce feelings of peace. Silence is an essential ingredient of mindfulness practice.

ART

Sister Wendy Beckett has assembled paintings reflecting the value of quiet contemplation in the section on silence in her *Book of Meditations.* In Rembrandt's portrait *Woman with a Pink,* silence is the way into the deep well of inner wisdom; the woman's attention is directed not at the flower she holds but on her own thoughts. The nourishing power of silence as part of the discipline of contemplative reading is depicted in Rogier van der Weyden's *The Magdalen Reading*. And in Raphael's *Saint Catherine of Alexandria*, we see the rapture that can come when our minds are stilled before God.

MUSIC

Van Morrison's jazzy chantlike rock song "Hymns to the Silence" on the CD of the same title describes the yearning of a person separated from his lover. In the emptiness and stillness of the night, he cries out, "When I'm away from you, I just have to sing, my hymns to the silence." He then retreats to the countryside where he connects with his soul and his feeling of oneness with God. Now he addresses his love, "Can you feel the silence?" In this song, silence is the seedbed for yearning, love, and union with the Divine.

SEE ALSO:

Devotion. Listening. Meaning. Peace. Questing. Transformation.

TEACHERS

THE BASIC PRACTICE

Whether they are called sages, masters, elders, crones, rebbes, gurus, shaikhs, ministers, or priests, teachers play an important part in our spiritual unfolding. They instruct directly and indirectly through stories, parables, koans, sermons, lectures, and personal example. They recommend readings in sacred texts, assign exercises and tasks to be accomplished, demonstrate devotional acts, and challenge us to reach the sacred fullness of our potential.

Of course, eventually in the spiritual life, there comes a point when we realize that everything we encounter and everyone we meet is a teacher. We can even learn from seemingly negative experiences, such as difficulties, personal warps, enemies, suffering, illness, and death. The first step in this practice, then, is to choose to see all of life as a classroom filled with spiritual lessons. Be a lifelong learner who walks in humility and with receptivity.

CATALYSTS, CONTRASTS, AND COMPANIONS

We hate to admit it, but we keep making the same mistakes over and over again. That is why the practice of teachers is so important and so insistent. These recurrent issues mean we still have something to learn. A major obstacle to this practice, then, is pride—thinking you already know it all, that you (and perhaps you alone) have it figured out.

The shadow side of teachers is surrendering your soul to a leader or cult and giving up personal responsibility for your spiritual development. A subtle symptom of this tendency is doubting your own judgment and needing the constant affirmation of others. A far better approach is to rejoice in the abundance of teachers, to seek their wisdom everywhere, and to have confidence that it is available and accessible to you.

PERSPECTIVES

I am sure that God has something to teach us in every situation in which we are put and through every person we meet; and once we grasp that, we cease to be restless and settle down to what we are.
–EVELYN UNDERHILL

Study your mistakes as if they were a secret code that can be broken, revealing deeper secrets about your hidden talents and desires. This awareness helps our errors become the seeds for more interesting futures than the one we habitually envision.
–BRADFORD KEENEY

Being a teacher is a worthwhile endeavor. That way you may find a good student, and learn a few things yourself.
–RABBI YITZCHAK MEIR OF GER

TEACHERS

Our teachers of this spiritual practice, understandably, come from different religious traditions and various occupations, reflecting the many ways we learn on the path of practice.

● Deng Ming-Dao, a teacher of Taoism, believes that the universe is set up to provide us with manifold lessons: "Everything we do is Tao," he writes. "Spirituality is not just 'out there.' It is also all around us and in us. If we understand that, no matter where we look, spiritual revelations abound." In *Everyday Tao: Living with Balance and Harmony*, he presents what it means to practice this ancient Eastern way. Starting with common Chinese ideograms, Deng offers readings of the teachings of a tree, a comb, a valley, a bowl, and much more. These musings are organized into 15 sections covering nature, silence, meditation, perseverance, simplifying, union, and other subjects.

● Buddhist teacher Pema Chödrön counsels us to stop running away from fear and to welcome chaos. The things we face in difficult times, she explains, may have the most to teach us. They certainly can open us up and soften our hearts. *When Things Fall Apart: Heart Advice for Difficult Times* is a series of lectures in which Chödrön discusses meditation, developing lovingkindness, the dharmic practice of reframing, poison as medicine, and the art of peacemaking. One of her key insights: "Nothing ever goes away until it has taught us what we need to know."

● Mark I. Rosen, a program director for the Jewish Healing Center of New England, wants us to recognize that all the people in our lives are our teachers. This understanding helps us improve and resolve even difficult relationships. *Thank You for Being Such a Pain: Spiritual Guidance for Dealing with Difficult People* advises that we see these individuals as "cosmic couriers" sent by God to refine our character and help us be more empathetic and compassionate. "The pain, frustration and suffering we experience with certain people are just as important for our personal and spiritual growth as love and joy." Rosen presents specific strategies for healing difficult relationships as we learn from them.

● Marie de Hennezel reveals the profound lessons she has learned from keeping company with those in the last stages of life. In *Intimate Death: How the Dying Teach Us How to Live,* she describes her experiences over a seven-year period on the staff of the first palliative care unit in a Paris hospital for people with a terminal illness. This is an emotionally affecting and edifying book with memorable epiphanies about the process of "diving into death" when patients decide to let go.

• Finally, on the spiritual journey it is important to have a teacher or guide who is knowledgeable about your own tradition. This was the experience of Evan Pritchard, who was tutored by one of his Micmac Algonquin elders in Native American wisdom. *No Word for Time: The Way of the Algonquin* is a lyrical summation of their myth, history, and philosophy. Pritchard's teacher shows him how to find the meanings in his experiences of fasting, his first sweat lodge, going on a vision quest, and receiving his spiritual name.

Pritchard adds texture to *No Word for Time* by comparing Algonquin teachings to other religions. As he notes, "The universe is big enough for all truth. We don't have to destroy someone else's to make room for our own." That's another good lesson.

VIDEOS

• *My Life as a Dog* is a Swedish coming-of-age drama set in the 1950s. The teacher here is childhood itself, when some of the most indelible and poignant events of our lives occur. This is when our values are deeply influenced by our relationships with family, friends, and community, and our attitudes are shaped by our first encounters with separation, sex, and death.

Twelve-year-old Ingemar goes to live with his uncle after his mother is afflicted with tuberculosis. There he interacts with all generations and squares off with a slew of troubles. His fierce and fragile hold on reality is tested again and again. This story vividly illustrates the invaluable lessons that come with life's pleasures and pains.

• The content of our characters is also shaped by the people who early in our lives teach us through their words and deeds what it means to be human. *Once Upon a Time . . . When We Were Colored* is a touching portrait of a young black boy's upbringing in Glen Allan, Mississippi, from 1946 to 1962. Clifton is raised by his grandfather, who gives him a keen sense of right and wrong. His great-aunt expands his horizons, and an iceman conveys to the boy how important it is to stand up for what he believes in. Mrs. Maybry, a white woman, introduces him to the wide world of literature. This vibrant film celebrates community as a workshop where young souls are forged.

• *The Power of One* is an inspiring film set in South Africa during the 1930s and 1940s. It pays tribute to the spiritual influence of three elders— a Zulu medicine man, a German concert pianist, and a black prisoner— on the character development of P.K., an English orphan who grows up to be a peacemaker and a leader in the fight against bigotry and violence. Each of his teachers has the wisdom he needs at key moments in his life; they show him how to find his courage, to look for answers in nature, to live with dignity, and to seek freedom.

Spiritual Exercises and Rituals

• As you go through your day, be alert to your teachers. Ask a challenge, a flower, a friend, or a passage from a sacred text, "What can I learn from you?" At bedtime, review your lessons.

• Choose an object that symbolizes a spiritual lesson you have learned and add it to your altar or keep it on your desk.

• Animals are recognized as teachers in many cultures. You can tap into this traditional wisdom by using *The Medicine Cards* by Jamie Sams and David Carson or a similar card system. The deck of cards contains pictures of animals, and a companion book explains the stories and myths from which the authors have derived specific teachings for each animal. Use the cards in a ritual, perhaps on your birthday, to seek the wisdom of totem animals.

Prayer or Mantra

One key to the spiritual practice of teachers is a willingness to learn.

> Breathing in: Teach me . . .
> Breathing out: I'm ready to learn.

Imagery Exercise

Colette Aboulker-Muscat, now in her nineties, has been teaching the use of imaginal techniques for healing and spiritual growth since she was a young woman in Algeria. Her experience with thousands of doctors, patients, and students lends authority to this exercise she created on the role of the teacher in the spiritual life.

Close your eyes and breathe out three times. See and know how it is possible to accept a direction from a teacher, a master, an analyst, a rabbi, a minister.

Breathe out one time. Sense how this accepted direction is freeing your mind, is permitting progress, development, and some cures.

Breathe out one time. Live how some destructive habits have been abandoned under the direction of a good teacher and a good example.

Breathe out one time. See and live how the example and teaching of a master in discipline is bringing you new energy and a new future.

Then open your eyes.

JOURNAL EXERCISE

Write about the most important spiritual teacher in your life. What did he or she do for you? Then listen to your inner teacher and write about what you have learned from your life experiences. Finally, think about your gifts as a spiritual teacher. When and where have you given back the wisdom? Where else can you teach?

DISCUSSION QUESTIONS, STORYTELLING, SHARING

• Talk about a person, an experience, an activity, or a thing that has been a spiritual teacher for you.

• Share a story about something you have learned from a difficult person or an enemy.

HOUSEHOLD, GROUP, AND COMMUNITY PROJECTS

• Work against your need to give the impression that you know it all. Encourage everyone to use the phrase "You may be right" often—make it your "slogan"—and see how that changes the atmosphere in your household or group.

• Play a game with your family and friends. Make up the faculty roster for the University of Life. Professors may be living or dead.

• In primal religions, ancestors and the elderly are treated with respect since they are repositories of wisdom for the tribe. Find more ways to tap into the spiritual wisdom of elders in your community. Involve young people in an oral history project where they tape elders talking about what they have learned in life. Keep the tapes at a local library or community center. Add a collection of stories, videos, and songs in which grandparents and elders are depicted as heroes.

FICTION, POETRY, OR CHILDREN'S BOOK

In *Father Melancholy's Daughter,* Gail Godwin explores all the teachers of Margaret Gower, the daughter of an Episcopalian priest who suffers from depression. During Easter week of her senior year in college, she witnesses the playing out of the passion story both communally and personally. Later, after a trip to England with an unlikely companion, Margaret discovers her calling. This deeply religious novel shows how the

Spirit constantly surprises us with new teachers and unpredictable teachings.

SPOKEN-WORD AUDIO

Death is a teacher not only to those who are dying but also to those who work with them. On *Being with Dying: Contemplative Practices and Teachings*, Joan Halifax brings over 25 years of experiences as an anthropologist, a health care professional, a student of shamanism, and a Buddhist lay priest to bear on this important rite of passage. She presents many techniques that have been used with the dying, such as the four basic principles of Native American council practice and death meditations.

ART

Judy Chicago's multimedia work *The Dinner Party* is designed to, in the artist's words, "forge a new kind of art expressing women's experience." It consists of a triangular dinner table on which are arranged 30 painted china plates dedicated to major historical and mythic women including Amazon, Kalki, Sojourner Truth, Susan B. Anthony, and others, each set on a richly embroidered runner faithful to the woman's era. This extraordinary work also includes a floor of 2,300 porcelain tiles with the names of 999 women of achievement from primeval times to 1979. *The Dinner Party* affirms the spiritual practice of honoring teachers—past, present, and future.

MUSIC

Many of the spiritual practices in this book—beauty, enthusiasm, imagination, joy, love, yearning—are part of Motown music. This soulful African-American musical genre is a good representative for the practice of teachers. *Motown 40 Forever* brings together many of the classics.

These songs about love sought and love lost tutor us in emotional intelligence. Mary Wells offers a tribute to faithfulness in "My Guy." Another singer wants her man to take their relationship seriously in "Stop! In the Name of Love" by Diana Ross & the Supremes. In "Neither One of Us (Wants to Be the First to Say Goodbye)" by Gladys Knight & the Pips, a woman confesses how difficult it is to admit responsibility for a failed relationship. In "What Becomes of the Brokenhearted," Jimmy Ruffin paints a poignant portrait of the deep feelings experienced in the "land of broken dreams." There are other lessons here about enjoying life.

Sometimes you just have to have some fun, singing and dancing "All Night Long," counsels Lionel Richie, another Motown teacher.

SEE ALSO:
Devotion. Meaning. Openness. Shadow. X—The Mystery. Zeal.

TRANSFORMATION

DAILY CUE, REMINDER, VOW, BLESSING

Watching ice melt into water is a cue for me to
practice transformation.

●

When I witness the movement from sickness to health, I am
reminded of the recuperative powers of spiritual transformation.

●

Looking at photographs of myself when I was younger, I vow to be
happy with all the changes I have undergone.

●

Blessed is the Sacred Source who lives in and through all
our transformations.

THE BASIC PRACTICE

The spiritual practice of transformation holds within its wide embrace
the personal renewals that come with a spiritual awakening, a conversion,
a mystical epiphany, or an enlightenment. It covers the deepening that
takes place when we get in touch with our Higher Self or Spirit.

Transformation usually involves the shedding of old ways, especially
those that have become burdens. This practice proclaims that no matter
who you are, no matter what has already happened to you, no matter what
you have done, it is still possible to be and do something new.

Transformation implies a marked change in your life, but you can practice it by making simple changes. Start by doing something differently—walk to work by a new route, answer the telephone with your other than usual hand. Break a habit, any habit. Signal Spirit that you are willing to accept change in your life and to be an agent of change in the world.

CATALYSTS, CONTRASTS, AND COMPANIONS

With transformation comes personal healing and growth. It's as if these possibilities have been in the wings all along, waiting for us to make room for them on stage.

Often, however, we aren't sure that we want this show to go on. The refusal to admit change in our lives is a major obstacle to transformation. We cling tenaciously to our habitual ways of doing things, thinking they are our only choices. We may resist anything new or different through indecisiveness. We waver, going back and forth between fear and doubt, fear that the change will be painful, doubt that it will make a difference in our lives.

There is also a shadow side of transformation—recklessness, where we keep pushing the edge. Here change becomes an addiction, and we race from one stimulus—or perceived panacea—to another.

PERSPECTIVES

Your possibility of transformation is your future. The past is dead and gone and finished. Bury it! It has no meaning anymore. . . . It is unnecessary luggage.
–OSHO

To live is to change and to be perfect is to have changed very often.
–JOHN HENRY CARDINAL NEWMAN

The world is new to us each morning—that is the Lord's gift, and we should believe we are reborn each day.
–BAAL SHEM TOV

TEACHERS

We prep ourselves for transformation by hearing the stories of what has happened to others. This is a classic form of spiritual transmission.

Accounts of transforming experiences abound in the holy scriptures of the world's religions and in the tales of the masters passed down through the generations. As our teachers of this spiritual practice reveal, these stories are also common in our day.

• In *Transformations: Awakening to the Sacred in Ourselves,* journalists Tracy Cochran and Jeff Zaleski present accounts of people who suddenly encounter "entirely new visions of themselves and their connection to reality" during near-death experiences, feelings of mystical awareness, and other life-altering happenings. Cochran reveals how a terrifying experience of being mugged led to her spiritual transformation, and Zaleski shares how his father's death reconnected him to "the incandescent sacredness" of his youth.

• In *Kitchen Table Wisdom: Stories That Heal,* Rachel Naomi Remen, M.D., a psycho-oncologist who counsels cancer patients and their doctors, writes about suffering and life-threatening diseases as doorways to transformation. "Life is known only by those who have found a way to be comfortable with change and the unknown. Given the nature of life, there may be no security, but only adventure."

This remarkable work contains a treasure trove of stories about courageous people who in the midst of crisis are able to find connection, sacred meaning, and personal renewal. Remen's own battle with a chronic progressive intestinal disease has given her a unique perspective on coping with pain. Her probes on the healing process contain insights into the power of belief, anger as a sign of engagement with life, and prayer as the movement from mastery to mystery. She concludes, "The things we cannot measure may be the things that ultimately sustain our lives."

• The arts and crafts have been known to trigger transformations and to reflect them. In *The Knitting Sutra: Craft as a Spiritual Practice,* Susan Gordon Lydon describes how knitting has played a major role in her spiritual journey as prayer, passion, stress reducer, way of service to others, and source of renewal. In *The Tao of Music: Sound Psychology, Using Music to Change Your Life,* John Ortiz outlines imaginative and practical exercises using sound and music as tools for change, creativity, and healing.

• Finally, the natural process of aging is seen as the setting for transformation in *Spiritual Passages: Entering Life's Sacred Journey* by Drew Leder, a professor of philosophy. He has chosen guides who exemplify the qualities needed for spiritual growth, especially in the second half of life: Buddha, an Aikido master, a Hindu sage, Jesus, the biblical Sarah, Scrooge, and a Native American.

VIDEOS

One of the most popular and timeless motifs in the movies is the story of how something happens and the character finds his or her life turned around. Some of these moments are immensely dramatic; others are as subtle as discovering a new way of being during a dreadful day.

● In *Phenomenon,* George is a big-hearted auto mechanic who is knocked over by a flash from the sky on his thirty-seventh birthday. Suddenly he can't sleep at night, he has telekinetic powers, he can read four books a day, and he is able to sense pre-earthquake activity. George's transformation into a wunderkind confounds and amazes his friends and new lover. But even more astonishing is the way he is revealed to be a deeply spiritual man who demonstrates selfless love, sees clearly, serves others, and honors the connections between all things.

● *Regarding Henry* is about an aggressive, successful, and amoral New York lawyer whose life is upended when he is shot in the head by a thief during a robbery. As he recovers, he has to relearn everything he does at home and at work. His vulnerability opens him up to the positive values of love, play, intimacy, tenderness, and conscience that were all absent in his previous existence. A catastrophe rearranges Henry's life, and he chooses to become a new person.

● *Groundhog Day* is a comic parable about the transformation of a repugnantly self-centered Pittsburgh TV weatherman who travels to Punxsutawney, Pennsylvania, to cover the Groundhog Day Festival. Bored with his life and holding a low regard for everyone else in the universe, Phil finds himself trapped in a rerun of his least favorite day of the year. Over and over again, he wakes up at 6:00 A.M. to the sound of Sonny and Cher's "I Got You Babe" and a series of encounters with his producer, his cameraman, and an awkward insurance salesman. This film challenges us to consider how the seeds for personal transformation lie dormant in the choices we make on ordinary—even terrible—days.

SPIRITUAL EXERCISES OR RITUALS

● Be on the lookout for symbols of transformation, such as a butterfly. When you find one that speaks to you, incorporate it as a motif in your daily life. Use it on notepads, checks, pins, or other items.

● Notice little rituals of transformation: cleaning the refrigerator, filling the car with gas, looking through a kaleidoscope. Create a ritual to mark your passage across a symbolic barrier, problem, or age into a new awareness.

PRAYER OR MANTRA

This mantra reminds us that transformation is both personal and public.

Breathing in: As Spirit transforms me, . . .
Breathing out: may I transform the world.

IMAGERY EXERCISE

Images of transformation are often idiosyncratic; what precipitates change for one person may not do the same for others. Here are three different exercises; the first was created by Colette Aboulker-Muscat and the other two by us. You can try any or all of them. The title reflects the intention.

"Opening to Possibilities." Close your eyes and breathe out three times. Find yourself in a cocoon, knowing how it feels to be in there and how much you can move around. Now break the cocoon and find your way out. Begin to stretch and with each movement emit a sound. Sense all the different ways your body is stretching and sounding. When you are finished, open your eyes.

"Getting Unstuck." Close your eyes and breathe out three times. See yourself stuck in a hole in the ground. Using a little golden spade, a golden shovel, or a golden backhoe (whatever you need), dig yourself out of that place. Then open your eyes.

"Changing Through Difficulties." Close your eyes and breathe out three times. See yourself as a gem being polished through friction. Know that through your trials and difficulties you are being made to shine. Then open your eyes.

Journal Exercises

• Draw a "Life Map" in your journal using any combination of straight, curved, solid, and broken lines. When do you turn or spiral back into an earlier pattern? Experiment with using different color pens for the various periods of your life. Include images to mark significant milestones on your journey as well as events you now recognize as stepping-stones to where you are now. Circle the major points of transition and put gold stars around transformations.

• List changes you would like to make. Then write a dialogue with a change trying to make its way into your life. Find out what it wants and express your reaction to the possibilities it offers you.

• Caroline Casey in *Making the Gods Work for You* describes one of the common side effects of transformation—the "sunset effect." As a pattern goes down, it glows most vividly. "Just before people are ready to change," she writes, "they often thrash around, saying, 'I've already worked through these issues, so why am I dealing with all this again?' The answer is, 'These issues are coming up again because you've *almost* resolved them.'" Look through your journal for examples of the sunset effect. What change was coming?

Discussion Questions, Storytelling, Sharing

• To open your discussion of this spiritual practice, point out that transformation means it is possible to do a "new thing." What would that be for each of you?

• Share the story of a transformative experience, one you came out of feeling like a different person. It might be an encounter with a person, a story, or a work of art; an occasion of intense joy, sorrow, or pain; or a time when you faced an illness or another challenge that resulted in your making changes in your life.

Household, Group, and Community Projects

• Many families and groups complain about always doing the same old things. To counter this pattern, practice breaking habits. Make small variations in your routine. For example, take a bath instead of a shower. Have green tea instead of coffee. Open your meeting five minutes earlier than the scheduled time. Sit in different chairs. The point is to dedicate such changes to the principle that transformation is possible.

• Invite a shaman to come to your community and speak on the rituals of transformation in contemporary life. These gifted individuals have been trained to explore alternate worlds and to practice the arts of healing and wholeness.

● There is a story told about Mahatma Gandhi. On his train trips he used to get off at every stop and collect money for the poor. A friend said of him, "If you want to see somebody consumed by greed, look no farther." Of course, instead of being greedy for himself, he was greedy for the poor. Meet with members of your community to determine what group flaw can be transformed into something positive.

FICTION, POETRY, OR CHILDREN'S BOOK

In *The Fatigue Artist* by Lynne Sharon Schwartz, Laura is a 40-year-old novelist living in Manhattan who comes down with chronic fatigue syndrome. The illness opens her up to new possibilities. In Tai Chi classes, she learns about flexibility and rooting herself in the Earth. She visits an herbalist and tries homeopathy. The illness is a catalyst to her transformation both as a woman and as an author.

SPOKEN-WORD AUDIO

On *The Way of Story: Myths and Stories for the Inner Life*, Jungian psychologist and lecturer Helen M. Luke examines the transforming powers of storytelling. She believes that literature can be a source of healing and personal renewal for those who take it seriously. To illustrate her point, she draws out the meanings of the novels of Charles Williams, the scriptural accounts of the Exodus and Saul, and her short stories.

ART

Jan Vermeer's *Young Woman with a Water Jug* portrays a woman standing beside a table that holds a pitcher and a bowl. The splendor of the light pouring through the partly open window seems to revitalize the woman and all the objects in the room. This evocative painting mirrors the illuminating powers of the spiritual practice of transformation.

MUSIC

Reggae is infectiously syncopated music that sets the soul in motion. In the beat lies movement toward transformation. Jimmy Cliff's *The Harder They Come* is reggae music at its best—angry and prophetic, hopeful and rebellious. The 12 selections make up the musical soundtrack for the film of the same title set in Jamaica. Listen particularly for the changes promised in "You Can Get It If You Really Want," "Rivers of Babylon," and "The Harder They Come."

SEE ALSO:
Attention. Hospitality. Listening. Meaning. Teachers.
X—The Mystery. Yearning.

UNITY

THE BASIC PRACTICE

Unity in this Alphabet refers to living in harmony with other people.
It means working for a common cause with those around the globe who
know that when one person gains, all gain, and when one fails, all fail. We
are crafting unity when we build communities.

The spiritual practice of hospitality helps us learn to respect differences and celebrate diversity in the Creation. Unity is about affirming
commonalities. This can be as simple as acknowledging how you are like

another person. It can lead to actions demonstrating your solidarity with others. Without unity, there is little hope for compassion, justice, or peace.

Catalysts, Contrasts, and Companions

Feeling lonely and isolated from other people are symptoms of a lack of unity in your life. Extreme manifestations are alienation and estrangement. Sometimes we deliberately cut ourselves off from others by our tyrannical and arrogant behavior. We may be very protective of our turf and highly individualistic, interested only in having our own way.

These same tendencies may lead us to build or support the walls that separate groups in our societies along economic, racial, ethnic, sexual, religious, or other lines. Gated, insular communities, where people show little interest in the outside world, are sure signs that unity needs to be practiced.

Unity is more than a passing acquaintance with our neighbors, a temporary agreement among parties, or a superficial feeling of community. Feelings of harmony run deeper and last longer. They broaden your spiritual life in all directions.

Perspectives

We all have the same color bones.
–Paul Reps

I am part and parcel of the whole and cannot find God apart from the rest of humanity.
–Mahatma Gandhi

Only the unity of all can bring out the well-being of all.
–Robert Muller

Teachers

● "The awareness of unity is the distinguishing mark of spiritual awareness," according to Eknath Easwaran, founder and director of the Blue Mountain Center of Meditation in Tomales, California. Born and raised in Mahatma Gandhi's India, he has been teaching in the United States for more than 30 years. *Your Life Is Your Message: Finding Harmony with Yourself, Others and the Earth* is addressed to "people changing the world by changing themselves."

Easwaran recalls that his grandmother, who was his spiritual teacher, once pointed to a tamarind tree, noting how its very small but densely packed leaves provided ample shade from the hot sun. "Little Lamp," she told him, "you don't have to look for big people. Look for little people like yourself, then band together and work together in harmony."

In a series of profound short essays, the author outlines the attitudes and practical steps for self-transformation to establish unity, including harnessing anger, slowing down, finding spiritual companions, and putting others first. He quotes the Bhagavad Gita: "They live in wisdom who see themselves in all and all in them." He suggests that recognizing the unity of life is a little like breaking a secret code: Once you realize you are at one with the natural world, strangers, and even inanimate objects, you will be more open to the expression of peace, love, meaning, beauty, and much more.

● Religions have an important role to play in promoting unity in our pluralistic world. *Yes to a Global Ethic: Voices from Religion and Politics*, edited by theologian Hans Kung, is a collection of essays by representatives of Christianity, Buddhism, Judaism, and Islam on the principles drawn up at the 1993 Parliament of the World's Religions. This global ethic offers a commitment to the culture of nonviolence and respect for life, to the aim of a just social and economic order, and to the ideal of equal rights and partnership between men and women. The essayists demonstrate solidarity in their hope for international cooperation to achieve a world order that will bring out the best in all human beings.

VIDEOS

● Music testifies to the value of harmony. *Paradise Road* is based on the true-life experiences of a group of European, Australian, and American women who are captured by the Japanese Army during World War II. In a jungle prison camp, they are subjected to a hellish existence of hard labor, little food, and a shortage of medical supplies.

In order to lift the women's spirits, a former missionary to China comes up with the idea of starting a vocal orchestra to sing classical compositions. The project creates an oasis of beauty and transcendence in an atmosphere of pain, grief, and death. Even the Japanese guards are moved by their harmonies. Art can tear down the barriers that separate people—even those created by war and hatred.

• Sometimes people just have to work together. That's the theme of *The Milagro Beanfield War*. The film is set in a small Hispanic town in northern New Mexico where a developer wants to build a resort. When a handyman from Milagro irrigates his half-acre beanfield with water controlled by the developer, he sets in motion a series of events that test everyone's ideas about place, progress, and civic solidarity.

The colorful cast of characters are a diverse lot: the oldest man in town, an angel, a community activist, a newspaper publisher, and a New York graduate student of indigenous cultures. This film celebrates the magical and often surprising ways in which people come together in a community—concrete expressions of the spiritual practice of unity.

SPIRITUAL EXERCISES AND RITUALS

• Use the phrase "just like me" to signify your unity with others. Whenever you find yourself making an assessment of another person, whether you are saying something critical or something complimentary, right after you think or say it, add the statement "just like me." For example, "My partner is so stubborn, just like me." "My friend is so generous with her time, just like me." "She holds too many grudges, just like me." "He is so creative, just like me."

• Create a ritual to express your appreciation of community life; it might emphasize interconnection (see the ritual with balls of yarn on page 483 of *Spiritual Literacy*), the strength that comes from working together (see page 476 of *Spiritual Literacy*), or another theme. Find or make a symbol of unity to give to those attending.

• The Maya say, "I am another one of Yourself." The next time you are on a bus or train, look around at your fellow passengers and repeat this phrase or the following mantra.

PRAYER OR MANTRA

These lines for meditation come from the Hindu and Taoist traditions.

> Breathing in: I am one with all . . .
> Breathing out: I am that.

IMAGERY EXERCISE

Eknath Easwaran suggests a spiritual exercise that he calls "watch your family grow." The idea is to extend the reach of your love to include more and more people. That is also the intention of the following imagery exercise. You can do it in two ways. First, while sitting, eyes closed, imagine yourself doing the suggested directional turns. Second, while standing, eyes open, physically turn your body for each part of the exercise.

Face the East. See the people of the East. Notice the shape of their eyes and the color of their skin, their clothes, their stance, their expression. What are they saying to you?

Face the South. See and observe the people of the South. What message are they sending to you?

Face the West. See and observe the people of the West. What are they knowing that you need to know?

Face the North. See and observe the people of the North. What are they saying to you?

JOURNAL EXERCISES

● Write about a time in your life when you felt lonely and a time when you felt part of a community.

● Recall a conversation during which you felt separated from someone else. Write down the script in your journal. Then change your own and the other's responses until you no longer feel separated. You may also do this in the form of an unsent letter.

DISCUSSION QUESTIONS, STORYTELLING, SHARING

● In Africa, the Xhosa tribe has a saying, "I am because we are." Share a story about a community where you have felt this way.

● What do you look for in a community? What do you expect to give in return?

● What blocks or obstacles most often keep you from feeling that you are one with others, especially those living in different countries?

HOUSEHOLD, GROUP, AND COMMUNITY PROJECTS

● Eat together with others regularly, even if you live alone. Take time to observe this most basic way of building community, no matter how hard it is to coordinate schedules.

● Take a tour of your house and note all the things you have that come from other places which now belong in yours. Talk about ways that you as a household can express your solidarity with people around the globe, such as buying crafts from artisans in developing countries.

● Inform your elected representatives, as well as the leaders of any groups to which you belong, of your support for organizations of international cooperation, such as the United Nations or the World Council of Churches. Your group may also want to look into establishing a local affiliate of, or raising money for, one of the private voluntary organizations working internationally, such as Amnesty International, Save the Children, World Watch, and CARE.

FICTION, POETRY, OR CHILDREN'S BOOK

● *To Every Thing There Is a Season* weds the sacred verses from the Book of Ecclesiastes in the Bible with the breathtaking artwork of illustrators Leo and Diane Dillon. Here is a global family album of the rhythms of life depicted through 16 different cultures and eras, including Celtic, Egyptian, Japanese, Mexican, Indian, Ethiopian, Chinese, Australian, Russian, and Inuit. Planting, plucking up, weeping, laughing, mourning, dancing, getting, losing, keeping, casting away, rending, sewing, keeping silence, speaking, loving, hating—these are universal experiences that unite people through time and space.

● Another global album is *Children Just Like Me* by Barnabas and Anabel Kindersley in association with UNICEF. A photographer and a teacher traveled to more than 30 countries to show that children all over the world are busy doing the same things. A different child is featured on each two-page spread with pictures and comments on his or her family, home, dress, toys, favorite activities, and more. The book's introduction sets the goal of this impressive project: "In *Children Just Like Me* you will meet children from all walks of life—from tiny rural communities to busy cities, from cold, snowy lands to the hot, humid tropics. You'll learn about these children's daily lives, their hopes and fears, and their dreams. And you'll discover how much these children have in common with each other—and with you!"

SPOKEN-WORD AUDIO

In *God and the Big Bang: Discovering Harmony Between Science and Spirituality,* Daniel C. Matt uses insights gleaned from his study of Kabbalah to shed light on the ethical implications of Big Bang cosmology. A professor of Jewish spirituality, Matt maintains that physics and mysticism, two tools for understanding, agree that a oneness undergirds all of life. The cosmos is vast and complex, but science and spirituality both underscore the commonalities of human experience.

ART

In his work from the early 1920s, French painter Fernand Léger created images of humans interacting with machines. Indeed, his bold block and cylindrical figures have a mechanical quality to them. By the 1930s and 1940s, however, the artist had moved on to depicting a different style of union—acrobats and divers with intertwined arms and limbs. See *Composition aux Deux Perroquets* (Composition with two parrots) and *Les Plongeurs* (The Divers) for very vivid, graphic, and startling images of human unity.

MUSIC

Mozart's *Symphony No. 41, in C,* known as the *Jupiter Symphony,* was the composer's last. It is an amazingly complex composition characterized by constant alterations of contrasting elements and styles, melodies and phrases that keep coming in and out and back together again. For all its diversity of musical expression, the *Jupiter* is comprehended as one harmonious whole. Unity does not come to us easily, but when it does, as here, there is nothing quite like it!

SEE ALSO:

Compassion. Connections. Faith. Hospitality. Justice.
Openness. Peace.

 VISION

DAILY CUE, REMINDER, VOW, BLESSING

Putting on my glasses is a cue to think seriously about my visions
of the future.

•

Using a microscope, a telescope, or a kaleidoscope, I am reminded
of the importance of different viewpoints.

•

Watching small children, I vow to make my vision of a better
world a reality.

•

Blessed is the Great Spirit who has given us vision so that we can
bring about change in the world.

THE BASIC PRACTICE

The spiritual practice of vision encompasses the discovery of fresh
insights about the way things are and the cultivation of different outlooks
on what can be. It is how you find your own wisdom and align yourself
with Spirit. Sometimes this process involves developing good judgment,
deliberative skills, and common sense. Other times you may experience
extraordinary perceptions, what are often called revelations.

Values and visions go hand in hand. That is why this practice is so
often associated with ethical decision making and social action. Begin by

reexamining the assumptions beneath your understandings of reality. Identify an area that you might see in a different way. This could be as simple as reframing a household task as an act of service or as complex as recognizing the common interests at the core of an international conflict. Seek and accept solutions.

CATALYSTS, CONTRASTS, AND COMPANIONS

Visionaries are called all kinds of names—dreamers, romantics, seers, utopians, altruists, reformers, cranks—and often the title is not meant as a compliment. But in the spiritual life, idealism is welcome. The regular practice of vision creates and supports idealists.

Realists and pragmatists, on the other hand, have difficulty with this practice. They are the kind of people who, when offered a new approach to a situation, request a feasibility study. They are not comfortable with unproven strategies. They tend to be shortsighted, preferring to consider immediate effects rather than long-range ones. If you lean in this direction, the practice of vision will give you a more balanced outlook on life.

PERSPECTIVES

The best success I can dream for my life: to have spread a new vision of the world.
–PIERRE TEILHARD DE CHARDIN

A very good vision is needed for life and the man who has it must follow it—as the eagle seeks the deepest blue of the sky.
–CHIEF CRAZY HORSE

If we want to live healthy lives, we have to build into our daily life moments of vision and then let our action be formed by that vision.
–BROTHER DAVID STEINDL-RAST

TEACHERS

• Christopher Childs spent many years working as a Greenpeace activist and spokesperson. He believes that genuine idealism is fueled by a clear vision of a desirable future. In *The Spirit's Terrain: Creativity, Activism and Transformation,* he writes: "The juxtaposition of what is and a clarified, deeply poetic vision of what can be lies at the heart of the creative process." Using such Greenpeace campaigns as saving the great whales and protesting the pollution of the Great Lakes, he demonstrates the important roles that intuition and creativity play in activism. It is not enough to claim to want a better future; we have to "take the time to envision how we want things to turn out, and to transmit that vision by every conceivable means to every available audience."

Where can we turn for help in initiating the spiritual practice of vision? Childs looks for mentors, people like Mahatma Gandhi, Dr. Martin Luther King, Jr., and Aung San Suu Kyi, who combine spirituality with activism. He salutes the importance of individual vision in Native American tradition and the value of collective vision in Tibetan Buddhism. Activists who want to affect the course of future events constructively must use patience, persistence, and compassion toward opponents.

Acknowledging the possibility of positive outcomes is also important. "When one is attempting to create and establish wholly new 'ways of doing business' on the planet, and even wholly new ways of thinking, it becomes critical not merely to identify the world's deficiencies, but to clearly identify also every significant step taken by a culture in the direction of creative change."

● For David Spangler, the New Age has been a seedbed for visionary change. *A Pilgrim in Aquarius* is a personal account of his involvement in this social and spiritual movement. As one of its most articulate and thoughtful philosophers, he outlines how New Age encompasses a planetary perspective, ecological awareness, new paradigms of science and technology, and insights into personal empowerment and responsibility.

The New Age, he writes, "lives in my imagination as an inspiration, in my mind as a set of principles and paradigms, in my heart as a spiritual connection and presence, and in my life as a guide for action. It is no longer a vision of the future. It is a vision of the present. The New Age is no longer something I believe in. It is something I practice."

VIDEOS

● *Thunderheart* is a remarkable video movie on the role of visions as bridges to reality in both the visible and the invisible worlds. Roy Levoi is a zealous FBI agent who is sent to investigate the murder of an Oglala Sioux in the Badlands of South Dakota. Although he has been chosen for the job because he's one-fourth Native American, Ray is embarrassed by his ethnic roots. But during the investigation he meets a medicine man who tells him that he has been summoned to the Badlands by the spirits.

Ray begins to have visions that lead him to a breakthrough in his investigation, enabling him to see what had been missed before. Equally important, the visions help him to connect with his ancestors. He gains a new understanding of who he is and what he must do.

● Once a person is seized by a vision of societal renewal, there is no turning back. *Romero* is a stirring biodrama about the martyred Archbishop of San Salvador who preached reform and tolerance and called for justice for all people in the midst of a violent civil war in El Salvador. He incurred the wrath of the military in the process. The drama conveys the changes in this man of God during the last three years of his life.

SPIRITUAL EXERCISES AND RITUALS

● Sacrifice is an important rite in many spiritual traditions. It is the ritual giving up of something for a purpose, such as a payment for sins, an expression of gratitude, a purgation in preparation of receiving a blessing, or an offering intended to evoke a response from the invisible world. Give up something, other than money and time, for a cause you believe in.

● Go on a vision quest. Denise Linn's *Quest: A Guide for Creating Your Own Vision Quest* is an accessible and insightful overview of modern variations on this ancient spiritual practice of going off alone to experience a vision. She writes: "When your heart is open and your intention is clear, your vision will come, no matter where you are." Go on an outdoor retreat or plan a day away where you can be by yourself. Spend the time examining your life and calling for a vision.

PRAYER OR MANTRA

Vision gives us new perspectives on our world and also shows us different ways of behaving. This mantra reinforces the second value.

> Breathing in: The vision . . .
> Breathing out: leads me on.

IMAGERY EXERCISE

To create new visions in imagination, we can use mirrors to reflect changes in the inner life. Gerald Epstein provides several examples of this in his book *Healing into Immortality.* He incorporates movement into these exercises, noting that movement from right to left pushes things into the past and movement from left to right is into the future. This exercise, "Changing the World," uses this technique.

Close your eyes. Breathe out three times, counting backward from three to one. At one, breathe out once more and see the one becoming a zero. See the zero growing in size a bit and becoming a circular mirror. Looking into the mirror, see a disturbing, damaging, or destructive situation happening in your community, the nation, or the world. Breathe out once, and wipe the image away, out of the mirror, from right to left, with your left hand.

Now turn the mirror over and see a positive change, movement, or construction happening in your community, the nation, or the world. Wipe that image away, out of the mirror, from left to right, with your right hand. After you finish, breathe out and open your eyes.

JOURNAL EXERCISES

● Having a vision of who you are and where you want to go is like having a blueprint for building a house. What are the cornerstones and building blocks of your vision? Make a sketch in your journal of your vision house.

● Use your journal to send an encouraging message to your "activist self." Make a list of changes in the world around you—developments in line with your vision of a better world—that have occurred in the last one to five years.

● Write forward-dated entries in your journal, perhaps annually on an anniversary or birthday. Put a date one to five years from today at the top of the page. Then write about what you want to have occurring in your life at this time. Christina Baldwin, who suggests this technique in her book *Life's Companion: Journal Writing as a Spiritual Quest*, explains: "Such writing is often the first glimpse we have of the solidity of our choices. . . . Writing the possible future helps us understand what desire and what action need to occur in order to support the vision."

DISCUSSION QUESTIONS, STORYTELLING, SHARING

● What contemporary artists, spiritual teachers, or social activists have provided you with an inspiring, soul-stirring vision of the future that you can align yourself with? In other words, who are your vision mentors?

● Have you ever had a "vision"? Share the story. (A vision can be a mystical experience or revelation, or it can be a dream for personal or group fulfillment.)

• One of Dr. Martin Luther King, Jr.'s most famous speeches was "I Have a Dream" given during the march on Washington for civil rights in 1963. On the national holiday celebrating his birthday, have a party during which you all share your dreams for our society.

HOUSEHOLD, GROUP, AND COMMUNITY PROJECTS

• Take a look at how you make decisions in your household. Does everyone have a say? Who is the ultimate authority? When there is a dispute, how is it resolved? Our homes are training grounds for our participation in the wider community.

• Organize a group in your community dedicated to effecting social change. Meet regularly to share ideas, exchange energy, and find concrete ways to act upon your vision. Christopher Childs in *The Spirit's Terrain* outlines a 12-step educational program to develop activism. Key steps include finding positive role models; identifying a desired, ideal, and long-term outcome; promoting your cause; and celebrating all significant positive results. Another book on this process is *Wisdom Circles: A Guide to Self-Discovery and Community Building in Small Groups* by Charles Garfield, Cindy Spring, and Sedonia Cahill. The authors see these groups as "places to share a vision, define a mission." They detail the basics of calling a circle together, creating rituals, sustaining the process, and rotating leaders.

FICTION, POETRY, OR CHILDREN'S BOOK

Revelations by Sophy Burnham is a novel about an Episcopal minister in the 1950s who has a vision of God. His congregation and the bishop are uncomfortable with his revised understanding of the Gospel. This story asks us to consider the meaning of visions, especially when they challenge conventional theology and ecclesiastical stability.

SPOKEN-WORD AUDIO

Black Elk Speaks as Told to John G. Neihardt is a classic account of Native American spirituality. Black Elk, an Oglala visionary and medicine man, recounts his life, his visions, and the tragedies that befell his people.

ART

In Paul Gauguin's compelling *The Vision After the Sermon*, a group of peasant women and a priest envision the biblical story of the battle between Jacob and the angel. Eyes down, heads bowed, the people are obviously seeing this scene in the inner world of the imagination where all visions are birthed. The drama of the battle appears close at hand, however, just on the other side of a tree trunk that cuts the picture in half. The strong red background contrasted with the white folds of the women's caps reinforces the vividness of the vision.

MUSIC

The overture for Gioacchino Rossini's opera *Guillaume Tell* (*William Tell Overture*) is music for visionaries. The opera recalls the hero's fight for freedom from political tyranny. Of course, we can't listen to it today without having visions from our childhood of the Lone Ranger—it was his theme song—coming to the rescue of desperate people. This is marching, galloping music that propels you to put energy into any endeavor, even the seemingly impossible ones. It is the sound of idealism.

For a particularly inspiring rendition of this overture, listen to the one played by the brass band in the video movie *Brassed Off*. They come from a North Yorkshire town in England that is about to lose its main employer when the government shuts down its coal pit. Determined to keep their spirits up, the miners' band enters a competition and makes it all the way to the final concert at Albert Hall. There it's the *William Tell Overture* that most expresses their determined vision of a better life.

SEE ALSO:
Hope. Imagination. Listening. Meaning. Openness.
Questing. Silence.

WONDER

THE BASIC PRACTICE

Wonder begins in the senses, comes alive in the imagination, and flourishes in adoration of the Divine. It arises from our natural curiosity about the great adventure of life. It increases our capacity to be a bold inner-space tripper and an avid explorer of the physical world.

There is no end to the things that can awaken our wonder, from the majesty of the night sky, to the smell of lilacs in the spring, to the turning of the leaves in the fall. And it is all right here, a feast of epiphanies and astonishments in the daily round of our lives.

The first step in this spiritual practice is to rejoice in the play of our senses: smell, touch, taste, hear, and see. Slow down and tune in to the varied world of this and that. You'll never get anywhere with this practice by rushing.

CATALYSTS, CONTRASTS, AND COMPANIONS

Indifference—that listless, blasé, and detached feeling—is the contrast to wonder. We can never be astonished or awestruck when we are either overwhelmed or underwhelmed. Feeling the first, we don't notice the subtle blessings in our surroundings; we don't take the time to stop and smell the roses. Feeling underwhelmed, we couldn't care less. "So what?" becomes our response instead of "Aha!" Wonder is an antidote to both conditions.

This spiritual practice spices up our lives with a constant parade of new delights. Most glorious of all, it enhances sensuousness, that elixir that keeps us forever young in spirit.

PERSPECTIVES

Wonder encourages us to stand humbly before the unfathomable mysteries of human life, trusting that, in them, we encounter God.
–MELANNIE SVOBODA

The tin foil collectors and the fancy ribbon savers may be absurd, but they're not crazy. They are the ones who still retain the capacity for wonder that is the root of caring.
–ROBERT FARRAR CAPON

I think we all have a core that's ecstatic, that knows and that looks up to wonder. We all know that there are marvelous moments of eternity that just happen. We know them.
–COLEMAN BARKS

TEACHERS

● Poet, essayist, and naturalist Diane Ackerman is a multitalented teacher of the spiritual practice of wonder. "How sense-luscious the world is," she writes in *A Natural History of the Senses*. "There is no way in which to understand the world without first detecting it through the radar-net of our senses. . . . We need to return to the feeling textures of life."

Drawing on a wealth of illustrations from science, history, anthropology, psychology, literature, and philosophy, Ackerman leads us on a dazzling and informative tour of smell, touch, taste, hearing, vision, and synesthesia (the interplay of the senses). The author's own sensory adventures, ranging from her backyard to all parts of the globe, serve as touchstones for her wonderstruck approach to the world. This is an ideal resource for those who want to savor the enchantments of the senses and incorporate such celebrations into their spiritual lives.

• Another teacher of wonder is Pulitzer Prize–winning poet Mary Oliver. In *New and Selected Poems*, which brings together three decades of work, she demonstrates her deep respect for the epiphanies of the natural world. As she notes in "The Summer Day": "I don't know exactly what a prayer is. / I do know how to pay attention, how to fall down / into the grass, how to kneel down in the grass, / how to be idle and blessed, how to stroll through the fields, / which is what I have been doing all day."

Oliver's exquisite poetry brings all our senses alive. She shows us how to be astonished by things we take for granted, including the sun and poppies. She finds within nature profound parables on living and dying. She demonstrates—again and again—how the spiritual practice of wonder is linked to reverence, imagination, openness, and hospitality. *New and Selected Poems* incarnates the art of long and loving looking.

VIDEOS

• Sam Keen coined the term "wonderosity," by which he means the fountain of wonder and curiosity inside us all. It may take a poet to make us aware of it. *Il Postino* (The Postman) is set in 1952 on an island off the coast of Naples where the world-famous poet Pablo Neruda is living after being exiled from his homeland of Chile. The local postmaster hires Mario, the son of a fisherman, to deliver mail to this famous outsider. Impressed by Neruda's worldwide popularity with women because of his love poems, Mario slowly develops a friendship with him. The poet encourages the postman to see the world with fresh eyes and to think metaphorically. Mario does and soon he is in love with Beatrice, a beautiful woman who works at a local inn.

Il Postino (The Postman) is an intimate film about the soulful dimensions of wonder and the ways it can serve as a spur to passion, meaning, and adventure. This faculty is a spiritual gift that can enrich the lives of all who use it.

• The world is filled with abundant marvels and delights. Yet we are often so busy and so distracted that we just don't notice them. It may take a journey to a strange place to wake up our wonder. In *Local Hero*, Felix Happer, the powerful chairman of the board of Knox Oil and Gas, sends Mac, an employee, to Ferness, a small Scottish fishing village. His mission is to convince residents to allow the American company to build a refinery there.

Mac, a confirmed city slicker, feels out of place in the small town. And he is not well acquainted with the natural world. One day he becomes so involved in gathering shells that he leaves his watch on a rock and the waters wash it away. Then Mac sees the aurora borealis, which takes his breath away. Wonder has worked its way into his soul, and he'll never be the same again.

Local Hero reveals the manifold blessings of what is too often an underutilized faculty. The film itself induces wonder in the viewer with its endearing look at nature, community, and human idiosyncracy.

SPIRITUAL EXERCISES AND RITUALS

• Notice marvels in your home or neighborhood and respond to them with "Ahhh!"

• The use of incense is mentioned over 100 times in the Bible. Many churches use it in their worship services. It is also frequently an element in Buddhist, Taoist, and Hindu devotions. Try burning various kinds of incense during your periods of prayer and meditation and sense its effects.

• Have a "Wonder Week." Each day concentrate on a different sense: Monday, smell; Tuesday, touch; Wednesday, taste; Thursday, seeing; Friday, hearing; and Saturday, synesthesia (the interplay of the senses). Notice what each sense is drawn to and irritated by. Try to expose your senses to new sensations. Go into a natural food store, where herbs and spices are stored in bulk, and see how many you can identify by smell alone. Walk barefoot. Assemble a platter of as many tastes as possible: salty, sweet, bitter, bland. Look for odd color combinations. Scan the stations on your radio, noticing types of music, modulations of voices, and more.

PRAYER OR MANTRA

Wonder yields new insights and sensations. Remember this as you pray.

> Breathing in: O let me sense . . .
> Breathing out: the world anew.

IMAGERY EXERCISE

Rumi's poetry is filled with reflections on the wonders of a world infused with the presence of the Beloved. This exercise is developed from the quatrain beginning "This moment this love comes to rest in me" in *The Essential Rumi*.

Breathe out three times. Pick up a grain of wheat. See it transform into a thousand stacks of wheat.

Breathe out one time. Take a stalk of wheat. See it become the eye of the golden needle.

Breathe out one time. Look into the needle's eye and see the night sky full of stars. Know there are many beings in One Being.

Then open your eyes.

JOURNAL EXERCISES

● Take an inventory of your awareness of each of your senses. Which is most dominant? Which is overlooked? Use the Wonder Week exercise above to develop your unused senses.

● Experiment with smells to see what memories you associate with them. Cigar smoke, cinnamon, coffee, and bleach are a few to try. Then write about the memory in your journal.

● If you have been keeping a journal for some time, read through old entries for experiences of wonder. Usually you will find they have sparked some of your most vivid descriptions.

DISCUSSION QUESTIONS, STORYTELLING, SHARING

● Share a story of some experience, event, or person that aroused or renewed your sense of wonder.

● What special places always bring out your wonder?

● Discuss the following: The closest some people get to wonder in our society is horror films, sci-fi thrillers, or movies about aliens.

● What aspects of the worship service in your religious tradition elicit your wonder?

HOUSEHOLD, GROUP, AND COMMUNITY PROJECTS

● Have members of your household go on a wonder hunt. Explore your neighborhood as if seeing it for the very first time. Make a list of wonders you discover that you have never seen before.

• Organize a poetry reading in your community. Concentrate on works from "wonder" poets such as Mary Oliver and Gary Snyder.

• Volunteer to be a guide for visitors to a botanical garden, a zoo, or an art museum, places known to evoke wonder.

• In many cultures, rituals are built around natural events that bring out people's wonder: a full moon, the annual meteor showers, blossoming trees and flowers in the spring. Plan a community-wide celebration of one such event. For example, encourage people to picnic under flowering trees in bloom or to gather in silence to gaze at the full moon.

FICTION, POETRY, OR CHILDREN'S BOOK

For *No Nature: New and Selected Poems*, Gary Snyder has chosen material from eight earlier collections. He possesses a watchful and elegant mind that has been tutored by Native American sensitivities, Zen proclivities, and wilderness experiences. The poems in this volume will teach you how to sit still, read signs, and sense in your bones the poetics of place. Snyder has crossed many borders, and these poems bring us fresh wonders.

SPOKEN-WORD AUDIO

Anne Morrow Lindbergh has a refined sense of wonder. Her diary of several months spent by the seaside, *Gift from the Sea*, provides ample testimony to her powers of observation. She is moved to poetic expression in the presence of so much natural beauty. A fine audio version of this spiritual classic is read by Claudette Colbert.

ART

When asked what they enjoy most about being in the presence of little children, many adults mention their unquenchable curiosity and sense of wonder. "Childlike" is almost synonymous with "filled with wonder." Our artist for this spiritual practice is both. Alexander Calder created witty drawings, jewelry, wire sculptures, and action toys, including a miniature circus. He invented the mobile, a sculpture consisting of disks in various shapes connected with rods and wire and balanced so that the elements move in relationship to each other.

Mostly, the artist said he was interested in creating art that made people happy. And the mobiles do that by tickling our senses. *Big Red* is painted a vibrant color that the artist adored. *Red Lily Pads* consists of more red disks floating above a stationary pond; it is especially delightful when viewed from above. *Lobster Trap and Fish Tail* is a witty and charming mobile that flutters on currents of air. To see how one of the mobiles looks in action, just flip the pages of the book *Alexander Calder and His Magical Mobiles*; the mobile *Dots and Dashes* will dance around at the top of the pages.

MUSIC

French composer Claude Debussy's *La Mer* engages more of our senses than just hearing. This piece consists of three "symphonic sketches" catching all the moods and sensual pleasures of the sea. We can see the changing light playing on the surface of the water in "From Dawn to Noon on the Sea." We can feel the rocking sensations and the tug of the currents in "Play of Waves." And in the last section, "Dialogue of the Wind and the Sea," we sense the power of the ocean, pushed onto the shore by the winds. Like the painters who were so popular in his time, Debussy created "impressions" with his music. Its effect is to draw out our wonder.

SEE ALSO:

Beauty. Grace. Imagination. Listening. Reverence.
X—The Mystery. Zeal.

X—THE MYSTERY

THE BASIC PRACTICE

To be spiritual is to have an abiding respect for the great mysteries of life—the profound distinctiveness of other souls, the strange beauty of nature and the animal world, the ineffable complexity of our inner selves, the unfathomable depths of the Inexplicable One. The wisdom traditions challenge us to live within a cloud of unknowing.

The first step in this practice is to cherish the baffling, curious, hidden, and inscrutable dimensions of your existence and the world around you.

Live with paradoxes. Give up the idea that you can always "get it." Be suspicious of all the "ologies" that try to explain everything—from astrology, to psychology, to theology. Whenever you are honestly stumped by the existence of evil, injustice, or suffering, resist the temptation to ask "Why?" And never be afraid to admit "I don't know."

CATALYSTS, CONTRASTS, AND COMPANIONS

The practice of mystery enhances our understanding of the complexity of reality. It is an affront to the modern need to have answers to every question and our tendency to create tidy systems with a cubbyhole for every problem and aspiration. Of course, some people simply ignore the mysterious because it lies outside the hallowed precincts of reason and logic.

The antidote to these reductionist approaches is to rest in the riddle of not knowing. If you sometimes think that answers are wisdom, it is time to try practicing mystery.

PERSPECTIVES

Our life is a faint tracing on the surface of mystery.
–ANNIE DILLARD

We never "catch up with" reality itself. The real nature of mystery always evades our attempts to conceptualize it, and escapes the nets of our language and symbolism. Its depths are never plumbed. Mystery is always linked to passion, enthusiasm and all great emotions, in short, to life's deepest and greatest impulses.
–LEONARDO BOFF

When we trust "Don't know" we do not cling to the past. We do not hold onto old points of view and stagnant opinions. When we trust "Don't know" we are open to being in process, with many possibilities and alternatives. We do not force things to happen. "Don't know" waits and explores, searches and considers, examines and trusts.
–JOYCE RUPP

TEACHERS

● In India they use the term "old soul" to describe someone who is ripe enough to experience the deepest mysteries. It applies to our teacher of mystery, best-selling author and psychologist Robert A. Johnson. In *Balancing Heaven and Earth: A Memoir of Visions, Dreams, and Realizations*, Johnson, writing with Jerry M. Ruhl, recounts the amazing twists and turns of his spiritual journey. His encounters with what Mircea Eliade called "the Golden World" have given him a great respect for the mysteries of ecstatic experiences.

Johnson's spiritual mentors have included Jiddu Krishnamurti, Fritz Kunkel, and Carl Jung. Throughout the book, he reflects upon the significant dreams in his life as pathways to discovery and personal renewal. He also ponders the important role India, friends, active imagination, music, and Eastern and Western religions have played in his quest for understanding. Johnson is a great exemplar of what it means to cherish the mysteries.

● Traditionally, mystics are the ones who tutor us in the art of being moved by that which we can never fully comprehend or control. In *Breakfast at the Victory: The Mysticism of Ordinary Life*, James P. Carse reflects upon happenings in his life that have been "bounded by the boundless." The author, who teaches literature and religion at New York University, battles with his false self, which is always looking for attention and acclaim. On the other hand, he finds moments to celebrate when the soul shows through and the ego is "naughted." He fondly recalls a night watch on a schooner in Lake Michigan when he felt at one with the boat, the stars, and the sea. And in the title piece essay, Carse lauds the ability of the one-legged owner of the Victory Luncheonette to so lose himself in what he is doing at the counter that it is no longer work but sheer flow. He concludes with a paean to mystery: "It is one thing to see something remarkable appearing inexplicably in the world. It is quite another to see the world is remarkable and all of existence as inexplicable."

VIDEOS

● Great movies often bring us into the presence of the inexplicable mysteries of the human heart. *The English Patient* is an enthralling Academy Award–winning film about the violent upheavals of World War II and the healing power of love. A badly burned patient is taken to an Italian monastery by Hana, a Canadian nurse. Her spirit has been shattered by the deaths of two people very close to her. In the silence and solace of this holy place, the text of the dying patient's life is slowly unraveled. A morphine addict turns up and develops a keen interest in his story. Another arrival on the scene, a Sikh bomb disposal expert, falls in love with Hana.

The monastery turns out to be a divine milieu where the healing balm of confession, compassion, forgiveness, and personal renewal are administered. Lives are changed but the reasons why and how are never quite explained. *The English Patient* pays homage to the mysteries of the human soul and its great powers of resiliency.

• One of the characters in *Household Saints* says, "You think you know how the game is going but you never do. At any moment God can deal you a wild card." The wild cards are mysteries.

This quirky and offbeat drama revolves around a lucky butcher who wins his wife's hand in marriage in a card game. They live with his pious Catholic mother and raise a very devout daughter, Teresa, who wants to serve God like Saint Thérèse of Lisieux. Then one day while ironing shirts she has a vision of Christ. She tries to tell her parents about it, but they send her to a Catholic institution for having, as one nun puts it, "temporarily lost touch with what we call reality." But yet another wild card is dealt. The upshot of Teresa's spiritual journey is that God moves mysteriously in our lives to work miracles while we are dealing with such seemingly insignificant matters as making sausages, ironing shirts, and scrubbing floors.

• Movies can transport us to a place where awe and wonder are the only appropriate responses to mysteries beyond our ken. One of the most impressive films of the modern era in this regard is *Close Encounters of the Third Kind.*

Roy Neary, a power repairman in Muncie, Indiana, has a series of close encounters with UFOs. As he tries to work out his feelings about these experiences, his life is completely upended. Alienated from his wife, who can't understand what he is going through, Roy teams up with a widow who has also seen UFOs and is looking for her missing son. The third major figure in this thriller is Claude Lacombe, a French scientist who is leading an international investigation of UFOs.

This extraordinary film asks us to reimagine the vastness of the universe and our small place within it. The drama affirms our impulse to believe in cosmic unity and downplays the idea of Earth chauvinism. But the main message of *Close Encounters of the Third Kind* is this: Openness to the unknown is the best policy; there are surely many more mysteries yet to come.

SPIRITUAL EXERCISES AND RITUALS

● Black is the color of mystery. It reveals no particular color but absorbs all others. Wear all black one day this week to signify your devotion to the manifold mysteries of life.

● Quit reading astrological, numerological, and other such forecasts that try to take the mystery out of the future.

● Find an artist in any creative medium who helps you deepen your sensitivity to the mysteries of the human soul, the natural world, your inner self, and God. Go to this spiritual resource whenever you feel the urge to try to explain everything.

● Rituals help to reinforce a spiritual practice by using heightened concentration, special settings, and symbolic objects. This is especially true for the practice of mystery. The Christian sacraments of baptism and Holy Communion, for example, are based on a belief in a mysterious activity of God moving through the ritual toward the individual and the community. Create a simple ritual in which you yield to "unknowing" and welcome the Mystery of God.

PRAYER OR MANTRA

This prayer is suggested by Joyce Rupp in her book of meditations *The Cup of Our Life.*

> Breathing in: O Mystery . . .
> Breathing out: alive in me.

IMAGERY EXERCISE

This exercise on being in the presence of the Mystery was designed by Colette Aboulker-Muscat. It gives you practice living with paradox.

Close your eyes and breathe out three times.

See yourself standing and kneeling at the same time.

Breathe out one time. Sense and feel your silent cry going out of yourself.

Breathe out one time. See and feel yourself dancing and standing still at the same time.

When you are finished, open your eyes.

JOURNAL EXERCISES

• Reflect upon the things you just can't explain in your daily life, especially ones that you are having difficulty leaving alone. Describe the mystery but don't try to add an explanation.

• Write about an experience that opened your eyes to the fact that we can never really know the heart of another person, even those who are closest to us. Express the feelings that come up when you accept this idea.

DISCUSSION QUESTIONS, STORYTELLING, SHARING

• Monks and nuns of all traditions have been called caretakers and preservers of God's mysteries. Who else performs that function today?

• So much has been made of the mystery of evil. Who or what has taught you about the mystery of good? For instance, how was this mystery revealed in the movie *Schindler's List*?

• Talk about what religious educators and spiritual teachers can do to insure that young people have a proper respect for the limits of reason and the bounties of mystery.

HOUSEHOLD, GROUP, AND COMMUNITY PROJECTS

• One of the best ways to practice mystery is for adults to model accepting it in the home. This means that parents, grandparents, and other significant figures in the lives of children make room for "not knowing" in their responses to difficult questions. Not everything can be answered or explained simply and quickly. Here are some common situations when "not knowing" would be appropriate. You see survivors of a natural disaster on television expressing their gratitude that their property was spared, while others lost everything, and a child wants to know who deserved what. One of your child's friends, a parent, or a pet dies, and your child wants to know why this happened. Somebody wins the lottery, and your child wants to know if that could happen to you.

• Volunteer to work in a hospital, a hospice, or a rehabilitation center where you will come face to face with suffering and death. Don't try to make rational sense out of what you witness.

FICTION, POETRY, OR CHILDREN'S BOOK

Mariette in Ecstasy by Ron Hansen tells the riveting story of a young nun whose stigmata brings disorder and doubt to her convent community in upstate New York in 1906. This brief novel sheds light on the difficulty some religious communities have living with the awesome burdens of mystery and the presence of individuals exhibiting ardent spirituality.

SPOKEN-WORD AUDIO

Novelist, poet, and essayist Ursula LeGuin has fashioned an elegant and lyrical interpretation of Lao Tzu's *Tao Te Ching*. In her audio reading of this ancient spiritual text, which is the most translated book in the world next to the Bible and the Bhagavad Gita, she conveys the feminine spirit of the Great Mystery that holds all things together. In addition, she emphasizes Taoism's respect for paradox—the use of opposites.

ART

The world is immersed in mystery, and the most spiritual approach is to revel in it rather than analyze it. That certainly was the approach of Vincent van Gogh, whose paintings honor the unknowable in human nature, in the natural world, and even in simple objects. In *A Pair of Shoes*, van Gogh conveys the sanctity of these dirty, worn-out tools of his working life. His respect for the mystery of the human personality comes through in portraits of a postman, *Portrait of Joseph Roulin,* and a physician, *Portrait of Doctor Gachet.* Two of his most powerful paintings pay tribute to the wild unsystematic energy of nature: *Branches with Almond Blossom* salutes new life, and *The Starry Night* vividly conveys the awesome quality of a turbulent sky.

MUSIC

Music is a very subjective experience; it speaks to us in mysterious ways. Just the sound of music can set in motion a complex series of responses that have just been awaiting activation. Moreover, the activation may be immediate, delayed, repressed, or even unrecognized. The mystery of music is the way it works us over and, on some occasions, connects with great power directly to our souls. One of the best descriptions of this phenomenon is

"Music" by John Miles on his album *Rebel*. This beautifully orchestrated five-minute masterpiece celebrates music as the magic that helps pull us through.

SEE ALSO:

Devotion. Grace. Imagination. Meaning. Reverence. Vision. Wonder.

YEARNING

DAILY CUE, REMINDER, VOW, BLESSING

The sight of a flower leaning toward the sun is my cue to practice yearning.

•

When I look at the moon, I am reminded of the great distances that can be traveled on the wings of our desire.

•

Reading a letter from an advocacy organization, I vow to make my yearnings into concrete demands for change.

•

Blessed is the Supreme One who dances with us in our yearning.

THE BASIC PRACTICE

Yearning is the force field of desire that draws us to God. It grows out of our sense of incompleteness and our deep need for something more that we know can only be met by the More. It is characterized by a restlessness in our souls. We desperately want to move beyond the petty wants of the ego and break out of the self-constructed prisons that confine us.

Yearning draws out the mystic inside us as we sense the Sacred Presence in the world and feel one with all that exists. By attending to this desire, we realize that it also fuels our drive for sexual fulfillment. Yearning reveals the sacramental dimensions of erotic love and makes it one of the most enthralling experiences of life.

Practice yearning by constantly rekindling your desire through seeking, study, and devotion. Notice who and what pulls you. Honor the fluid, boundless, and timeless qualities of this faculty. Allow yourself to reach for fulfillment.

CATALYSTS, CONTRASTS, AND COMPANIONS

A block to the practice of yearning is being stuck in the status quo, unwilling or unable to move. We may be satisfied with the way things are, but that does not mean that everything is hunky-dory. No, our world is probably too small; we don't realize there is a much bigger one available to us.

We may also stifle our yearning out of a need for stability. We may be too cynical or pessimistic to believe that any life other than the one we are used to is possible. We've seen these same tendencies get in the way of other spiritual practices in this Alphabet. The mystics see them, too, and they are not daunted. Come, they say, join us in the ecstatic life.

PERSPECTIVES

When we were given the capacity to love, to speak, to decide, to dream, to hope and create and suffer, we were also given the longing to be known by the One who most wants to be completely known. It is a longing woven into the very fabric of the image in which we were made.
–ROBERT BENSON

He finds God quickest whose concentration and yearning are strongest.
–SRI RAMAKRISHNA

It is exactly through desire that we discover what animates and moves in us.
–DAVID WHYTE

TEACHERS

• Jelaluddin Rumi is the best teacher you could ever find of the spiritual practice of yearning. "The wakened lover speaks directly to the beloved. / 'You are the sky my spirit circles in, / the love inside love, the resurrection-place. / Let this window be your ear. / I have lost consciousness many times / with longing for your listening silence, / and your life-quickening smile.' " The poetry of this great thirteenth-century Persian mystic continues to enchant, inspire, and enlighten Muslims, Jews, Christians, Hindus, Buddhists, and others. He composed 3,500 odes, 2,000 quatrains, and an epic six-volume poem titled *Mathnawi*.

In *The Essential Rumi*, Coleman Barks presents the best of his translations of this Sufi master's ecstatic poetry and stories. He has organized this diverse material under 27 headings and offers brief meditations on such recurring motifs as the tavern, emptiness and silence, feeling separation, being a lover, and much more. Many of the verses express a desire for union. "I am filled with you. / Skin, blood, bone, brain, and soul. / There's no room for lack of trust, or trust. / Nothing in this existence but that existence."

Rumi's intoxicating love of God comes across as central. "I belong to the beloved, have seen the two worlds as one," writes this doctor of yearning. Yet there is also his sensual, celebratory, and pensive desire for the bounties of everyday life: "Love's secret is always lifting its head / out from under the covers, / 'Here I am!' " Rumi's spiritual largess is awesome—everything is taken into his embrace.

• According to Andrew Harvey, mystical moments bring us "a sense of wonder, a freedom from time's fury and anxiety, and a growing revelation of a far larger and more marvelous universe and a far vaster identity than anything we could begin to intuit with our ordinary senses and consciousness." As editor of *The Essential Mystics: Selections from the World's Great Wisdom Traditions*, Harvey has brought together a broad range of writings that express the soul's yearning for such experiences.

There are selections from tribal cultures in "Voices of the First World." Other chapters are "Taoism: The Way of the Tao," "Hinduism: The Way of Presence," "Buddhism: The Way of Clarity," "Judaism: The Way of Holiness," "Ancient Greece: The Way of Beauty," "Islam: The Way of Passion," and "Christianity: The Way of Love in Action."

Throughout the book, Harvey expresses a yearning for the Sacred Feminine, the motherhood of God in all of the traditions. Like the great Bede Griffiths, he is convinced that this connection is desperately needed in our times as a source of compassion, imagination, and transformation.

VIDEOS

• A fine way to continue your exploration of yearning via mystical poetry is to watch the video *Rumi: Poet of the Heart*, a 58-minute documentary written, produced, and directed by Haydn Reiss. Narrator Debra Winger and world religion expert Huston Smith present a brief profile of this scholar and teacher who was living in what is now Konya, Turkey, when his life was transformed by a mysterious itinerant dervish, Shams of Tabriz. Together, in an extended mystical conversation, they explored the secrets of the Beloved. Poet Robert Bly talks about the special meaning of this soulful friendship.

Coleman Barks, accompanied by a variety of musicians, reads many selections of Rumi's poetry, which he sees as a passport into the vastness of the inner world. Mythologist and storyteller Michael Meade offers interpretations of other poems. Best-selling author Deepak Chopra probes Rumi's great contribution to our understanding of the spiritual dimensions of love. This edifying and entertaining documentary perfectly captures and conveys the fragrance of Rumi's poetry, spirituality, and yearning for the Beloved.

● Desire can take us far beyond the familiar neighborhoods of our lives. And sometimes it even enables us to transform ourselves completely. In *Shall We Dance?* Shohei is a middle-aged Japanese accountant who lives with his wife and daughter in a comfortable suburban area. One day while riding the train home from work, he notices a beautiful woman looking out the window of a rundown building. Overwhelmed by his desire to find out more about her, Shohei enters the place and discovers it is a dance school.

He starts taking lessons, keeping them a secret from his wife and co-workers. A wonderful teacher helps him discover how to enjoy the music and relax into the movements. By letting himself go, Shohei is liberated from his malaise. He learns to live in the moment, to trust his body, and to flow with the magic élan of dance. This marvelous Japanese film celebrates the spiritual uplift of desire.

● Often we do not have words powerful enough to convey our yearning. Certainly this is true when it comes to sexual desire, passion, and love that will not let us go. All of these are part of the drama in *The Piano*, an Australian film filled with unforgettable and startling imagery.

Ada, a nineteenth-century Scottish mute woman, arrives in New Zealand with her nine-year-old illegitimate daughter to marry Stuart, a man chosen by her father. Although she uses sign language to speak, her soul is expressed through playing the piano. Ada's relationship with Stuart never works, and she falls in love with Baines, his illiterate estate manager.

At one point Baines says to her, "I am unhappy because I want you, because my mind has seized on you and thinks of nothing else. This is how I suffer. I am sick with longing." Eventually Ada, too, is transported by her desire. *The Piano* is an exotic and erotic film that boldly explores the connections among yearning, passion, and rapture.

SPIRITUAL EXERCISES AND RITUALS

● Read selections from *The Song of Songs* in the Bible aloud with your partner. This poetry expresses the relationship between humans and the Divine in erotic imagery. Give voice to your yearning; hear it in each other.

● Design a ritual to express your boundless desire for God. Use water or fire to symbolize your yearning.

PRAYER OR MANTRA

This breath prayer is given by Joyce Rupp in her guide to spiritual growth *The Cup of Our Life.*

> Breathing in: Thirsting, thirsting . . .
> Breathing out: for you, God.

IMAGERY EXERCISE

In *Sadhana: A Way to God,* Anthony de Mello recalls a phrase used by the founder of the Jesuit Order, Ignatius of Loyola—"prayers and holy desires"—by which he meant to encourage young priests to do great things for God and for the good of the community. This exercise catches both kinds of desire.

Place before God the desires you have for each one of the people you wish to pray for. . . . See each one of them as having the things you desire for them. . . . You need not make an explicit prayer for them. It is enough to expose God to your holy desires . . . and to see those desires fulfilled.

What you have done for individuals, do now for families and groups and communities. . . . Have the courage to overcome all defeatism and pessimism, and desire and hope for great things . . . and see these great things as actually fulfilled by the mighty power of God.

Now place before God the desires you have for yourself. Expose him to all the great things you desire to do in his service. . . . The fact that you will never actually do them, or that you feel incapable of doing them, is irrelevant. . . . What is important is that you gladden the heart of God by showing him how immense your desires are even though your strength is very small. . . . It is thus that lovers speak when they express the immensity of their desires, which far outdistance their limited capacity.

JOURNAL EXERCISES

● Use your journal to explore your heart's desires. What do you most want? Whom do you want? Do a brief history of your yearnings and see how they have evolved or changed over the years.

● Write a dialogue between Your Self and Your Desire. Discuss how they each limit and expand the other.

DISCUSSION QUESTIONS, STORYTELLING, SHARING

● Share a story about the ways in which your desire has expressed itself in a relationship, in a creative project, or at work.

● What recent experiences, books, or workshops have enabled you to see more clearly the connections between sexuality and spirituality?

● Have you ever had an experience of ecstasy, other than a sexual one? What was it like?

● Nowadays people talk about desire as a key to inner growth. What were you taught about your desires when you were young? How has your view of yearning changed over the years?

HOUSEHOLD, GROUP, AND COMMUNITY PROJECTS

● Incorporate little rituals into your activities that enable you to freely express your desires. Wish on birthday candles or the last bite of pie. Build a "wishing wall" in your community where people add a stone to symbolize something they yearn for. Explain that the desire can be individual or communal but joining your desires to others may make its fulfillment more likely.

● One of the ways groups in society make their desires known to the authorities is through petitions. Draft a petition expressing what your group wants to have happen in your community—a new political party, a park, silent zones around religious institutions and schools, or other such developments. Get as many signatures as possible to support your yearning.

FICTION, POETRY, OR CHILDREN'S BOOK

Some heroic figures in religion speak to those of us who yearn to express ourselves creatively in the name of God. *The Journal of Hildegard of Bingen* by Barbara Lachman is a fictional work that imagines a year in the life of this highly gifted twelfth-century abbess who founded an autonomous community of Benedictine nuns. In these pages, Hildegard comes across as a prolific composer of liturgical songs, an accomplished healer, and a reflective spiritual leader. All of this grows out of her constant yearning to do God's will.

SPOKEN-WORD AUDIO

The Art of Sexual Magic by Margot Anand is an audio workshop on the art of tapping into sexual energy as a sacred practice. She believes that tantra, the ancient Indian practice of generating powerful sexual energies and funneling them into the expansion of consciousness, can also be used to bring passion and pleasure into everyday life. Anand presents erotic rituals and meditations that can draw couples closer together in a fusion that is mystical and mutually fulfilling.

ART

Our boundless desire keeps us crossing borders and looking for new possibilities. In Thomas Gainsborough's *Chasing the Butterfly,* two little girls are in pursuit of this magical and elusive creature. In Andrew Wyeth's *Christina's World,* a young woman whose body has been twisted by polio lies in a field stretching toward her house on the horizon. This painting depicts yearning as an emotion capable of taking us beyond ourselves.

MUSIC

Bruce Springsteen's pulsating rock music is filled with powerful expressions of all the yearnings that animate the hearts and souls of restless youth. He's known for his songs about city streets, fast cars, sexual adventure, and walks on the wild side. Some of his best urban anthems are "Born to Run," "Badlands," "Darkness on the Edge of Town," "The Promised Land," and "No Surrender!" For Springsteen, the status quo is never enough. There are better things to be had, and we have to dare to desire them.

SEE ALSO:

Compassion. Imagination. Love. Questing. Transformation. You.

YOU

THE BASIC PRACTICE

Each of us is a work-in-progress. The spiritual practice of you challenges us to become all we can be as God's beloved sons and daughters. We are, after all, cocreators of the Great Work of the Universe. By attuning ourselves to what in different traditions has been called the image of God, the everlasting soul, or the higher self, we are able to fulfill our mission in life.

All the world's religions refer to the civil war that rages inside us when self-absorption meets self-regard and selfishness clashes with selflessness.

The spiritual life requires that we think enough of ourselves to believe we can serve others without putting ourselves above them. It's sometimes a tricky balance to maintain.

Begin with what is right in front of you. Have both pride and humility. Be assertive and yielding. You are much more and much less than you probably think you are. Relax. This, the Creator reminds us, is good.

CATALYSTS, CONTRASTS, AND COMPANIONS

We can be our own worst enemies. We commit acts of sabotage by doubting our own competence. Because we lack self-esteem, we close off avenues that could lead to personal growth. Due to feelings of inferiority, we put ourselves down; because of grandiosity, we put others down. Aiming for perfection, we are not satisfied with anything we do. None of these approaches is part of the spiritual practice of you, which banishes woe-is-me and I-am-the-master-of-the-universe mood swings.

The ideal is to live with both our strengths and our weaknesses. The spiritual practice of you is the prescription to help you find and express your authentic self.

PERSPECTIVES

It is a glorious destiny to be a member of the human race. . . . Now I realize what we all are. And if only everybody could realize this! But it cannot be explained. There is no way of telling people that they are all walking around shining like the sun.
–THOMAS MERTON

The older I get, the more convinced I am that every human life is an evolutionary process during which the Creator offers to the creature an experience of divinity, an opportunity, great or small, to share in the ongoing act of creation.
–MORRIS WEST

I am vast as God; there is nothing in the world.
O miracle:—that can shut me up in myself.
–ANGELUS SILESIUS

TEACHERS

● The spiritual practice of you demands that we cherish what is distinctive about ourselves. To do so we must heed our calling. James Hillman, the father of archetypal psychology, teaches us how. In *The Soul's Code: In Search of Character and Calling,* he writes: "There is more in a human life than our theories of it allow. Sooner or later something seems to call us onto a particular path. You may remember this 'something' as a signal moment in childhood when an urge out of nowhere, a fascination, a peculiar turn of events struck like an annunciation: This is what I must do, this is what I've got to have. This is who I am."

Presenting his "acorn theory" of human nature, Hillman contends that every person has a unique character and destiny that cannot be stifled by genetic makeup, environmental factors, or parental influences. Using illustrative material from the lives of Eleanor Roosevelt, Josephine Baker, Judy Garland, and others, Hillman celebrates "the remarkable singularity of individuals" who live out their calling no matter what. Throughout this brilliant work, the author pays tribute to the acorn's resistance to reduction and its ability to make the most of imagination, intuition, and "the purposeful eye."

● "Each of us has access codes to the many stations of our being. Our tendency is to forget to update them and to tune ourselves day after day to the same old programs. And yet the reality waves that move through us are filled with extraordinary stories and ideas, even connection to the Ultimate Program, the greatest show in the universe." This observation is from Jean Houston in *A Passion for the Possible: A Guide to Realizing Your True Potential.* This bellwether book draws together the major motifs in her teaching as a philosopher and cultural historian over the past 30 years. "The complexity of our time," she notes, "requires a greater and wiser use of our capacities."

Houston shows how to tap the resources of our soul by activating four realms of experience. In a section on the sensory world, she profiles Helen Keller and lays out exercises and projects designed to open new doors of perception. She explores the psychological realm with commentary on memory, creativity, and joy. Houston hits high stride with a chapter on myth; she uses the transforming journey of Luke Skywalker as a template for the hero's journey. Rumi and Roshi Dogen are the guides for the final section on spiritual quest. Through this accessible and enthusiastic guide, Houston enables us to see all the wild possibilities in being human.

VIDEOS

● The spiritual practice of you is not a smooth road paved with gold but a bumpy one that requires patience and persistence. *Strictly Ballroom* is a zany and inspiring Australian film about two daring ballroom dancers who break new ground by expressing their authentic selves. Scott Hastings has been preparing for the Australian Ballroom Dance Federation Championships since he was six. His manipulative mother and the local dance hall academy are shocked when he chooses Fran, an awkward and inexperienced dancer, to be his new partner. But she is a soul mate who shares Scott's eagerness to try new steps. This movie says: Don't let fear shut you down. Take a chance and be yourself.

● Finding one's calling is part of the spiritual practice of you. In *Ruby in Paradise,* a sensitive young woman moves to a beach town in Florida after fleeing rural Tennessee. She finds work in a souvenir shop. Raised in a fundamentalist Christian home, she is ready to break some rules and to test her wings in several relationships with men. But what she is really interested in is finding her destiny.

Ruby processes all of her experiences through her diary. She writes about her feelings and ideas about care, desire, loneliness, fear, intimacy, independence, and loss. At one point, Ruby asks a friend what she would teach children. She replies: "How to survive with your soul intact." This unusual and compelling film charts one young woman's spiritual journey as she tries to find meaningful work, examines her relationships, contemplates her experiences, discovers her own authority, and learns how to survive in the new world she has chosen. For Ruby, being who she is meant to be is a spiritual practice.

SPIRITUAL EXERCISES AND RITUALS

● The next time you tell a story about yourself, instead of saying "I am" substitute the phrase "Part of me is."

● In a situation where you are inclined to put yourself first, seek the subordinate position instead and see what happens. For example, give up your place at the head of the line.

● Practice being less reactive, especially to other people's actions and attitudes toward you. Do not let anything that happens outside of yourself determine whether you are happy or sad, grateful or moody.

• Macrina Wiederkehr celebrates her birthday once a month by honoring those who have loved her and sustained her ministry. Find ritual ways to do this for yourself. At least once a year throw a party on your birth date for the people who make it possible for you to be your best self.

PRAYER OR MANTRA

This mantra is inspired by some advice given by actor Sidney Poitier, when he accepted the Lifetime Achievement Award from the American Film Institute.

> Breathing in: May I be true to myself . . .
> Breathing out: and useful to the journey.

IMAGERY EXERCISE

"We are aided on our journey by inner guides, or archetypes, each of which exemplifies a way of being on the journey," writes Carol S. Pearson in *Awakening the Heroes Within: Twelve Archetypes to Help Us Find Ourselves and Transform Our World*. This exercise works with four of the archetypes.

Close your eyes and breathe out three times. In the safety and security of the inner garden, see the Innocent filled with excitement and optimism. Become the Innocent on the journey from dependence through adversity to wise trust without denial.

Breathe out one time. On the inner battlefield, see the courageous and disciplined Warrior preparing to fight enemies to protect others and his or her own boundaries. Become the Warrior devising a plan to confront a great challenge. Live and know how to claim power.

Breathe out one time. In the inner chamber of the heart, see and sense the Lover feeling his or her body's passion for a person, an activity, or a cause. Become the Lover following your bliss, bonding with your love, and connecting with the greater universe.

Breathe out one time. At the inner hearth, see the Sage getting ready to teach the wisdom of the ages. Become the Sage learning from objective observations, from subjective feelings, and by letting go of the ego. Live and know how you are a source of wisdom.

When you are finished, open your eyes.

JOURNAL EXERCISES

● Write a brief meditation on the meaning of the following rabbinic understanding: Every time we walk down the street, we are preceded by hosts of angels singing "Make way, make way, make way for the image of God."

● Identify your special gifts and the talents or skills you have developed. Our gifts—what we are naturally good at—and our talents—what we have chosen to improve—are clues to our calling, what in religious terminology is called God's will for us. Reflect on how well you are fulfilling your destiny.

● Draw pictures of some of the masks you tend to wear, the outer expressions of your inner selves. Choose the one you would most like to present to the world.

DISCUSSION QUESTIONS, STORYTELLING, SHARING

● Who has helped you feel most positive about yourself?

● Are you more relaxed and familiar with your public or private self? Can you identify a point in your life when you accepted yourself just as you are? What precipitated that realization?

● Why do you think so many people are resistant to the idea that they have a divine spark within them and that they are signs of God's glory in the world?

HOUSEHOLD, GROUP, AND COMMUNITY PROJECTS

● Try the Hindu ritual in which all the members of the household are led to a mirror and reminded that the face they see there is the Lord's.

● In Pueblo festivals, people are allowed to be whichever of their personalities they want to be. This allows all to celebrate parts of themselves not usually acknowledged. Have a celebration with your group during which you act out your secret selves.

FICTION, POETRY, OR CHILDREN'S BOOK

One way to practice you is by celebrating birthdays. *On the Day You Were Born* by Debra Frasier is a beautiful picture book that sets the coming of an infant into the world in the context of the responses from migrating animals, the flaming sun and the glowing moon, the spinning Earth and the glittering stars, the rising tide and the falling rain, the growing trees and the rushing air, and a circle of singing people. The Earth community provides us with a divine milieu where we can flourish all the days of our lives.

Spoken-Word Audio

Matthew Fox's *Original Blessing* is a pathbreaking reimagining of Christianity. He outlines a spirituality based not on a fall-redemption model, where humans come into this world burdened with original sin, but one centered on life as a blessing. Passion, humility, eros, pleasure, and beauty are important elements of Creation Spirituality. God is an artist and humans are partners in creating. This mystical view encompasses a deep respect for the royal personhood of all human beings. Fox's good news makes the spiritual practice of you a high and holy calling.

Art

The whimsical art of Jean Dubuffet demonstrates that the human spirit cannot be categorized and classified. Dubuffet thumbed his nose at the artistic establishment with his paintings of crude figures—reminders to us at least of our start as primitives. *Figure in Red* looks like a child's drawing with its big head, red cheeks, and inquisitive look—there is an inner child in all of us. The same playfulness is evident in the artist's pictures in flattened dimensions (*Corps de Dame: Blue Short Circuit, Hilarious Figure*) and in his choice of mediums, even throwing botanical elements like leaves into the mix (*Tobacco Man with Goatee*).

Dubuffet's "Hourloupe" series evolved from ball-point pen doodles, a motif eventually used on large three-dimensional sculptured forms covered with cells of various shapes and sizes outlined in red, white, blue, and black. Looking at human forms depicted in this style (*Fiston la Filoche, Bidon l'Esbroufe*), we are reminded that we are all complex and unpredictable beings—one of the key lessons of the spiritual practice of you.

Music

Singer and songwriter Harry Chapin fulfilled his special destiny as a troubadour. He had an uncanny ability to make the human situation touching and meaningful through his folk-tinged story ballads. Many of his best song-poems convey people's deep desire to find their own place in the world and to grow in love. *Harry Chapin: The Gold Medal Collection* gathers together some of his most heart-affecting work, such as "Taxi," "Cat's in the Cradle," "Mr. Tanner," "Better Place to Be," "She Sings

Songs Without Words," and "Circle." Also listen to his album *Portrait Gallery*, if just for one song that expresses the very essence of the spiritual practice of you: "Someone Keeps Calling My Name."

SEE ALSO:
Meaning. Nurturing. Questing. Shadow. Teachers. Transformation. X—The Mystery.

 ZEAL

THE BASIC PRACTICE

The spiritual practice of zeal means being fully aroused by life. We
tap into the divine energy that pulsates within us and around us. We are
ready for anything that comes our way, and every moment is a golden
gateway to new possibilities.

This spiritual practice includes a wholehearted delight in the senses
and a passionate love for who we are and what we have been given. We
are encouraged in its pursuit by our companions on the path and the
countless teachers who stretch our souls. Our zeal moves us to live com-

---

passionately and to serve others. It shows up in our prayers, rituals, family life, and community activities.

Zeal is the last practice in our Alphabet, and appropriately it incorporates many of those that have come before it. Zeal means living abundantly—and we are more likely to do so when we can pay attention, live in the present, have gratitude, and experience wonder. Zeal is an energetic and committed response to opportunities and challenges that come our way. How much more likely that is to be when we have regular practices of devotion, when we are committed to justice, when we have a faith relationship with Spirit, and when we see life as a quest.

Zeal is the essence of the meaningful life. As a wise teacher said long ago, the last shall be first.

CATALYSTS, CONTRASTS, AND COMPANIONS

It's a terrible feeling—the sense that your life is passing you by, the awareness that your unique self has not come forth. How does it happen? And what countermeasures can you take?

We forfeit life by denying the spirit that is within us. We throw away everything when we don't join the parade because we are too busy, too tired, or too jaded. The unlived life is one we have squandered by passivity, by only trying to prove ourselves to others, or by only seeking to fulfill societal expectations.

In contrast to all this, there is the passionate life. Practice zeal and embrace all that comes your way with an open and full heart.

PERSPECTIVES

The glory of God is the human person fully alive.
–IRENAEUS

True spirituality is the rebirth of the full and undivided love of life.
–JURGEN MOLTMANN

Don't ask yourself what the world needs. Ask yourself what makes you come alive, and go do that, because what the world needs is people who have come alive.
–HOWARD THURMAN

TEACHERS

● One of the best teachers of zeal is Scott Russell Sanders. He has published several soul-stirring collections of essays, all of which reveal a man with a heightened appreciation for the fullness of life. Our Sanders collection includes *Secrets of the Universe, Writing from the Center, Hunting for Hope: A Father's Journey,* and *Staying Put: Making a Home in a Restless World.* In the latter, he explores his delight in "the vast shining dance" of life and in the pleasures of being rooted firmly in one place. The author resides in Bloomington, Indiana, where he teaches literature at Indiana University. He is proud of what he calls the virtue and the discipline of staying put.

In one leisurely essay, Sanders shows how the investment of love and care can make a house into a home. In another, he savors the voluptuousness of the natural world. And in a third, he quotes from works by Gary Snyder, Wendell Berry, Bruce Chatwin, and Barry Lopez, who have all written about the importance of intimately knowing a particular place.

One magisterial essay revolves around Sanders's visit to an Ohio neighborhood he knew as a boy, recalling vividly seven mysteries—death, life, animals, food, mind, sex, and God—connected with the place. "Pilgrims often journey to the ends of the Earth in search of holy ground," he writes, "only to find that they have never walked on anything else." He spies the holy in the Creation: "One time it glowed from a red carnation, incandescent in a florist's window. Once it shimmered in drifting pollen, once in a sky needled with ice. I have seen it wound in a scarf of dust around a whirling pony. I have seen it glinting from a pebble on the slate bed of a creek. I have slipped into that secret place while watching hawks, while staring down the throat of a lily, while brushing my wife's hair. Metaphors are inexact." Yes, perhaps, but they do teach us about zeal.

● Another ardent teacher of the art of being aroused by life is Ernesto Cardenal, a Nicaraguan priest and poet. *Abide in Love* is a lyrical and enthralling paean of praise to God's presence in our world. Cardenal mines nature for its meanings and exalts the mysteries that link us to sea, stone, sand, and sky.

Cardenal is zealous about love of the world and God. "Each of us is irreplaceable. We are all unique collector's pieces because God is an artist who never repeats or copies. No two leaves are alike, no two fingerprints are the same, and even less are any two souls identical." The author's blazing sacramental vision finds signs and symbols of the Divine everywhere. *Abide in Love* is an invitation to sample the smorgasbord of the

Creation and to taste the infinite variety of life. It is the ultimate love letter to God.

VIDEOS

● *Zorba the Greek* is the best video movie about zeal. A blocked English writer is traveling to Crete to take over an abandoned mine owned by his father. He meets the itinerant Zorba while waiting for a boat to the island. This adventurer convinces the writer to take him along to oversee the reconstruction of the mine.

Whereas "the Boss" passively reacts to life, Zorba zestfully lives every day to its fullest. He tackles his work with enthusiasm and laughs at his blunders. While the Boss hesitates in visiting an attractive widow who shows an interest in him, Zorba immediately plunges into an intimate relationship with a dying French courtesan who owns the hotel in the poverty-stricken town.

Zorba's passion for life often leads him into folly, but he doesn't care for his heart is always in the right place. And when it is time to square off against death and the craziness of a full catastrophe, there is only one thing to do—dance. As Zorba tells the Boss, a man needs a little madness to be free.

● It takes many of us a long time to reconnect with the zest for life we had when we were young. The lead character in *Shirley Valentine* is a frustrated and isolated middle-aged Liverpool matron. Duty and attending to the needs of others have consumed her life. Shirley receives little support or affection from her husband and two grown children. Encounters with a snooty neighbor and an old classmate do little to relieve her depression.

Then a divorced friend wins a two-week vacation to Greece in a magazine contest and asks Shirley to accompany her. After much soul searching, she leaves her husband behind and heads off for the sun-drenched islands. The trip puts Shirley in touch with her unlived life and steers her into an inward journey of self-renewal. It is never too late to be aroused by life!

SPIRITUAL EXERCISES AND RITUALS

● Start your day with the affirmation "I am vibrantly alive!" Say it enough times so that it sinks into your consciousness and seeps into your body. Whenever your energy feels depleted during the day, repeat the affirmation. In the last hours of the evening, let your "I am vibrantly alive" extend outward to support others through your prayers.

● Drop a habit or a pattern that keeps you from being fully aroused by life.

● Memorize the e. e. cummings poem "I thank You God for this most amazing day." Put a copy on your refrigerator or desk. Create your own illustration of it. Then recite it aloud whenever you need to renew your zeal.

PRAYER OR MANTRA

Saint Francis of Assisi gives us this mantra about the basis of zeal.

Breathing in: My God . . .
Breathing out: and my all.

IMAGERY EXERCISE

Throughout the mystical poetry of the fifteenth-century Indian poet Kabir there are numerous calls to "Jump into experience while you are alive." A set of these poems appears in *The Soul Is Here for Its Own Joy,* edited by Robert Bly. This exercise, "Waking Up," is based on the images in some of them.

Breathe out three times. Sense and know that it is morning. Wake up!

Breathe out one time. See a clay jug before you. Know how it contains canyons and pine mountains and the maker of canyons and pine mountains. Sense how there are seven oceans inside and hundreds of millions of stars.

Breathe out one time. Know and see how the wheel of love turns in the sky and the spinning seat is made of the sapphires of work and study.

Breathe out one time. See a leaf floating on the water. Know that we live as the great One and the little one. Feel and know that the river inside you is flowing into the ocean.

Breathe out one time. Plunge into the Truth. Find out who the Teacher is. Believe in the Great Sound.

Then, breathe out and open your eyes.

JOURNAL EXERCISES

● The Japanese have a phrase in which they commend a person for "the nobility of failure." According to Caroline Casey, what they are doing is honoring the effort. We can look at the great things at which someone has failed and see the energy that is behind it. Even to fail, one has to be truly alive. Reframe a recent failure as evidence of your zest for life.

● Make a list of "Life Lessons." Be extravagant in your learning. Cover every period of your life so far and imagine lessons to come in the years ahead.

DISCUSSION QUESTIONS, STORYTELLING, SHARING

● Share a story about a time when you felt, in mythologist Joseph Campbell's words, "the rapture of being alive."

● Share another story about a time in your life when you practiced the shadow side of zeal. It might be your participation in a vindictive, narrow-minded, or wrong-headed crusade that was not life-affirming. It might be your involvement in a group or a project that consumed all your energy so that you had no time to care for yourself or others.

● Who are the most vibrantly alive people you know? What are the keys to their vitality?

HOUSEHOLD, GROUP, AND COMMUNITY PROJECTS

● On Old Year's Night or New Year's Day, gather with family and friends to share stories of your "Life High Points" during the previous year. When did you feel most fully alive? Who encouraged you in your zeal? Make this an annual ritual, and watch for high points to share throughout the year. Record or videotape your sharing as a record of your experiences on the path of spiritual practice.

● Another way to learn where you come alive is to play a game like LifeStories, which is designed to facilitate storytelling about experiences and different points of view. The Transformation Game allows you to choose an area of life you would like to change, or a dream you want to come true, and see what kind of feedback you get from the game and other players. Again, recording and taping the fun is recommended.

● Plan a "Toast to Life" celebration for your group or extended community. Have each person come prepared to talk about a vivid experience of being fully aroused by life. Also have each person bring a special goblet, glass, or mug to the gathering. Gather in a circle, bless your goblets, and fill them with celebratory liquids. After each person shares his or her story, all raise your glasses and toast "To Life!"

FICTION, POETRY, OR CHILDREN'S BOOK

● All of the spiritual traditions agree that the best way to stay aroused to life is to dance to the music of the Blessed One. In *Women in Praise of the Sacred: 43 Centuries of Spiritual Poetry by Women*, editor and poet Jane Hirshfield has gathered an incredibly diverse anthology of hymns, poetry, prayers, and songs. Each of the 70 women represented here has found her own special way of practicing zeal. Among those singing these sacred tunes are Rabi'a, Hadewijch of Antwerp, H.D., Emily Dickinson, and Nelly Sachs.

● Editor Robert Bly has assembled an excellent anthology of poems about the twists and turns of the spiritual path in *The Soul Is Here for Its Own Joy*. Rumi, Kabir, Lalla, Anthony Machado, Rainer Maria Rilke, and others give us plenty of reasons to practice zeal.

SPOKEN-WORD AUDIO

For more than 30 years, Ram Dass, whose name means "Servant of God," has expressed his zeal in the study of spiritual matters, his explorations of Eastern religions, his explanation of compassionate service, and his recent advocacy of conscious aging. This respected teacher mirrors many of the interests of seekers. *Experiments in Truth* by Ram Dass is a collection of eight classic lectures delivered from 1969 to 1995. He talks about his spiritual journey, suffering, the essence of love, the prison of the ego, honoring the body, and how to use truth to change your life.

ART

Umberto Buccioni's celebrated sculpture *Unique Forms of Continuity in Space* evokes the dynamism and movement of a human form through a forward-striding figure. According to the spiritual practice of zeal, to be aroused by life is to be on the move and open to change. Here movement is celebrated, even lionized.

MUSIC

In the original Broadway cast recording of the classic musical *Fiddler on the Roof*, the most buoyant and rousing number is "To Life." At a local inn in a small Russian town, a group of hardworking Jews sing: "God would like us to be joyful even when our hearts lie panting on the floor." A wedding is on the horizon and so in great conviviality they exchange toasts. The magic moment comes when they conclude: "And if our good fortune never comes, here's to whatever comes!" That is the heart and soul of the spiritual practice of zeal. Drink deep and experience the passion of truly being alive no matter what happens.

SEE ALSO:
Being Present. Enthusiasm. Gratitude. Joy. Play. Teachers. You.

PASSAGES IN *SPIRITUAL LITERACY*

Our book *Spiritual Literacy: Reading the Sacred in Everyday Life* contains more than 650 passages that show how contemporary writers and artists do spiritual practices. These brief excerpts—most of them are one or two paragraphs—put flesh on our Alphabet. On the pages that follow here, we have listed the page numbers in *Spiritual Literacy* where you can find good illustrations of each practice. Reviewing them, you will probably notice some familiar voices and meet others you have never heard of. All of them were chosen because they provide very concrete and practical examples of spiritual living.

Reading these passages is a quick way to jump into a variety of experiences and see the possible applications of each practice. They supplement what the teachers tell us through their books and what you can learn from doing the exercises and projects we suggest. They will give you a better sense of whether a particular practice is for you.

ATTENTION

Numerous passages in *Spiritual Literacy: Reading the Sacred in Everyday Life* illustrate the practice of attention. Our meditation on attention, informed by teachers from different religions, appears on pages 52–53. The story of Auggie Wren's photography project from the movie *Smoke* (page 27) illustrates the rewards of a life of attention. So do examples given by Ken Wilbur (page 35), Anthony de Mello (page 190), and Normandi Ellis (page 378). For examples of mindfulness, see Bettina Vitell on washing the dishes (page 236), Stephen Levine on having a cup of tea (page 231), and Marc David on eating dinner (page 535). The need to be attentive to other people is the subject of stories by Bonnie Friedman (page 378) and Glen A. Mazis (page 437). The importance of details is evident in the passages on observing your body by Linda Weltner (page 372), digging in the garden by Deborah Tall (page 107), and being in a flower garden by Alan Epstein (page 161). Frederic Brussat's poem about the speed skater (page 255) identifies single-mindedness as key to a sport. Timothy Miller reveals how breath awareness helped him enjoy the opera (page 301). James Hillman explores the implications of paying attention to things (page 70), and Robert Sardello applies an attentive eye to a building (page 532). Finally, we pay tribute to a friend who practices attention in her relationships (page 457).

BEAUTY

Our meditation on beauty, with quotations from Thomas Merton, D. H. Lawrence, and Buddha, appears on pages 64–65. Bonnie Friedman sees beauty in a flock of pigeons (page 171), and Laurens van der Post contemplates it in a rhinoceros (page 199). Kathleen Norris seeks beauty on the High Plains (page 87), and Frederick Buechner finds it in traffic (page 529). Macrina Wiederkehr is impressed by the inner beauty of a little girl (page 328). Madeleine L'Engle relates how her marriage was enriched by a shared love of beauty (page 429). Anthony Lawlor describes the unusual beauty of a Japanese teahouse (page 140), and David Reynolds celebrates the simplicity of the tea ceremony (page 234). Kenneth Leong explains how flying kites can be an aesthetic experience (page 250). Megan McKenna tells a story about how beauty can be found in imperfection (page 55). Desmond Tutu believes we are made to enjoy beauty and make the world more hospitable to it (page 275).

BEING PRESENT

Our exploration of being present appears on pages 66–67. Being here is illustrated in passages by Anne Morrow Lindbergh (page 84), Scott Russell Sanders (page 111), Wendy Wright (page 526), and a story about feeling at home (page 94). The now is experienced by David Reynolds at the beach (page 141), Bettina Vitell while cooking (page 219), Mary Ann Brussat while snokeling (page 251) and typing (page 309), Marjory Zoet Bankson while working with clay (page 293), Barbara Crafton while sewing (page 294), Michael Jones while playing the piano (page 300), Bettyclare Moffatt while walking (page 384), and Zorba the Greek while kissing a woman (page 425). Robert Fulghum (page 249), James Carse (page 306), Elizabeth Berg (page 333), Jean Shinoda Bolen (page 456), and Gary Paulsen (page 535) give other examples. Natalie Kusz (page 390)

FAITH

Various aspects of faith are emphasized in quotations from theologians and religious leaders in our meditation on pages 152–153. A deer reminds Karen Karper of faith (page 172); a hermit thrush has that effect on John Hay (page 174). Gunilla Norris contemplates faith as trust (page 133) while watching falling leaves. Edward Hays explores faith as letting go in a piece on the Prayer of Napping (page 262). A trusting relationship with God is mirrored in the dialogue of a father and daughter in a novel by Reynolds Price (page 446).

FORGIVENESS

We discuss the various kinds of forgiveness on pages 154–155. Donna Schaper (page 294) likens personal forgiveness to stripping paint off an old chair. Stories by Dan Millman (page 427) and Ram Dass (page 449) reveal how people have been able to give up feelings of anger and frustration. In a passage from a novel, Hilma Wolitzer (page 431) points to the role of forgiveness in marriage. Renee Beck and Sydney Barbara Metrick describe a ritual a separating couple used to symbolize mutual forgiveness (page 438). Finally, Sister Helen Prejean (page 501) pays tribute to a father who was able to forgive the man who murdered his son.

GRACE

Rumi, Ramakrishna, Saint Paul, Thomas Aquinas, John Wesley, and other more contemporary writers have been teachers to us about grace, as our meditation on pages 182–183 reveals. Grace is experienced by Frederick Buechner sitting in his car (page 46), Andrew Greeley hearing the sounds of passing trains (page 47), Patsy Neal playing basketball (page 254), and Robert Fulghum getting a snack (page 542). In a poem, May Sarton embraces the grace of being able to let go (page 399). Characters in a short story by Wendell Berry (page 264) and novels by Lorene Cary (page 464) and Anne Tyler (page 480) recognize grace as it happens to them. We recall scenes from two television dramas that touched us as grace moments (page 289). G. K. Chesterton turns the story of Santa Claus into a tribute to God's grace (page 267). Dorothy Day uses the donation of a diamond ring to teach about God's generosity (page 352). Ernesto Cardenal looks at the world around him and sees only grace (page 47). We recognize it in the presence of a friend in our lives (page 466). Finally, three poems by Rumi (pages 179, 228, 390) and another by Denise Levertov (page 252) convey the essence of grace.

GRATITUDE

We join Sufi, Jewish, Muslim, and Christian writers in praising the practice of gratitude on pages 184–185. David K. Reynolds (page 63) and Dawna Markova (page 63) express appreciation for little things. Timothy Miller is grateful for an old chair (page 57), Shaun McNiff for a pair of slippers (page 68), Richard Foster for a fireplace (page 101), Frederic Brussat for a beach cabana (page 105), Edward Hays for office equipment (page 315), and Laura Green for a bed (page 541). Robert Coles recalls his parents' gratitude for books (page 241), a sentiment seconded by Frederic Brussat (page 243), and Macrina Wiederkehr treasures letters (page 462). Laurie Colwin (page 223), Naomi Shihab Nye (page 225), and Anne Scott (page 229) praise food. Holly L. Rose outlines a housewarming ritual for a new home (page 98). We describe one of our gratitude rituals (page 441), as do Peter Matthiessen (page 114) and Alan Epstein (page 490). The body's gifts are the subjects of thanksgiving by Buson (page 375), Robin Morgan (page 376), John Cowan (page 376), and Thich Nhat Hanh (page 377). People are cause for gratitude by Nancy Burke (page 303), Kay Hardie (page 328), William Stafford (page 455), and Holly Bridges Elliott (page 505). Gratitude finds unusual expression in stories by Garrison Keillor (page 263) and Anthony de Mello (page 429). Barbara Kingsolver (page 125) and Jamie Sams (page 180) write about the importance of gratitude in Native American spirituality.

HOPE

Our reflection on different manifestations of hope appears on pages 194–195. Sara Maitland gets an image of hope in a dream (page 281); Oliver Sacks feels it while listening to music (page 301); Linda Hogan finds a symbol of hope in seeds (page 162); and Macrina Weiderkehr compares hope to baking powder (page 221). A woman is inspired to hope by a quotation during a health crisis (page 395). While she is undergoing treatment for cancer, Nancy Burke receives the gift of hope from a child (page 336). Kathleen Norris talks about the stories of hope heard in a small town (page 529). Megan McKenna tells a classic tale about hope for the future (page 490), and Parker Palmer relates a story about hope from Dorothy Day (page 352). We admit that we have been inspired to hope by rock and reggae music (page 302) and by fund-raising letters received from organizations doing good work around the world (page 358).

HOSPITALITY

We discuss the tradition of hospitality, particularly in Christianity and Buddhism, on pages 196–197. David Whyte's story about Saint John of the Cross (page 342) underlines its importance. Mary Ann Brussat considers the relevance of the classic story about Saint Francis and the Wolf of Gubbio to a situation in her neighborhood (page 498). Natalie Goldberg recalls how an Israeli landlady practiced hospitality (page 424), and James Kavanaugh describes how he experienced it from a couple at his local grocery store (page 428). A ritual to convey that your home is a place of welcome is suggested by Dolores Ashcroft-Nowicki (page 99). Frederic Brussat explains how he practices hospitality as a "Film Recommender" (page 286). Finally, two different ways to look at hospitality to criticism are revealed in stories by Benjamin Hoff (page 425) and Anthony de Mello (page 426).

IMAGINATION

Our exploration of the spiritual practice of imagination appears on pages 232–233. Imagination is stirred by the arts, according to George Leonard (page 300), W. A. Mathieu (page 456), Thomas Moore (page 291), and Shaun McNiff (page 241). Stories reflect creative thinking—see Anthony de Mello (page 277) and Elie Wiesel (page 199)—and have the power to instruct—see Joan Halifax (pages 173 and 279), Stephen King (page 287), Wendell Berry (page 489), and Barry Lopez (page 538). Mary Ann Brussat considers the importance of stories at holiday time (page 267), and Frederic Brussat comments on their value during illness (page 387); we also comment on the power of books to stimulate dreaming (page 62). Examples of imaginative reframings are Eda LeShan on friendship (page 465), Lynne Sharon Schwartz on her bed (page 61), James Hillman on street litter (page 68), Linda Hogan on a rake (page 528), and Mary Ann Brussat on her rocking chair (page 57). The imagination resonates with symbolism—see Phil Cousineau on the fingers (page 378) and Scott Russell Sanders on the four elements (page 135). Imagination is at home in the kitchen with Nancy Willard (page 226), in a cemetery with Robert Fulghum (page 400), and with an elderly couple Deena Metzger meets (page 430). Finally, Lynda Sexton (page 74) and Annie Dillard (page 378) prove that children are great exemplars of this spiritual practice.

JOY

Sufi, Jewish, Buddhist, and Christian teachers help us salute the spiritual practice of joy in our essay on pages 244–245. Poet Anne Sexton relishes the joys in her home (page 97), and poet Mary Oliver muses on the happiness of a nail (page 74). Clarissa Pinkola Estés contemplates the natural joy of the body (page 370). Frederic Brussat (page 369) and Ronald Grimes (page 369) describe joyful dancers. Lynne Sharon Schwartz observes the joy of children learning to ride a bike (page 252). Frederic Brussat recognizes it on the face of a slalom skier (page 255), and George Sheehan experiences it while running (page 525). Henri J. M. Nouwen discovers joy at a birthday party (page 265) and in caring for a handicapped man (page 337). Ram Dass and Mirabai Bush encourage us to find ways to both enjoy ourselves and serve others (page 329). Gertrud Mueller describes a family's celebration of a church festival (page 266), and a character in the movie *A Thousand Clowns* encourages us to make up our own holidays (page 265).

JUSTICE

Our meditation on justice in which we quote some great justice-seekers appears on pages 246–247. Macrina Wiederkehr is shaken by the injustices in the world while reading the newspaper (page 524), and David Wolpe shares a story about God's response to such a lament (page 327). The need to take personal responsibility is echoed by the mystic Mechtild of Magdeburg (page 502). Parker Palmer salutes a friend's contributions to justice projects (page 358). Corinne McLaughlin and Gordon Davidson look at the health care system through the lens of justice (page 389). Joanna Macy relates how a group of people created a Council of Beings to express the justice demands of plants and animals (page 513).

KINDNESS

Our thoughts on the value of kindness appear on pages 260–261. Kindness is advocated in a poem by John Wesley (page 360) and in stories shared by Megan McKenna (page 331), Caryl Hirshberg and Marc Ian Barasch (page 344), Andrew Harvey (page 343), Gerald Epstein (page 340), and Howard Thurman (page 340). Joan Chittister (page 490) and Thomas Moore (page 500) assess the value of kindness in our troubled world. Ram Dass and Paul Gorman identify little ways to help people (page 329). Maxine Dennis gives examples from her work as a cashier (page 318). Jean Shinoda Bolen (page 486) and Bob Libby (page 341) remember kind people. Sue Bender describes her son's kindness to his grandmother (page 453). Other authors write about specific acts reflecting thoughtfulness and respect: David K. Reynolds to things (page 113), Robert Sardello to a meeting room (page 112), Scout Cloud Lee to flowers (page 156), James Carse to ants (page 190), Andrew Rooney to his car (page 532), and Gunilla Norris to crumbs of food (page 536). Eduardo Rauch observes the kindness of a guide dog (page 186). Scott Russell Sanders relays examples of reciprocal acts of kindness between humans and birds (page 190). Mary Ann Brussat and Joseph Bruchac recall men who were kind to toads (pages 208–209). An excerpt from a Nancy Willard novel reveals kindness to the dead (page 318).

LISTENING

Spiritual teachers from different traditions are quoted in our meditation on listening that appears on pages 282–283. W. A. Mathieu muses on all the music in our lives (page 299). Burghild Nina Holzer listens to her flesh during a massage (page 371); Ronald Blythe, to plant crops (page 156); Linda Hogan, to the wind (page 158); and Frederic Brussat, to car alarms (page 72). Carla Needleman notes that craftsmen listen to their material (page 72), and we meet a repairman who listens to machines (page 69). In poetry, Chief Dan George and Helmet Hirnschall (page 126) and William Stafford (page 208) praise how nature speaks to us. In another poem, John Fox catches the significance of feeling deeply listened to (page 454). Natalie Goldberg recalls the significance of listening to the rain in ninth grade (page 465). David Ariel (page 177) and Frederick Buechner (page 511) tell stories about how sounds connect us to God. Morton Kelsey listens to his dreams (page 542) and to God in the middle of the night (page 286).

LOVE

Our discussion of love appears on pages 284–285. For Robert A. Johnson, love is like stirring the oatmeal (page 441); for Kuan Tao-Sheng, it is symbolized by two clay statues (page 423); for another individual, it is represented by two stones smoothed out over time (page 437). Love is felt in many situations: looking at one's place (page 110), swimming with dolphins (page 193), being with cats (page 186), drawing (page 290), in a hospital (page 333), seeing roses (page 401), in an all-night diner (page 482), and playing with a dog (page 525). Love is important during illness (page 391), a bout of depression (page 336), and a period of grief (page

405). The enduring qualities of family love are described by Daniel Mark Epstein (page 442), David J. Wolpe (page 447), Celeste Snowber Schroeder (page 449), Richard Ford (page 450), Andrew Harvey (page 451), Philip Roth (page 403), Gabriel Horn (page 407), Barbara Cawthorne Crafton (page 524), and in two vigils by Noela Evans (page 453). The love of friends is conveyed through stories by Anthony de Mello (page 458), Madeleine L'Engle (page 427), and Frederic Brussat (page 455). The varied expressions of love in marriages and partnerships are described by Alan Watts (page 384), Edward Hays (page 425), Henri J. M. Nouwen (page 429), Eda LeShan (page 436), Andre Dubus (page 524), Kent Nerburn (page 541), Jane Smiley (page 431), and Anne Tyler (page 439). Edward Hays explains the positive sides of the love of money (page 314). Kahlil Gibran in *The Prophet* presents work as love made visible (page 305).

MEANING

Our meditation on the spiritual practice of meaning appears on pages 296–297. Earlier we describe the various meanings we read into an empty city lot (pages 39–40). A Hasidic tale relates the meanings of three familiar objects (page 45). The symbolic significances assigned to other things are noted by Fulton Sheen on a ring (page 45), Frederic Brussat on a painting (page 51), John Aurelio on a couple's gifts (page 58), Megan McKenna on baklava (page 229), Rami Shapiro on a jigsaw puzzle (page 239), William Bryant Logan on fingers (page 377), David Spangler on an old hymnal (page 479), Laura Green on socks (page 526), and Joseph Epstein on books (page 536). Found objects have significance for Burghild Nina Holzer (page 148) and Roger B. Swain (page 533). A Native American perspective is revealed by Scout Cloud Lee on a ceremonial object (page 49), Lame Deer on a pot of soup (page 222), and Linda Hogan on an eagle feather (page 50). Places have special meaning to John Updike (page 88), Sam Keen (page 103), and Tom Adams's mother (page 104). Jacob Needleman comments on money's value (page 314). Kat Duff (page 386), Mary Ann Brussat (page 388), Anatole Broyard (page 388), and Max Lerner (page 398) reveal their interpretations of illnesses. Meanings pop up on Mary Ann Brussat's computer screen (page 315). Finally, Jewish sage Ben Hei Hei gives an exposition on the big picture (page 353).

NURTURING

Our discussion of the various ways to practice nurturing appears on pages 310–311. Nurturing relationships are described by Anne Morrow Lindbergh (page 423), William Betcher (page 441), Frederic Brussat (page 448), and Toni Morrison (page 456). The arts are often sources of nourishment—see John Fox on poetry (page 280), Brigid O'Shea Merriman on Dorothy Day's use of books (page 242), and Brenda Peterson on musical tapes (page 534). Places are nourishing, according to Sallie Tisdale on the West (page 89); Ellen Gilchrist (page 96) and Theo Pelletier (page 97) on home; Linda Weltner on her house (page 96); Joseph Rael on his village (page 114); Frederic Brussat (page 102), Jo Ann Passariello Deck (page 102), and Gunilla Norris (page 522) on kitchens; Marilyn Barrett on her garden (page 527); and Macrina Weiderkehr on a healing rock (page 534). Thomas Moore praises the nourishment of ordinary arts such as doing dishes (page 536). A story about Rabbi Hillel recognizes taking a bath as a religious obligation (page 374). Time away from work and regular responsibilities is lauded by Peg Thompson (page 253), Robert Fulghum (page 256), Sue Bender (page 257), Maya Angelou (page 258), Sy Safransky (page 259), and the haiku poet Issa (page 263).

OPENNESS

Our essay on openness with insights from Taoism, Native American spirituality, Sufism, Judaism, Christianity, and Buddhism appears on pages 334–335. The value of cross-cultural encounters is illustrated in stories told by Deena Metzger (page 279) and Dawna Markova (page 412). Ram Dass confesses how difficult it can be to practice openness toward someone with apparently different beliefs (page 493). Edward Hays (page 243) explains how he remains open to the ideas of other writers. Stephanie Kaza reaches out to a tree (page 147) and demonstrates empathy. Frederic Brussat goes out for a walk in New York to practice openness toward people, buildings, things, and other aspects of city life.

PEACE

Our meditation on the spiritual practice of peace appears on pages 348–349. The importance of practicing peace at home is discussed by Stephen and Ondrea Levine (page 448). Thich Nhat Hanh finds peace in his backyard (page 148). Linda Hogan pays tribute to a peace worker in Ireland (page 356). Angeles Arrien relates an example of peacemaking by a woman and a boy on a skateboard (page 493). Another comes from a movie about a boy determined to stop nuclear war (page 331). Edward Hays suggests a very basic step individuals can take toward disarmament (page 540). Megan McKenna tells a story about a woman unwilling to make sacrifices for peace (page 359). Brother David Steindl-Rast recalls a time when a community stopped a ritual to think of peace (page 148), and Fran Peavey shares a powerful image of the whole world longing for peace (page 353).

PLAY

We express our love of play on pages 350–351. Two passages from William Betcher's book *Intimate Play* reveal how couples use nicknames and games to liven up their relationships (pages 69, 440). A character in a Nancy Willard novel takes a lighthearted approach to her cooking pots (page 69), and Laurie Colwin attributes her love of corn to its associations with recreation (page 224). Matthew Fox learns about play from his dog (page 181). Harold Kushner admires the effortlessness of two children's play at the beach (page 424), and Sue Monk Kidd shares a story about her grandfather's effortless fishing. Eduardo Galeano reminds us that the body is meant to play (page 369). Eda LeShan (page 257) enjoys riding on a carousel (page 257), Mary Ann Brussat relishes the playful dimensions of an art exhibit (page 292), and Rick Bass describes the sublime pleasures of ice skating (page 250). Joseph Campbell concludes that his work is play (page 103), and Marilyn Gustin proclaims that God is present in our recreation (page 537). At a monastery, Kathleen Norris tunes in to the monks' sense that life itself is a sign of God's play with us (page 481).

QUESTING

We explore the different meanings and purposes of questing on pages 380–381. The value of questing for young and old alike is revealed in stories by David Wolpe (page 128), Willigis Jager (page 303), and John Sanford (page 144). How the environment shapes a pilgrimage is revealed by Terry Tempest Williams discussing deserts (page 84), Joan Halifax on mountains (page 84), and Bede Griffiths on forests (page 128). Kent Nerburn outlines the many benefits of travel (page 259), and Cathy Johnson recommends wandering around (page 533). Finally, William Guion describes how the search for a good photograph helped him focus on his career choices (page 137), and William Stafford reveals how a morning run can be an adventure (page 248).

REVERENCE

Our essay on reverence appears on pages 392–393. Terry Tempest Williams (page 207) demonstrates reverence for a dead swan. Joan Halifax (page 145) and David Suzuki and Peter Knudtson (page 205) describe how indigenous peoples show respect for animals. Sue Hubbell (page 177) admires bees, and Noel Perrin, cows (page 189). Reverence is part of household tasks for David Adam (page 221), Mary Hayes-Grieco (page 224), William McNamara (page 234), Aryeh Kaplan (page 235), and Brenda Peterson (page 526). Weeds deserve respect, say Frederic Brussat (page 157) and Linda Weltner (page 527); so does a pebble on the beach (page 149). Even things should be honored (page 71). The sacred as being full of awe is contemplated by Sara Maitland (page 316). We are awed by the sights of a grand old tree (page 147), a colorful coral reef (page 150), and a flock of pigeons (page 171); Annie Dillard, by a glimpse of a muskrat (page 200); and Thich Nhat Hanh, by the knowledge of an orchid and a snail (page 207). Gary Paul Nabhan (page 86), Wendell Berry (page 105), and Macrina Wiederkehr (page 539) understand that the Earth is holy. Reverence for the dead is conveyed in stories by Jeff Friedman (page 401) and from the TV series *Picket Fences* (page 404). Finally, John Cowan (page 319) and Megan McKenna (page 492) remind us to acknowledge the divinity in each other.

SHADOW

We discuss the signs and symptoms of shadow in our essay on pages 408–409. Aspects of shadow are revealed in illustrations by Mary Ann Brussat (page 55), Anne Scott (page 134), Robert A. Johnson (page 191), Sheldon Kopp (page 281), Mary José Hobday (page 379), and Anthony de Mello (page 495), and in a story about Nasruddin (page 430) and one about Saint Francis and the Wolf of Gubbio (page 498). Sy Safransky (page 345), Robert Coles (page 346), Ram Dass and Paul Gorman (page 346), and Jean Vanier (page 494) explore the shadow side of organizations. David Hilfiker (page 347), Daniel Berrigan and Margaret Parker (page 498), and Patricia J. Williams (page 495) examine how the shadow manifests in American society. Henri J. M. Nouwen (page 458), Lewis Smedes (page 459), and Joseph Goldstein (pages 345, 481) discover qualities in themselves they have tried to deny. A couple has the good sense to say "shadow vows" before their wedding (page 437). Wendell Berry (page 71) and Shaun McNiff (page 71) notice signs of shadow in our use of things, and Lewis Thomas sees it in our attitude toward germs (page 387). An oil slick is evidence of the shadow for Corinne McLaughlin and Gordon Davidson (page 158), and a character in a William Boyd novel would agree (page 159). Rick Bass (page 157), Terry Tempest Williams (page 191), and Mary Oliver (page 192) meditate on the shadow in the natural world. A poem by Leonard Cohen reminds us that it is through the cracks in our lives that the light gets in (page 56).

SILENCE

Our consideration of silence, revolving around definitions from writers, poets, and religious teachers, appears on pages 410–411. The gifts arising out of silence are revealed in stories by Anthony de Mello (page 142), Sri Chinmoy (page 178), and Edward Hays (page 178). Wayne Muller explores the benefits of quiet for busy people (page 313). Mary José Hobday reflects on the importance of silence in Native American spirituality (page 218). Sue Bender comes to a new understanding of the "immensity within ourselves" at a museum (page 291). Kathleen Norris enjoys silence while hanging up laundry (page 238). Mary Anthony Wagner recommends setting up a hermitage within your home (page 538). Henri J. M. Nouwen recalls how he and a friend shared silence during a period of grief (page 458). Sue Monk Kidd discovers while sitting with a stunned bird that in stillness is healing (page 198).

TEACHERS

We consider the importance of teachers on pages 432–433. We are encouraged to recognize teachings all around us by Namkhai Norbu (page 179), Zen Master Eihei Dogan (page 131), and a Ute prayer (page 162). Lessons come to Mark Gerzon from his body (page 371), to Gretel Ehrlich from an illness (page 394), and to Wayne Muller from suffering (page 389). Frederic Brussat is instructed in life by a hotel maid (page 375) and a critical woman at a film discussion (page 288). Micheal Elliott recalls what he has learned from homeless children (page 337), and Joan Chittister describes a burial ritual honoring a sister's teachings (page 406). Insights come to Macrina Wiederkehr from a tree (page 132), to Joan Halifax from poisonous plants (page 206), and to Octavio Paz from a handmade object (page 49). Frederic Brussat explains how hobbies are teachers (page 239). Sewing projects yield lessons for Phyllis Tickle's father (page 295) and Debra Farrington (page 298). Mary Ann Brussat discovers how animals can be teachers (pages 187, 189), as do Loren Eiseley (page 175), Edward Hays (page 175), Francis Ponge (page 187), Italo Calvino (page 188), and Anne Scott (page 395).

TRANSFORMATION

Our meditation on personal and societal transformation appears on pages 434–435. Clarissa Pinkola Estés (page 276) and Kent Nerburn (page 320) reflect on the transformative power of creativity. Anthony Lawlor (page 237) and Gail Godwin (page 237) feel the same effect from cleaning. Robert MacNeil finds transformation by going to the sea (page 523); James Cowan, at a waterfall (page 85); and Frederick Buechner, during a rainstorm (page 137). Shaun McNiff notes symbols of transformation among the things in our homes (page 54); a bell is one of those for W. A. Mathieu (page 51), as is a glass ball for Christopher De Vinck (page 54). Tom Driver recalls inventing a ritual of transformation (page 523). Noela Evans offers vigils for moving into a new home (page 99) and changing jobs (page 312), and Kathleen Wall and Gary Ferguson describe a ritual for the end of a relationship (page 438). Wendell Berry finds a symbol of change in nature (page 134), Edward Hays notices it looking into a mirror (page 398), and Thich Nhat Hanh reminds us that everything is in transformation (pages 134, 538).

UNITY

Various affirmations from world leaders about the value of unity are included in our discussion of this practice on pages 444–445. Several excerpts present interesting reminders of unity in everyday life: photographs of the Earth from space (page 83), eating rituals (page 217), raindrops merging on a window (page 422), a puzzle (page 422), a web of yarn (page 483), letters (page 537), and popcorn (page 537). The power of people working together is the theme of the examples cited by Ram Dass and Mirabai Bush (page 342), stories from the Hasidic tradition (pages 476, 502), a story from Africa related by Clarissa Pinkola Estés (page 476), and a childhood incident recalled by poet Pablo Neruda (page 488). A movie about a long-distance friendship of two book lovers sparks a meditation by Mary Ann Brussat on the friends she has made through e-mail (page 462). Dan Wakefield shares how going to church gives him a sense of living in a larger context (page 478), and Scott Russell Sanders experiences that from relating to his neighborhood (page 528). Finally, several poets address the theme of unity: James A. Autry (page 317), Sheila Cassidy (page 355), Marge Piercy (page 475), and Mary Oliver (page 514).

VISION

We open with a passage from the Hebrew Bible and add definitions of vision from a variety of teachers in our essay on pages 460–461. Vision's role in creative problem-solving is revealed in passages by Joseph Goldstein (page 277) and Anthony de Mello (page 278). Scott Russell Sanders shares his views on what makes a house a home (page 95). Joan Sauro describes an unusual outlook from a bus window (page 510). Vision often involves reframing our experiences; examples are Brenda Peterson on housework (page 236), Corinne McLaughlin and Gordon Davidson on politics (page 330), and Joan Chittister on various kinds of work (page 312). Sedonia Cahill and Joshua Halpern describe a ritual that signified a visionary commitment to confront violence (page 501). Finally, a trio of passages by Lawrence Kushner (page 354), Soozi Holbeche (page 354), and Willigis Jager (page 512) make the connection between our vision of the Creation and the actions needed to repair it.

WONDER

Wonder's many gifts are noted by D. H. Lawrence, Joan Miró, Lily Tomlin, Sam Keen, and others in our essay on pages 484–485. Thomas Mann shares a story about a child's sense of wonder (page 447). Richard Solly (page 451) and Graziano Marcheschi (page 278) remark on the power of the senses to bring back memories. Places evoke wonder for Annie Dillard (page 86), Mary Ann Brussat (page 89), Valerie Andrews (page 107), and Gretel Ehrlich (page 110). Terry Tempest Williams marvels at seashells (page 60), Joyce Rupp at frost on the windowpane (page 133), Mary Ann Brussat at trees growing on a city rooftop (page 148), and Diane Ackerman at monarch butterflies (page 204). Ernesto Cardenal finds wonders all around us in nature (page 130); so do Wendell Berry (page 129) and Mary Ann Brussat (page 136). William Bryant Logan meditates on the message of the biblical story of Moses and the burning bush—that the very ground is holy (page 130). Mary Oliver knows that from sleeping in the forest (page 128).

X—THE MYSTERY

The many mysteries of life and the Great Mystery are the focus of our reflection on pages 496–497. Anthony de Mello proposes a riddle that points to the need to honor mystery (page 299). A sense of mysterious presences and energies is reported by David A. Cooper (page 112) and Lyall Watson (pages 62, 112). Mystery is experienced in a hospital by Suzanne Guthrie (page 87). Encounters with wild animals are represen-tatives of mysteries to Jane Kenyon (page 172) and Charles Bergman (page 201) and to us watching the movie *The Bear* (page 200). We also relate how we were surprised by the mysterious travels of a plastic duck reported by CBS News (page 60). Daphne Rose Kingma notes that sex brings people in touch with the mystery of embodied spirit (page 383). Edith Sullwold tells a story about Jung's respect for the unknown in dreams (page 281). Eduardo Galeano (page 50) and Brother David Steindl-Rast (page 452) describe rituals designed to help children learn to love mystery.

YEARNING

Yearning as an expression of boundless desire is the focus of our essay on pages 506–507. We share three illustrations that capture the desire to have a different kind of life (page 373). Dan Wakefield recalls his child-hood yearning for spiritual refreshment (page 127). Jack Kornfield notes that most people have a deep longing to give back to the Earth and other people (page 327). Robert Farrar Capon uses cooking as a metaphor for the expression of a desire for God (page 220). Sex is sacred in a story told by Edward Hays (page 383). Desire plays an important role in a sick person's healing (page 397). It is at the center of a powerful ritual attended by Terry Tempest Williams in Spain (page 483). Finally, three poems by Rumi demonstrate an intense longing for the Beloved (pages 173, 227, 516).

YOU

We consider the implications of the spiritual practice of you on pages 508–509. Different understandings of human nature are revealed in sto-ries from *Peacemaking Day by Day* (page 36) and by Mark Link (page 38) and Bede Griffiths (page 421). Dawna Markova (page 220) and Jean Houston (page 226) use food images to convey the complexity of the soul. The body reveals a great deal about you—see Virginia Satir (page 373), Frederic Brussat (page 373), Buson (page 375), Bonnie Friedman (page

382), Nancy Mairs (page 382), Marsha Sinetar (page 385), Wataru Ohashi (page 391), and Brenda Peterson (page 539). Frederic Brussat (page 193) and Maya Angelou (page 466) receive lessons in self-esteem. Caretakers recognize the worth of sick people in emotionally powerful passages by Richard Solly (page 338), Sheila Cassidy (page 396), and Dawna Markova (page 396). The contribution of others to our sense of self is explored by Robert Fulghum (page 482) and Madeleine L'Engle (page 289). Marianne Williamson (page 317) and Lawrence Kushner (page 309) write about the purpose of an individual's life. Two poems, by Naomi Shihab Nye (page 73) and Thich Nhat Hanh (page 502), pay tribute to the many facets of the human personality.

ZEAL

We review all the ways to be aroused to life in our essay on zeal appearing on pages 530–531. Animals are teachers of zeal for Gunilla Norris (page 186) and Sue Hubbell (page 174). Marc David affirms eating as a celebration of existence (page 217). Mary Ann Brussat recognizes zeal in her mother's passion for learning (page 241). Eduardo Galeano sees it at a pantomine performance (page 289). Jonathan Kozol (page 487) and John R. Aurelio (page 413) admire people with *joie de vivre*. Frederick Buechner regards each new dawn as a time to be aroused to life (page 521). Brother David Steindl-Rast defines spirituality as "coming alive" (page 29), and Thich Nhat Hanh gives us the good news that we all can have it (pages 543–544).

THE *SPIRITUAL RX*
RESOURCE COLLECTION

On these pages we give source information for all the resources for your spiritual life recommended in *Spiritual Rx*. They are listed alphabetically by medium. The spiritual practice with which we suggest you use them is given in brackets at the end of the listing.

When *Spiritual Rx* went to press, all the books and music listed here were available in libraries and stores or could be easily ordered through online stores. Videos were in distribution and could be rented at local video stores or through one of the online services. Most of the art could be found easily in books. For your convenience, we provide links to sources and a gallery of the art on our World Wide Web site at www.spiritualrx.com.

We are very cognizant, however, of the fact that books go out of print and music and videos are pulled from wide distribution. We will continue to monitor the availability of the titles and watch for new releases by our teachers. If necessary, we will recommend additional titles through our web site.

The "*Spiritual Rx* Resource Collection" is an ongoing selection of the finest resources on spiritual practices. We urge you to use those listed below and to find additional ones through www.spiritualrx.com.

ART

Aboriginal Art.
Photographs of ancient and contemporary Aboriginal art in *Wisdom from the Earth: The Living Legacy of the Aboriginal Dreamtime* by Anna Voight and Neville Drury (Boston: Shambhala, 1998). [Openness]

Allston, Washington.
Landscape with a Lake. 1804. Painting in Museum of Fine Arts, Boston. Photograph of painting in *The Art Book* (London: Phaidon, 1996). [Peace]

Boccioni, Umberto.
Unique Forms of Continuity in Space. 1913. Bronze sculpture in the Museum of Modern Art, New York. Photograph of sculpture in *An Invitation to See: 150 Works from the Museum of Modern Art* edited by Helen M. Franc (New York: The Museum of Modern Art, 1992). [Zeal]

Calder, Alexander.
Lobster Trap and Fish. 1939. Mobile in Museum of Modern Art, New York. Photograph of mobile in *Alexander Calder and His Magical Mobiles* by Jean Lipman with Margaret Aspinwall (New York: Hudson Hill Press, 1981). [Wonder]

Calder, Alexander.
Red Lily Pads. 1956. Mobile in Guggenheim Museum, New York. Photograph of mobile in *Alexander Calder and His Magical Mobiles* by Jean Lipman with Margaret Aspinwall (New York: Hudson Hill Press, 1981). [Wonder]

Calder, Alexander.
Big Red. 1959. Mobile in Whitney Museum of American Art, New York. Photograph of mobile in *Alexander Calder and His Magical Mobiles* by Jean Lipman with Margaret Aspinwall (New York: Hudson Hill Press, 1981). [Wonder]

Calder, Alexander.
Dots and Dashes. 1959. Mobile in private collection. Photographs of mobile on flip pages in *Alexander Calder and His Magical Mobiles* by Jean Lipman with Margaret Aspinwall (New York: Hudson Hill Press, 1981). [Wonder]

Carravaggio, Michelangelo Merisi da.
Calling of Saint Matthew. 1600. Painting in San Luigi dei Francesi, Rome, Italy. Photograph of painting in *Sister Wendy Beckett's Grand Tour: Discovering Europe's Great Art* (New York: Stewart, Tabori & Chang, 1994). [Listening]

Cassatt, Mary.
On a Balcony. 1879. Painting in the Art Institute of Chicago. Photograph of painting in *Mary Cassatt: Modern Woman* Exhibition catalog organized by Judith A. Barter for the Art Institute of Chicago (New York: Harry N. Abrams, 1998). [Nurturing]

Cassatt, Mary.
The Garden. 1880. Painting in the Metropolitan Museum of Art, New York. Photograph of painting in *Mary Cassatt: Modern Woman* Exhibition catalog organized by Judith A. Barter for the Art Institute of Chicago (New York: Harry N. Abrams, 1998). [Nurturing]

Cassatt, Mary.
The Bath. 1891. Painting in the Art Institute of Chicago. Photograph of painting in *Mary Cassatt: Modern Woman* Exhibition catalog organized by Judith A. Barter for the Art Institute of Chicago (New York: Harry N. Abrams, 1998). [Nurturing]

Cassatt, Mary.
The Child's Bath. 1893. Painting in the Art Institute of Chicago. Photograph of painting in *Mary Cassatt: Modern Woman* Exhibition catalog organized by Judith A. Barter for the Art Institute of Chicago (New York: Harry N. Abrams, 1998). [Nurturing]

Chagall, Marc.
I and the Village. 1911. Painting in the Museum of Modern Art, New York. Photograph of painting in *Chagall: A Retrospective* edited by Jacob Baal-Teshuva (New York: Hugh Lauter Levin Associates, 1995). [Love]

Chagall, Marc.
The Birthday. 1915. Painting in the Museum of Modern Art, New York. Photograph of painting in *Chagall: A Retrospective* edited by Jacob Baal-Teshuva (New York: Hugh Lauter Levin Associates, 1995). [Love]

Chagall, Marc.
Abraham and the Three Angels. 1960. Painting in Musée National Message Biblique Marc Chagall, Nice. Photograph of painting in *Chagall: A Retrospective* edited by Jacob Baal-Teshuva (New York: Hugh Lauter Levin Associates, 1995). [Love]

Chagall, Marc.
Noah and the Rainbow. 1966. Painting in Musée National Message Biblique Marc Chagall, Nice. Photograph of painting in *Chagall: A Retrospective* edited by Jacob Baal-Teshuva (New York: Hugh Lauter Levin Associates, 1995). [Love]

Chagall, Marc.
Moses Receiving the Tablets of the Law. 1960. Painting in Musée National Message Biblique Marc Chagall, Nice. Photograph of painting in *Chagall: A Retrospective* edited by Jacob Baal-Teshuva (New York: Hugh Lauter Levin Associates, 1995). [Love]

Chicago, Judy.
The Dinner Party. 1974–1979. Mixed media traveling exhibition. Photographs of work by Donald Woodman in *The Dinner Party: A Symbol of Our Heritage* by Judy Chicago. (New York: Viking Press, 1996). [Teachers]

Constable, John.
The Cornfield. 1826. Painting in National Gallery, London. Photograph of painting in *Sister Wendy's Book of Meditations* (New York: Dorling Kindersley, 1998). [Peace]

Delaunay, Sonia.
Flamenco Singer. 1916. Painting in Centre d'Art Moderne, Lisbon. Photograph of painting in *Delaunay* by Hajo Duchting (Köln, Germany: Benedikti Taschen Publisher, 1994). [Enthusiasm]

Dubuffet, Jean.
Hilarious Figure. 1947. Painting in the Stedelijk Museum, Amsterdam. For photograph of painting, check books on Dubuffet. [You]

Dubuffet, Jean.
Corps de Dame: Blue Short Circuit. 1951. Painting in the Museum of Modern Art, New York. For photograph of painting, check books on Dubuffet. [You]

Dubuffet, Jean.
Tobacco Man with Goatee. 1959. Work consisting of botanical elements in private collection. For photograph of piece, check books on Dubuffet. [You]

Dubuffet, Jean.
Figure in Red. 1961. Painting in the Museum of Modern Art, New York. For photograph of painting, check books on Dubuffet. [You]

Dubuffet, Jean.
Fiston la Filoche. 1967. Sculpture in private collection. For photograph of sculpture, check books on Dubuffet. [You]

Dubuffet, Jean.
Bidon l'Esbroufe. 1967. Sculpture in the Solomon R. Guggenheim Museum, New York. For photograph of sculpture, check books on Dubuffet. [You]

Dürer, Albrecht.
Young Hare. 1502. Painting in Albertina Museum, Vienna. For photograph of painting, check books on Dürer. [Reverence]

Dürer, Albrecht.
The Little Owl. 1508. Painting in Albertina Museum, Vienna. For photograph of painting, check books on Dürer. [Reverence]

Dürer, Albrecht.
Three Linden Trees. Painting in Kunsthalle, Bremen. For photograph of painting, check books on Dürer. [Reverence]

Gainsborough, Thomas.
Chasing the Butterfly. 1756. Painting in National Gallery, London. Photograph of painting in *Sister Wendy's Book of Meditations* (New York: Dorling Kindersley, 1998). [Yearning]

Gauguin, Paul.
The Vision After the Sermon. 1888. Painting in National Gallery of Scotland, Edinburgh. Photograph of painting in *Sister Wendy's The Story of Painting: The Essential Guide to the History of Western Art* (New York: Dorling Kindersley, 1994). [Vision]

Haindl, Hermann.
Haindl Tarot Cards. Stamford, CT: U.S. Games Systems, Inc. 1990. [Imagination]

Icons.
Various photographs of icons in *Praying with Icons* by Jim Forest (Maryknoll, NY: Orbis, 1997). [Devotion]

Kiff, Ken.
Flower and Black Sky. 1988. Painting in Marlborough Fine Art Ltd., London. Photograph of painting in *Sister Wendy's Book of Meditations* (New York: Dorling Kindersley, 1998). [Hope]

Klee, Paul.
Genie Serving a Light Breakfast. 1920. Painting in Sprengel Museum, Hanover. Photograph of painting in *Klee: Great Modern Masters* edited by José María Faerna (New York: Cameo/Abrams, 1996). [Play]

Klee, Paul.
Dance, You Monster, to My Soft Song! 1922. Painting in the Solomon R. Guggenheim Museum, New York. For photograph of painting, check books on Klee. [Play]

Klee, Paul.
The Creator. 1934. Painting in private collection. Photograph of painting in *Paul Klee* by Katalin de Walterskirchen (New York: Rizzoli, 1975). [Play]

Klee, Paul.
A Child's Game. 1939. Painting in Felix Klee Collection, Berne. For photograph of painting, check books on Klee. [Play]

Koff-Chapin, Deborah.
Soul Cards. Langley, WA: The Center for Touch Drawing, 1995. [Imagination]

Kollwitz, Käthe.
Chalk drawings, *Plowing.* 1906. Drawing in National Gallery of Art, Washington, D.C. *Municipal Lodging.* 1926. Drawing in National Gallery of Art, Washington, D.C. Photographs of drawings in *Prints and Drawings of Käthe Kollwitz* selected by Carl Zigrosser (New York: Dover Publications, 1969). [Compassion]

Kroyer, Peter Severin.
Summer Evening on the Southern Beach. 1893. Painting in Skagens Museum, Skagen, Norway. Photograph of painting in *The Art Book* (London: Phaidon, 1996). [Peace]

Léger, Fernand.
Composition aux deux perroquets (Composition with two parrots). 1939. Painting in the Centre Georges Pompidou, Paris. For photograph of painting, check books on Léger. [Unity]

Léger, Fernand.
Les Plongeurs (The Divers). 1942. Painting at the Museum of Modern Art, New York. For photograph of painting, check books on Léger. [Unity]

Matisse, Henri.
Dance. 1909. Painting in the Museum of Modern Art. Photograph of painting in *An Invitation to See: 150 Works from The Museum of Modern Art* edited by Helen M. Franc (New York: The Museum of Modern Art, 1992). [Joy]

Matthews, Caitlin.
The Celtic Book of the Dead. New York: St. Martin's Press, 1992. [Imagination]

Monet, Claude.
Waterlily Pond. 1899. Painting in the National Gallery, London. For photographs of waterlily paintings, check books on Monet. [Gratitude]

Neve, Margaret.
By Moonlight. 1994. Painting in private collection. Photograph of painting in *Sister Wendy's Book of Meditations* (New York: Dorling Kindersley, 1998). [Joy]

Nevelson, Louise.
Sky Cathedral. 1958. Sculpture in Albright-Knox Art Gallery, Buffalo, New York. For photograph of sculpture, check books on Nevelson. [Hospitality]

O'Keeffe, Georgia.
Paintings of giant flowers. Photographs of paintings in *One Hundred Flowers* edited by Nicholas Callaway (New York: Alfred A. Knopf, 1989). [Beauty]

Oldenberg, Claes.
Clothespin. 1976. Public sculpture located in central Philadelphia, Pennsylvania. For photographs of sculpture, check books on Oldenberg. [Connections]

Picasso, Pablo.
Guernica. 1937. Painting in Prado, Madrid. Photograph of the painting in *Art of the Western World* by Bruce Cole and Adelheid Gealt (New York: Summit Books, 1989). For other photographs, check books on Picasso. [Compassion]

Picasso, Pablo.
Weeping Woman. 1937. Painting in Tate Gallery, London. Photograph of painting in *Sister Wendy Beckett's The Story of Painting: The Essential Guide to the History of Western Art* (New York: Dorling Kindersley, 1994). Also in *The Art Book* (London: Phaidon, 1996). [Compassion]

Pissarro, Camille.
Landscape at Chaponval. 1880. Painting in Musée d'Orsay, Paris. Photograph of painting in *The Art Book* (London: Phaidon, 1996). [Peace]

Pollack, Rachel.
The Shining Woman Tarot Cards. London: The Aquarian Press, 1992. [Imagination]

Pollock, Jackson.
Numbered "drip" paintings. 1947–1950. Several paintings in the Museum of Modern Art, New York. Photographs of paintings in *An Invitation to See: 150 Works from The Museum of Modern Art* edited by Helen M. Franc (New York: The Museum of Modern Art, 1992). Also in *The Art Book* (London: Phaidon, 1996). [Being Present]

Raphael.
Saint Catherine of Alexandria. 1507. Painting in National Gallery, London. Photograph of painting in *Sister Wendy's Book of Meditations* (New York: Dorling Kindersley, 1998). [Silence]

Rembrandt.
The Return of the Prodigal Son. 1662. Photograph of the painting in *The Return of the Prodigal Son* by Henri J. M. Nouwen (New York: Image Books/Doubleday, 1994). [Forgiveness]

Rembrandt.
Woman with a Pink. 1669. Painting in Metropolitan Museum of Art, New York. Photograph of painting in *Sister Wendy's Book of Meditations* (New York: Dorling Kindersley, 1998). [Silence]

Remington, Frederic.
The Unknown Explorers. 1905. Color illustration in *Collier's Magazine*, archived at the Remington Art Memorial Museum, Ogdensburg, New York. For photograph of illustration, see books on Remington. [Questing]

Renoir, Pierre-Auguste.
Dance at Bougival. 1883. Painting in the Museum of Fine Arts, Boston. For photograph of painting, check books on Renoir. [Grace]

Renoir, Pierre-Auguste.
In the Meadow. 1890. Painting in the Metropolitan Museum of Art, New York. For photograph of painting, check books on Renoir. [Grace]

Renoir, Pierre-Auguste.
Shepherd Boy. 1911. Painting in the Museum of Art, Rhode Island School of Design. For photograph of painting, check books on Renoir. [Grace]

Renoir, Pierre-Auguste.
Woman with a Parasol. 1877. Painting in the Museum of Fine Arts, Boston. For photograph of painting, check books on Renoir. [Grace]

Rivera, Diego.
The Flower Carrier. 1935. San Francisco Museum of Modern Art. Photograph of painting in *The Gaze of Love* by Sister Wendy Beckett (San Francisco: HarperSanFrancisco, 1993). [Kindness]

Rothko, Mark.
Untitled. 1968. Painting in the National Gallery of Art, Washington, D.C. Photograph of painting on page 217 of *Mark Rothko* by Jeffrey Weiss (Washington, D.C.: National Gallery of Art, published in association with the Yale University Press, 1998). [Shadow]

Rothko, Mark.
Untitled (Black on Gray). 1969–1970. Painting in Solomon R. Guggenheim Museum, New York. Photograph of painting on page 239 in *Mark Rothko* (Washington, D.C.: National Gallery of Art, published in association with the Yale University Press, 1998). [Shadow]

Rouault, Georges.
Joan of Arc. 1951. Painting in private collection. For photographs of painting, check books on Rouault. [Faith]

Segal, George.
Bus Riders. 1924. Sculpture in Hirshhorn Museum and Sculpture Garden, Washington. Photograph of sculpture in *The Art Book* (London: Phaidon, 1996). [Meaning]

Siqueiros, David Alfaro.
From the Dictatorship of Porfirio Diaz to the Revolution. 1965. Mural in the National History Museum, Chapultepec Castle, Mexico City. Photograph of mural in *Mexican Muralists: Orozco, Riviera, and Siqueiros* by Desmond Rochfort (San Francisco: Chronicle Books, 1998). [Justice]

Van der Weyden, Rogier.
The Magdalen Reading. 1445. Painting in National Gallery, London. Photograph of painting in *Sister Wendy's Book of Meditations* (New York: Dorling Kindersley, 1998). [Silence]

van Gogh, Vincent.
A Pair of Shoes. 1887. Painting in the Baltimore Museum of Art, Baltimore. For photograph of painting, check books on van Gogh. [X—The Mystery]

van Gogh, Vincent.
Portrait of Joseph Roulin. 1888. Painting in the Museum of Fine Arts, Boston. For photograph of painting, check books on van Gogh. [X—The Mystery]

van Gogh, Vincent.
The Starry Night. 1889. Painting in the Museum of Modern Art, New York. For photograph of painting, check books on van Gogh. [X—The Mystery]

van Gogh, Vincent.
Branches with Almond Blossom. 1890. Painting in the Rijksmuseum, Amsterdam. For photograph of painting, check books on van Gogh. [X—The Mystery]

van Gogh, Vincent.
Portrait of Doctor Gachet. 1890. Painting in the Musée d'Orsay, Paris. For photograph of painting, check books on van Gogh. [X—The Mystery]

Vermeer, Jan.
Young Woman with a Water Jug. 1662. Painting in the Metropolitan Museum of Art, New York. Photograph in *Sister Wendy's Book of Meditations* (New York: Dorling Kindersley, 1998). [Transformation]

Vogel, Karen.
Motherpeace Round Tarot. Stamford, CT: U.S. Games Systems, Inc., 1983. [Imagination]

Wyeth, Andrew.
Christina's World. 1948. Painting in the Museum of Modern Art, New York. Photograph of painting in *An Invitation to See: 150 Works from the Museum of Modern Art* edited by Helen M. Franc (New York: The Museum of Modern Art, 1992). [Yearning]

BOOKS

A Day in the Life . . . Registered trademark of HarperCollins Publishing, Inc. Individual editions of the series published by various imprints of HarperCollins. Check the photography section of bookstores and libraries. [Attention]

Abrams, Jeremiah, ed.
The Shadow in America: Reclaiming the Soul of a Nation. Novato, CA: Nataraj, 1994. [Shadow]

Ackerman, Diane.
A Natural History of the Senses. New York: Vintage, 1991. [Wonder]

Angell, Carole S.
Celebrations Around the World: A Multicultural Handbook. Golden, CO: Fulcrum Publishing, 1996. [Openness]

Artress, Lauren.
Walking a Sacred Path: Rediscovering the Labyrinth as a Spiritual Tool. New York: Riverhead, 1966. [Questing]

Bateson, Mary Catherine.
Peripheral Visions: Learning Along the Way. New York: HarperCollins, 1994. [Openness]

Bender, Sue.
Plain and Simple: A Woman's Journey to the Amish. San Francisco: HarperSanFrancisco, 1991. [Questing]

Berling, Judith A.
A Pilgrim in Chinese Culture: Negotiating Religious Diversity. Maryknoll, NY: Orbis, 1998. [Hospitality]

Berrigan, Daniel.
And the Risen Bread: Selected Poems, 1957–1997. New York: Fordham University Press, 1998. [Peace]

Berry, Wendell.
A Timbered Choir: The Sabbath Poems 1978–1997. Washington, D.C.: Counterpoint, 1998. [Reverence]

Bly, Robert, ed.
The Soul Is Here for Its Own Joy: Sacred Poems from Many Cultures. Hopewell, NJ: ECCO Press, 1995. [Zeal]

Boff, Leonardo.
Cry of the Earth, Cry of the Poor. Maryknoll, NY: Orbis, 1997. [Justice]

Bolen, Jean Shinoda.
Crossing to Avalon: A Woman's Midlife Pilgrimage. San Francisco: HarperSanFrancisco, 1994. [Questing]

Borg, Marcus.
The God We Never Knew: Beyond Dogmatic Religion to a More Authentic Faith. San Francisco: HarperSanFrancisco, 1998. [Faith]

Bridges, Holly.
A Circle of Prayer: Coming Together to Find Spirit, Caring, and Community. Berkeley, CA: Wildcat Canyon Press, 1997. [Devotion]

Brisson, Pat.
Wanda's Roses. Honesdale, PA: Boyds Mills Press, 1994. [Enthusiasm]

Broomfield, John.
Other Ways of Knowing: Recharting Our Future with Ageless Wisdom. Rochester, VT: Inner Traditions, 1997. [Connections]

Brown, Margaret Wise.
The Runaway Bunny. Pictures by Clement Hurd. New York: HarperCollins, 1972. [Love]

Bruchac, Joseph.
The Arrow over the Door. Pictures by James Watling. New York: Dial Books for Young Readers, 1998. [Silence]

Brussat, Frederic and Mary Ann.
Spiritual Literacy: Reading the Sacred in Everyday Life. New York: Touchstone, 1998. [Passages in *Spiritual Literacy*]

Buechner, Frederick.
Listening to Your Life: Daily Meditations with Frederick Buechner. San Francisco: HarperSanFrancisco, 1992. [Grace]

Bulkeley, Kelly.
Spiritual Dreaming: A Cross-Cultural and Historical Journey. Mahwah, NJ: Paulist Press, 1995. [Imagination]

Burnham, Sophy.
Revelations. New York: Ballantine, 1992. [Vision]

Byrd, Baylor.
I'm in Charge of Celebrations. Illustrations by Peter Parnall. New York: Charles Scribner's Sons, 1986. [Joy]

Byrd, Baylor.
The Way to Start a Day. Illustrations by Peter Parnall. New York: Charles Scribner's Sons, 1978. [Joy]

Cardenal, Ernesto.
Abide in Love. Maryknoll, NY: Orbis, 1995. [Zeal]

Carse, James P.
Breakfast at the Victory: The Mysticism of Ordinary Experience. San Francisco: HarperSanFrancisco, 1995. [X—The Mystery]

Carver, Raymond.
"A Small Good Thing." *Cathedral.* New York: Vintage Books, 1989. [Compassion]

Casey, Caroline W.
Making the Gods Work for You: The Astrological

Language of the Psyche. New York: Harmony, 1998. [Transformation]

Childs, Christopher.
The Spirit's Terrain: Creativity, Activism, and Transformation. Boston: Beacon Press, 1998. [Vision]

Chittister, Joan.
A Passion for Life: Fragments of the Face of God. Maryknoll, NY: Orbis, 1996. [Enthusiasm]

Chödrön, Pema.
Start Where You Are: A Guide to Compassionate Living. Boston: Shambhala, 1994. [Compassion]

Chödrön, Pema.
When Things Fall Apart: Heart Advice for Difficult Times. Boston: Shambhala, 1999. [Teachers]

Christ, Carol P.
Rebirth of the Goddess: Finding Meaning in Feminist Spirituality. New York: Addison-Wesley Publishing Co., 1997. [Nurturing]

Cleary, Thomas.
The Lively Garden Prayer Book. Leavenworth, KS: Forest of Peace Books, 1997. [Gratitude]

Cochran, Tracy, and Jeff Zaleski.
Transformations: Awakening to the Sacred in Ourselves. New York: Bell Tower, 1995. [Transformation]

Coelho, Paulo.
The Alchemist: A Fable About Following Your Dream. San Francisco: HarperSanFrancisco, 1995. [Questing]

Conlon, James.
Ponderings from the Precipice. Leavenworth, KS: Forest of Peace Books, 1998. [Peace]

Cooper, Rabbi David A.
God Is a Verb: Kabbalah and the Practice of Mystical Judaism. New York: Penguin USA, 1998. [Faith]

Cousineau, Phil.
The Art of Pilgrimage: The Seeker's Guide to Making Travel Sacred. Berkeley, CA: Conari Press, 1998. [Questing]

Dass, Ram, and Mirabai Bush.
Compassion in Action: Setting Out on the Path of Service. New York: Bell Tower, 1995. [Compassion]

Davies, Robertson.
The Cunning Man. New York: Penguin, 1996. [Meaning]

de Caussade, Jean-Pierre.
The Sacrament of the Present Moment. New York: HarperCollins, 1966. [Being Present]

de Hennezel, Marie.
Intimate Death: How the Dying Teach Us How to Live. New York: Knopf, 1998. [Teachers]

de Mello, Anthony.
Sadhana: A Way to God: Christian Exercises in Eastern Form. Liguori, MO: Liguori/Triumph, 1998. [Silence]

Deng, Ming-Dao.
Everyday Tao. San Francisco: HarperSan-Francisco, 1996. [Teachers]

Dillon, Leo, and Diane Dillon.
To Every Thing There Is a Season. New York: The Blue Sky Press/Scholastic, 1998. [Unity]

Dossey, Larry.
Meaning & Medicine. New York: Bantam, 1991. [Meaning]

Easwaran, Eknath.
Your Life Is Your Message: Finding Harmony with Yourself, Others, and the Earth. New York: Hyperion, 1996. [Unity]

Eck, Diana L.
Encountering God: A Spiritual Journey from Bozeman to Banaras. Boston: Beacon Press, 1994. [Hospitality]

Einstein, Patricia.
Intuition: The Path to Inner Wisdom. Rockport, MA: Element, 1997. [Listening]

Elffers, Joost.
Play with Your Food. New York: Stewart, Tabori & Chang, 1997. [Play]

Ellsberg, Robert, ed.
All Saints: Daily Reflections on Saints, Prophets, and Witnesses for Our Time. New York: Crossroad, 1997. [Enthusiasm]

Fellowship in Prayer.
The Gift of Prayer: A Treasury of Personal Prayer from the World's Spiritual Traditions. New York: Continuum, 1995. [Devotion]

Fleischman, Paul R.
Cultivating Inner Peace. New York: Jeremy P. Tarcher/Putnam, 1997. [Peace]

Ford, Debbie.
The Dark Side of the Light Chasers: Reclaiming Your Power, Creativity, Brilliance, and Dreams. New York: Riverhead, 1998. [Shadow]

Forster, E. M.
Howards End. New York: Penguin Signet Classics, 1998. [Connections]

Foster, Richard J.
Prayer: Finding the Heart's True Home. San Francisco: HarperSanFrancisco, 1992. [Devotion]

Fox, John.
Poetic Medicine: The Healing Art of Poem-Making. New York: Jeremy P. Tarcher/Putnam, 1997. [Listening]

Fox, Matthew.
A Spirituality Named Compassion. San Francisco: Harper & Row, 1990. [Compassion]

Fox, Matthew.
In the Beginning There Was Joy. New York: Crossroad, 1995. [Joy]

Frasier, Debra.
On the Day You Were Born. San Diego: Harcourt Brace Jovanovich, 1991. [You]

Gaines, Ernest J.
A Lesson Before Dying. New York: Vintage, 1994. [Justice]

Garfield, Charles, Cindy Spring, and Sedonia Cahill.
Wisdom Circles: A Guide to Self-Discovery and Community Building in Small Groups. New York: Hyperion, 1998. [Vision]

Glassman, Bernie.
Bearing Witness: A Zen Master's Lessons in Making Peace. New York: Bell Tower, 1998. [Peace]

Godwin, Gail.
Father Melancholy's Daughter. New York: Avon, 1991. [Teachers]

Gray, Dorothy Randall.
Soul Between the Lines: Freeing Your Creative Spirit Through Writing. New York: Avon Books, 1998. [Hope]

Greeley, Andrew M.
Windows: A Prayer Journal. New York: Crossroad, 1995. [Devotion]

Hansen, Ron.
Mariette in Ecstacy. New York: HarperPerennial, 1992.

Harvey, Andrew, ed.
The Essential Mystics: Selections from the World's Great Wisdom Traditions. San Francisco: HarperSanFrancisco, 1997. [Yearning]

Hass, Robert, ed.
The Essential Haiku: Versions of Basho, Buson, and Issa. Hopewell, NJ: The Ecco Press, 1994. [Being Present]

Havel, Vaclav.
The Art of the Impossible: Politics as Morality in Practice: Speeches and Writings, 1990–1996. Translation by Paul Anson. New York: Fromm International, 1998. [Hope]

Hays, Edward.
Prayers for the Domestic Church: A Handbook for Worship in the Home. Leavenworth, KS: Forest of Peace Books, 1979. [Devotion]

Hays, Edward.
Prayers for a Planetary Pilgrim: A Personal Manual for Prayer and Ritual. Leavenworth, KS: Forest of Peace Books, 1989. [Devotion]

Heidish, Marcy.
Who Cares? Simple Ways You Can Reach Out. Notre Dame, IN: Ave Maria Press, 1996. [Listening]

Hillman, James.
The Soul's Code: In Search of Character and Calling. New York: Warner Books, 1998. [You]

Hirshfield, Jane, ed.
Women in Praise of the Sacred: 43 Centuries of Spiritual Poetry by Women. New York: HarperPerennial, 1995. [Zeal]

Hogan, Linda.
Solar Storms. New York: Scribner, 1997. [Openness]

Hogan, Linda, Deena Metzger, and Brenda Peterson.
Intimate Nature: The Bond Between Women and Animals. New York: Fawcett Columbine, 1998. [Reverence]

Houston, Jean.
A Passion for the Possible: A Guide to Realizing Your True Potential. San Francisco: HarperSanFrancisco, 1998. [You]

Howatch, Susan.
Absolute Truths. New York: Knopf, 1995. [Grace]

Irving, John.
A Prayer for Owen Meany. New York: Ballantine Books, 1997. [Faith]

Johnson, Robert A.
Balancing Heaven and Earth: A Memoir of Visions, Dreams, and Realizations. San Francisco: HarperSanFrancisco, 1998. [X—The Mystery]

Joosse, Barbara M.
Mama, Do You Love Me? Illustrations by Barbara Lavallee. San Francisco: Chronicle Books, 1991. [Love]

Keen, Sam.
To Love and Be Loved. New York: Bantam, 1997. [Love]

Kelly, Marcia, and Jack Kelly.
100 Graces: Mealtime Blessings. New York: Bell Tower. 1997. [Gratitude]

Kelsey, Morton.
The Other Side of Silence: Meditation for the Twenty-First Century. New York: Paulist Press, 1997. [Silence]

Kindersley, Barnabas, and Anabel Kindersley.
Children Just Like Me. New York: Dorling Kindersley, 1995. [Unity]

Kingma, Daphne Rose.
A Lifetime of Love. Berkeley, CA: Conari Press,
1998. [Love]

Kingsolver, Barbara.
Animal Dreams. New York: HarperPerennial,
1991. [Hope]

Kolbenschlag, Madonna.
Eastward Toward Eve: A Geography of Soul.
New York: Crossroad, 1996. [Openness]

Krauss, Ruth.
The Carrot Seed. New York: Harper & Row,
1945. [Enthusiasm]

Kung, Hans, ed.
*Yes to a Global Ethic: Voices from Religion and
Politics.* New York: Continuum, 1996. [Unity]

Kushner, Harold S.
*How Good Do We Have to Be? A New
Understanding of Guilt and Forgiveness.* Boston:
Little Brown & Co., 1997. [Forgiveness]

Kushner, Lawrence.
*Invisible Lines of Connection: Sacred Stories of the
Ordinary.* Woodstock, VT: Jewish Lights, 1996.
[Connections]

Lachman, Barbara.
The Journal of Hildegard of Bingen. New York:
Crown, 1995. [Yearning]

Lawrence of the Resurrection, Brother.
The Practice of the Presence of God. Washington,
D.C.: ICS Publications, 1991. [Being Present]

Leder, Drew.
*Spiritual Passages: Embracing Life's Sacred Jour-
ney.* New York: Jeremy P. Tarcher/Putnam,
1997. [Transformation]

Leighton, Taigen Daniel.
*Bodhisattva Archetypes: Classic Buddhist Guides
to Awakening and Their Modern Expression.* New
York: Penguin Arkana, 1998. [Enthusiasm]

L'Engle, Madeleine.
*Glimpses of Grace: Daily Thoughts and Reflec-
tions.* San Francisco: HarperSanFrancisco,
1996. [Grace]

L'Engle, Madeleine.
*Time Trilogy: A Wrinkle in Time, A Wind in the
Door, A Swiftly Tilting Planet.* New York:
Farrar Straus Giroux, 1988. [Shadow]

Lerner, Michael.
*The Politics of Meaning: Restoring Hope and
Possibility in an Age of Cynicism.* New York:
Addison-Wesley, 1997. [Justice]

Linn, Denise.
*Quest: A Guide for Creating Your Own Vision
Quest.* New York: Ballantine Books, 1998.
[Vision]

Lionni, Leo.
Frederick. New York: Pinwheel Books/Knopf/
Pantheon, 1973. [Nurturing]

Lopez, Barry.
*About This Life: Journeys on the Threshold of
Memory.* New York: Alfred A. Knopf, 1998.
[Reverence]

Lopez, Barry.
Crow and Weasel. Berkeley, CA: North Point
Press, 1990. [Questing]

Lydon, Susan Gordon.
The Knitting Sutra: Craft as a Spiritual Practice.
San Francisco: HarperSanFrancisco, 1997.
[Transformation]

Macy, Joanna, and Molly Young Brown.
*Coming Back to Life: Practices to Reconnect Our
Lives, Our World.* Stony Creek, CT: New
Society Publishers, 1998. [Justice]

Magida, Arthur J., ed.
*How to Be a Perfect Stranger: A Guide to Eti-
quette in Other People's Religious Ceremonies.*
Woodstock, VT: Jewish Lights, 1996.
[Hospitality]

Marty, Martin, and Micah Marty.
*When True Simplicity Is Gained: Finding Spiri-
tual Clarity in a Complex World.* Grand Rapids,
MI: William B. Eerdmans, 1998. [Beauty]

Marzollo, Jean, and Walter Wick.
I Spy Gold Challenger! A Book of Picture Riddles.
New York: Scholastic/Cartwheel Books, 1998.
[Attention]

Mathieu, W. A.
The Musical Life: Reflections on What It Is and How to Live It. Boston: Shambhala, 1994. [Listening]

Matlins, Stuart M., and Arthur J. Magida. *How to Be a Perfect Stranger, Vol. 2: A Guide to Etiquette in Other People's Religious Ceremonies.* Woodstock, VT: Jewish Lights, 1997. [Hospitality]

McNiff, Shaun.
Trust the Process: An Artist's Guide to Letting Go. Boston: Shambhala, 1998. [Play]

Miller, D. Patrick.
A Little Book of Forgiveness: Challenges and Meditations for Anyone with Something to Forgive. Berkeley, CA: Fearless Book, 1999. [Forgiveness]

Miller, Timothy.
How to Want What You Have: Discovering the Magic and Grandeur of Ordinary Experience. New York: Avon Books, 1996. [Gratitude]

Moore, Thomas.
Care of the Soul: A Guide for Cultivating Depth and Sacredness in Everyday Life. New York: HarperPerennial, 1994. [Imagination]

Moore, Thomas.
The Re-Enchantment of Everyday Life. New York: HarperPerennial, 1997. [Imagination]

Moore, Thomas.
Soul Mates: Honoring the Mysteries of Love and Relationship. New York: HarperPerennial, 1994. [Imagination]

Muller, Wayne.
How, Then, Shall We Live? New York: Bantam, 1996. [Kindness]

Nhat Hanh, Thich.
The Long Road Turns to Joy. Berkeley, CA: Parallax Press, 1996. [Attention]

Nhat Hanh, Thich.
The Miracle of Mindfulness: A Manual on Meditation. Boston: Beacon Press, 1987. [Attention]

Nhat Hanh, Thich.
Present Moment, Wonderful Moment. Berkeley, CA: Parallax Press, 1990. [Attention]

Nhat Hanh, Thich.
Teachings on Love. Berkeley, CA: Parallax Press, 1997. [Love]

Needleman, Jacob.
A Little Book on Love. New York: Dell, 1998. [Meaning]

Needleman, Jacob.
Money and the Meaning of Life. New York: Currency/Doubleday, 1994. [Meaning]

Needleman, Jacob.
Time and the Soul. New York: Currency/Doubleday, 1998. [Meaning]

Nouwen, Henri, and John Dear, ed.
The Road to Peace: Writings on Peace and Justice. Maryknoll, NY: Orbis Books, 1998. [Peace]

Okri, Ben.
The Famished Road. Landover Hills, MD: Anchor, 1993. [Imagination]

Oliver, Mary.
New and Selected Poems. Boston: Beacon Press, 1992. [Wonder]

Oman, Maggie, ed.
Prayers for Healing: 365 Blessings, Poems, and Meditations from Around the World. Berkeley, CA: Conari Press, 1997. [Connections]

Ortiz, John M.
The Tao of Music: Sound Psychology, Using Music to Change Your Life. York Beach, ME: Samuel Weiser, Inc., 1997. [Transformation]

Paley, Vivian Gussin.
The Kindness of Children. Cambridge, MA: Harvard University Press, 1999. [Kindness]

Pearson, Carol S.
Awakening the Heroes Within: Twelve Archetypes to Help Us Find Ourselves and Transform Our World. San Francisco: HarperSanFrancisco, 1991. [You]

Pritchard, Evan T.
No Word for Time: The Way of the Algonquin

People. Tulsa, OK: Council Oak Books, 1997. [Teachers]

Remen, Rachel Naomi.
Kitchen Table Wisdom: Stories That Heal. New York: Riverhead, 1997. [Transformation]

Rosen, Mark I.
Thank You for Being Such a Pain: Spiritual Guidance for Dealing with Difficult People. New York: Harmony Books, 1998. [Teachers]

Roth, Gabrielle.
Sweat Your Prayers: Movement as Spiritual Practice. New York: Jeremy P. Tarcher/Putnam, 1998. [Joy]

Rumi, Jelaluddin.
The Essential Rumi. Translations by Coleman Barks. San Francisco: HarperSanFrancisco, 1995. [Yearning]

Rupp, Joyce.
The Cup of Our Life: A Guide for Spiritual Growth. Notre Dame, IN: Ave Maria Press, 1997. [Listening]

Salzberg, Sharon.
A Heart as Wide as the World: Living with Mindfulness, Wisdom, and Compassion. Boston: Shambhala, 1999. [Compassion]

Salzberg, Sharon.
Lovingkindness: The Revolutionary Art of Happiness. Boston: Shambhala, 1997. [Compassion]

Sams, Jamie, and David Carson.
Medicine Cards: The Discovery of Power Through the Ways of Animals. Santa Fe, NM: Bear & Company, 1988. [Teachers]

Sanders, Scott Russell.
Hunting for Hope: A Father's Journeys. Boston: Beacon Press, 1998. [Zeal]

Sanders, Scott Russell.
Secrets of the Universe. Boston: Beacon Press, 1992. [Zeal]

Sanders, Scott Russell.
Staying Put: Making a Home in a Restless World. Boston: Beacon Press, 1994. [Zeal]

Sanders, Scott Russell.
Writing from the Center. Bloomington, IN: Indiana University Press, 1997. [Zeal]

Sasso, Sandy Eisenberg.
In God's Name. Woodstock, VT: Jewish Lights, 1994. [Devotion]

Schaper, Donna.
Sabbath Sense: A Spiritual Antidote for the Overworked. Philadelphia: Innisfree Press, Inc., 1997. [Nurturing]

Schroeder, Celeste Snowber.
Embodied Prayer: Harmonizing Body and Soul. Liguori, MO: Triumph Books, 1995. [Devotion]

Schwartz, Dannel I., and Mark Hass.
Finding Joy: A Practical Spiritual Guide to Happiness. Woodstock, VT: Jewish Lights, 1998. [Joy]

Schwartz, Lynne Sharon.
The Fatigue Artist. New York: Scribner, 1996. [Transformation]

Shapiro, Rabbi Rami M.
Minyan: Ten Principles for Living a Life of Integrity. New York: Bell Tower, 1997. [Kindness]

Singer, Daniel, and Marcella Bakur Weiner.
The Sacred Portable Now: The Transforming Gift of Living in the Moment. Rocklin, CA: Prima Publishing, 1997. [Being Present]

Sluyter, Dean.
Why the Chicken Crossed the Road and Other Hidden Enlightenment Teachings from the Buddha to Bebop to Mother Goose. New York: Jeremy P. Tarcher/Putnam, 1998. [Play]

Snyder, Gary. *No Nature: New and Selected Poems.* New York: Pantheon Books, 1993. [Wonder]

Spangler, David.
A Pilgrim in Aquarius. Forres, Scotland: Findhorn, 1996. [Vision]

Steindl-Rast, Brother David.
Gratefulness: The Heart of Prayer. New York: Paulist Press, 1990. [Gratitude]

Strand, Clark.
Seeds from a Birch Tree: Writing Haiku and the Spiritual Journey. New York: Hyperion, 1997. [Being Present]

Streep, Peg.
Altars Made Easy: A Complete Guide to Creating Your Own Sacred Space. San Francisco: HarperSanFrancisco, 1997. [Devotion]

Taylor, Barbara Erakko.
Silence: Making the Journey to Inner Quiet. Philadelphia: Innisfree Press, 1997. [Silence]

Teresa, Mother, and Becky Benenate and Joseph Durepos, eds.
Mother Teresa: No Greater Love. Novato, CA: New World Library, 1997. [Love]

Trott, Susan.
The Holy Man. New York: Berkeley, 1996. [Hospitality]

Tuan, Yi-Fu.
Passing Strange and Wonderful: Aesthetics, Nature and Culture. New York: Kodansha, 1995. [Beauty]

Tyler, Anne.
Saint Maybe. New York: Ballantine Books, 1996. [Forgiveness]

Wallis, Jim.
The Soul of Politics: Beyond "Religious Right" and "Secular Left." Eugene, OR: Harvest, 1995. [Hope]

Westwood, Jennifer.
Sacred Journeys: An Illustrated Guide to Pilgrimages Around the World. New York: Henry Holt, 1997. [Questing]

Whitcomb, Holly W.
Feasting with God: Adventures in Table Spirituality. Cleveland: United Church Press, 1996. [Play]

Whitman, Walt, and Stephen Mitchell, ed.
Song of Myself. Boston: Shambhala, 1998. [Beauty]

Wiederkehr, Macrina.
The Song of the Seed: The Monastic Way of Tending the Soul. San Francisco: HarperSanFrancisco, 1995. [Listening]

Williams, Terry Tempest.
Refuge: An Unnatural History of Family and Place. New York: Vintage Books, 1992. [Reverence]

Williamson, Marianne.
The Healing of America. New York: Simon & Schuster, 1997. [Justice]

Wilson, Colin.
The Atlas of Holy Places & Sacred Sites. New York: DK Publishing, 1996. [Questing]

Wood, Douglas.
Old Turtle. Watercolors by Cheng-Khee Chee. Duluth, MN: Pfeifer-Hamilton Publishers, 1992. [Devotion]

IMAGERY EXERCISES

The imagery exercises suggested for each of the spiritual practices have been collected from several sources, including Mary Ann's imagery teachers Colette Aboulker-Muscat and Gerald Epstein. These general instructions for their way of doing imagery should be helpful to those just starting this type of practice.

Begin any imagery exercise by stating an intention. In the case of those included in *Spiritual Rx*, the intention is to experience one or more aspects of a spiritual practice.

Go to a relatively quiet place where you will not be bothered by irritating noises. Sit upright in a chair, keeping your back straight and placing your arms on its armrests, palms open and down. Your feet should be uncrossed and firmly placed on the floor.

Close your eyes and breathe rhythmically for a few minutes—out long, slow exhalations through your mouth and in normal inhalations through your nose. This signals your mind and body to relax deeply and to be ready to receive images. You will notice that many of the exercises in this book begin with the instruction to breathe out three times at the beginning, and more breathing instructions may follow at transition points. Always remember to breathe out before breathing in on each count.

You may want to tape record some of the exercises, using your own voice as the instructor. Leave a space of silence to do the exercise, then say to breathe out and open your eyes. You will discover the pacing that feels most natural to you. For shorter exercises, you can read the instructions first, then do the breathing, and recall the instructions as you do the exercise.

Let the images come to you. Don't try to anticipate or think them up to match a symbolic meaning you have read about. If you repeat the exercise, you may get entirely different images. Over time, you will become adept at reading what your images mean in the context of your spiritual life. Keeping a notebook where you both write a narrative of your experience and draw key images is a helpful way to discover patterns.

The following books give more information on imagery practice along with many more exercises.

Epstein, Gerald.
Climbing Jacob's Ladder: Finding Spiritual Freedom through Stories of the Bible. New York: ACMI Press, 1999. $14.95 plus $3.50 shipping. Available through the author: 16 E. 96 St., #1A, New York, NY 10128

Epstein, Gerald.
Healing into Immortality: A New Spiritual Medicine of Healing Stories and Imagery. New York: ACMI Press, 1997. $10.95 plus $3.50 shipping. Available through the author at the address above.

Epstein, Gerald.
Healing Visualizations: Creating Health Through Imagery. New York: Bantam, 1989.

Naparstek, Belleruth.
Staying Well with Guided Imagery. New York: Warner Books, 1995.

Naparstek, Belleruth.
Your Sixth Sense: Unlocking the Power of Your Intuition. San Francisco: HarperSanFrancisco, 1997.

JOURNAL EXERCISES

Throughout *Spiritual Rx*, we suggest journal exercises specific to each practice. You may also want to keep a special journal to keep track of your experiences with the book and its recommended activities. After watching a video, looking at a work of art, and listening to a piece of music, write your reactions in your journal. After trying a spiritual exercise for a week,

comment on how it has affected your attitudes and behavior. Keep notes of key ideas you learn from the books and audios, making a point of writing when one of them proves to be especially illuminating on your path.

The following titles are our favorite general books on journals.

Baldwin, Christina.
Life's Companion: Journal Writing as a Spiritual Quest. New York: Bantam Books, 1991.

Klug, Ronald.
How to Keep a Spiritual Journal: A Guide to Journal Keeping for Inner Growth and Personal Discovery. Minneapolis: Augsburg Books, 1993.

Rainer, Tristine.
The New Diary: How to Use a Journal for Self-Guidance and Expanded Creativity. New York: Jeremy P. Tarcher, 1978.

MUSIC

Bach, Johann Sebastian.
The Goldberg Variations. Recommended: Glenn Gould, piano. [Attention]

Barber, Samuel.
Adagio for Strings, Op. 11. Recommended: *Barber's Adagio.* BMG Classics. [Reverence]

Beatles, The.
"All You Need Is Love." [Love]

Beethoven, Ludwig van.
Symphony No. 6 in F Major, Op. 68, Pastoral Symphony. [Being Present]

Beethoven, Ludwig van.
Symphony No. 9 in D Minor, Op. 125, "Ode to Joy." [Joy]

Bock, Jerry, music; and Sheldon Harnick, lyrics.
"To Life" in *Fiddler on the Roof.* [Zeal]

Britten, Benjamin.
War Requiem. [Compassion]

Cage, John.
4' 33". [Hospitality]

Chapin, Harry.
The Gold Medal Collection. WEA/Elektra. [You]

Chapin, Harry.
"Someone Keeps Calling My Name" on
Portrait Gallery. WEA/Elektra. [You]

Chicago.
"You're the Inspiration." [Love]

Cliff, Jimmy.
"You Can Get It If You Really Want," "Rivers
of Babylon," and "The Harder They Come"
on *The Harder They Come*. PGD/Mango.
[Transformation]

Cocker, Joe.
"You Are So Beautiful." [Beauty]

Cooke, Sam.
"You Send Me." [Love]

Copland, Aaron.
"Appalachian Spring" on *The Aaron Copland
Collection*. Recommended: the complete original
version by Atlantic Sinfonietta; Andrew
Schenck, conductor. Koch International
Classics. [Grace]

D'Agostino, Peppino.
"Higher Connections" on *Close to the Heart*.
Mesa Records/Rhino. [Connections]

Debussy, Claude.
La Mer. [Wonder]

Dion, Celine.
"The Power of Love." [Love]

Dylan, Bob.
"If Not for You." [Love]

Dylan, Bob.
"I Shall Be Released." [Hope]

Everly Brothers.
"Let It Be Me." [Love]

Freyda.
Globallullabies. Music for Little People. [Nur-
turing]

Gaynor, Gloria.
"I Will Survive." [Hope]

Girls of Angeli.
The New Voice of North. Innovator Series/
Finlandia Records. [Openness]

Harrison, George.
"Be Here Now" on *Living in the Material
World*. [Being Present]

Hollies, The.
"The Air That I Breathe." [Love]

Isbin, Sharon, Paul Winter, and Thiago de
Mello.
Journey to the Amazon. Teltec Classics.
[Openness]

Kenton, Stan.
Kenton in Hi-Fi. Capitol Jazz. [Play]

Khechog, Nawang.
Sounds of Peace. Sounds True. [Peace]

Lennon, John.
"Imagine." [Imagination]

Lennon, John.
"Give Peace a Chance." [Peace]

Mahler, Gustav.
Das Lied von der Erde. The Song of the Earth.
[Meaning]

Melanie.
"Peace Will Come" on *Best of Melanie*. WEA/
Atlantic/Rhino. [Peace]

Melrose, Ron.
The Missing Peace. Judy Malloy, singer and
storyteller. Sons of Sound. [Questing]

Miles, John.
"Music" on *Rebel*. [X—The Mystery]

Morrison, Van.
"Hymns to the Silence" on *Hymns to the
Silence*. Polydor/PolyGram Records. [Silence]

Mozart, Amadeus.
Symphony No. 41 in C, Jupiter Symphony.
[Unity]

Nash, Johnny.
"I Can See Clearly Now." [Hope]

Nelson, Willie.
"Loving Her Was Easier Than Anything I'll
Ever Do Again." [Love]

Newton-John, Olivia.
"I Honestly Love You." [Love]

Penderecki, Krzysztof.
Threnody to the Victims of Hiroshima, on *Matrix 5*. Recommended: Polish Radio National Symphony Orchestra. EMI Classics. [Forgiveness]

Powers, Chet.
"Get Together." Recommended: rendition by The Youngbloods. [Kindness]

Rolling Stones.
"Sympathy for the Devil" on *Beggars Banquet*. [Shadow]

Ronstadt, Linda.
Dedicated to the One I Love. Elektra. [Nurturing]

Rossini, Gioacchino.
Guillaume Tell, William Tell Overture. [Vision]

Sayer, Leo.
"When I Need You." [Love]

Seeger, Pete.
Where Have All the Flowers Gone: The Songs of Pete Seeger. Appleseed Recording. [Justice]

Simon and Garfunkel.
"Bridge Over Troubled Water." [Kindness]

Sisters of Glory, The.
Good News in Hard Times. Warner Bros. [Enthusiasm]

Sly and the Family Stone.
"You Can Make It If You Try." [Hope]

Springsteen, Bruce.
"Badlands" and "Darkness on the Edge of Town" on *Darkness on the Edge of Town*. Sony Music. [Yearning]

Springsteen, Bruce.
"Born to Run" on *Born to Run*. Sony Music. [Yearning]

Springsteen, Bruce.
"No Surrender" on *Born in the U.S.A.* Sony Music. [Yearning]

Stevens, Cat.
"Peace Train." [Peace]

Tavener, John.
Akathist of Thanksgiving. Recommended: Westminster Abbey Choir and BBC Singers, BBC Symphony Orchestra, Martin Neary, conductor. Sony Classical. [Gratitude]

Three Dog Night.
"Joy to the World" on *The Best of Three Dog Night*. UNI/MCA. [Joy]

Various Artists, including the songs "My Guy" by Mary Wells; "Stop! In the Name of Love" by Diana Ross & the Supremes; "Neither One of Us (Wants to Be the First to Say Goodbye)" by Gladys Knight & the Pips; "What Becomes of the Brokenhearted" by Jimmy Ruffin; and "All Night Long" by Lionel Richie, on *Motown 40 Forever*. Motown. [Teachers]

Various Artists.
B'ismillah: Highlights from the Fes Festival of World Sacred Music. Sounds True. [Devotion]

Various Artists.
Hamdulillah, Vol. 2: Highlights from the Fes Festival of World Sacred Music. Sounds True. [Devotion]

Various Artists.
Wade in the Water: African American Spirituals: The Concert Tradition (Vol. 1). Smithsonian/Folkways Recordings. [Enthusiasm]

Various Choirs.
African American Congregational Singing: Nineteenth-Century Roots (Vol. 2). Smithsonian/Folkways Recordings. [Enthusiasm]

Williams, Ralph Vaughan.
The Lark Ascending. Recommended: London Chamber Orchestra. Virgin Classics. [Faith]

Winter, Paul.
Earth: Voices of a Planet. Living Music Records. [Listening]

Winter, Paul.
Wolf Eyes: A Retrospective. Living Music Records. [Listening]

Yindi, Yothu.
Tribal Voice. Hollywood Records. [Openness]

SPOKEN-WORD AUDIOS

Anand, Margot.
The Art of Sexual Magic. Six cassettes. Sounds True, 1996. [Yearning]

Arrien, Angeles.
Walking the Four-Fold Way. One cassette. New Dimensions, 1993. [Openness]

Black Elk.
Black Elk Speaks as Told to John G. Neihardt. Three cassettes. Audio Literature, 1994. [Vision]

Borysenko, Joan.
Seventy Times Seven: On the Spiritual Art of Forgiveness. Two cassettes. Sounds True, 1996. [Forgiveness]

Buber, Martin.
The Legend of the Baal-Shem. Two cassettes. Audio Literature, 1992. [Faith]

Chavis, Melody Ermachild.
Starting in Your Own Backyard. One cassette. New Dimensions, 1998. [Hope]

Chödrön, Pema.
Awakening Compassion: Meditation Practice for Difficult Times. Six cassettes. Sounds True, 1995. [Compassion]

Counts, Alex, and Muhammad Yunus.
The Micro-Lending Revolution. One cassette. New Dimensions, 1998.

Dass, Ram.
Experiments in Truth: A Collection of Classic Lectures from the '60s to the '90s. Six cassettes. Sounds True, 1998. [Zeal]

Dogen, Zen Master.
Edited by Kazuaki Tanahashi; selected from *Moon in a Dewdrop* and read by poet Gary Snyder. Two cassettes. Audio Literature, 1992. [Being Present]

Estés, Clarissa Pinkola.
The Faithful Gardener. One cassette. Sounds True, 1995. [Connections]

Flinders, Carol.
Enduring Grace: The Lives of Six Women Mystics from the Age of Faith. Two cassettes. Sounds True, 1995. [Grace]

Fox, Matthew.
Original Blessing. Two cassettes. Audio Literature, 1997. [You]

Fulghum, Robert.
All I Really Need to Know I Learned in Kindergarten. One cassette. Random House Audio, 1988. [Kindness]

Halifax, Joan.
Being with Dying: Contemplative Practices and Teachings. Six cassettes. Sounds True, 1997. [Teachers]

Hillman, James.
Beauty Without Nature: Refounding the City. Two cassettes. Spring Audio, 1998. [Beauty]

Holbrook, Hal.
Mark Twain Tonight. Two cassettes. Publishing Group West Audio, 1988. [Joy]

Kabat-Zinn, Jon.
Wherever You Go, There You Are: Mindfulness Meditations in Everyday Life. Three cassettes. Audio Renaissance, 1994. [Silence]

Keating, Thomas.
Contemplative Prayer. Three cassettes. Sounds True, 1996. [Devotion]

Kornfield, Jack.
Your Buddha Nature: Teachings on the Ten Perfections. Six cassettes. Sounds True, 1998. [Peace]

Le Guin, Ursula.
Lao Tzu: Tao Te Ching. One cassette. Shambhala Lion Editions, 1998. [X—The Mystery]

Levine, Stephen.
A Year to Live. Two cassettes. Sounds True, 1997. [Gratitude]

Lindbergh, Anne Morrow.
Gift from the Sea, read by Claudette Colbert. Two cassettes. Random House Audio, 1986. [Wonder]

Luke, Helen M.
The Way of Story: Myths and Stories for the

Inner Life. Two cassettes. Parabola, 1995. [Transformation]

Markham, Beryl.
West with the Night. Unabridged on six cassettes. Audio Partners, 1992. Abridged on two cassettes, read by Julie Harris. Spoken Arts, 1996. [Questing]

Matt, Daniel C.
God and the Big Bang: Discovering Harmony Between Science and Spirituality. Two cassettes. Audio Literature, 1998. [Unity]

Merton, Thomas.
The Seven Storey Mountain. Three cassettes. Audio Literature, 1998. [Meaning]

Mitchell, Stephen, assembler.
Bestiary: An Anthology of Poems About Animals. One cassette. Audio Literature, 1997. [Reverence]

Naparstek, Belleruth.
Health Journeys. Guided imagery tape series with 31 titles. Time Warner AudioBooks, 1992–2000. [Nurturing]

Nhat Hanh, Thich.
The Art of Mindful Living. Two cassettes. Sounds True, 1991. [Attention]

Nisker, Wes "Scoop."
Crazy Wisdom. Two cassettes. Ten Speed Press Audio, 1993. [Play]

Richards, M. C.
Living the Creative Life with M. C. Richards. One cassette. New Dimensions, 1997. [Imagination]

Schroeder-Sheker, Therese.
Musical Midwifery for the Dying. One cassette. New Dimensions, 1997. [Listening]

Sinetar, Marsha.
The Mentor's Spirit: Life Lessons on Leadership and the Art of Encouragement. Two cassettes. Sounds True, 1998. [Enthusiasm]

Smith, Huston.
Religions of the World. Ten cassettes. Sounds True, 1995. [Hospitality]

Twist, Lynne.
The Soul of Money. One cassette. New Dimensions, 1997. [Justice]

Welwood, John.
Journey of the Heart: Intimate Relationship and the Path of Love. Three cassettes. Audio Literature, 1994. [Love]

Zweig, Connie, and Steve Wolf.
Romancing the Shadow: Illuminating the Dark Side of the Soul. Simon & Schuster Audio, 1997. [Shadow]

VIDEOS

The Accidental Tourist.
Lawrence Kasdan, director. 1988. Warner Home Video. [Enthusiasm]

The Accompanist.
Claude Miller, director. 1992. Columbia TriStar Home Video. [Beauty]

Alice.
Woody Allen, director. 1990. Orion Home Video. [Meaning]

Amadeus.
Milos Forman, director. 1984. HBO/Cannon Video. [Gratitude]

Antonia's Line.
Marleen Gorris, director. 1996. BMG Independents Video. [Hospitality]

Awakenings.
Penny Marshall, director. 1990. Columbia TriStar Home Video. [Gratitude]

Babe.
Chris Noonan, director. 1996. MCA/Universal Home Video. [Kindness]

Babette's Feast.
Gabriel Axel, director. 1987. Orion Home Video. [Grace]

Baraka.
Ron Fricke, director. 1992. MPI Video. [Devotion]

The Bear.
Jean-Jacques Annaud, director. 1989. RCA/
Columbia Pictures Home Video. [Nurturing]

Beyond Rangoon.
John Boorman, director. 1995. Columbia Tri-
Star Home Video. [Beauty]

The Big One.
Michael Moore, director. 1997. Miramax
Home Entertainment. [Justice]

Black Robe.
Bruce Beresford, director. 1992. Vidmark
Video. [Faith]

Brassed Off.
Mark Herman, director. 1997. Miramax Home
Entertainment. [Vision]

Brother Sun, Sister Moon.
Franco Zeffirelli, director. 1973. Paramount
Home Video. [Devotion]

Central Station.
Darrell James Roodt, director. 1999. Sony
Pictures Classics. [Compassion]

Chariots of Fire.
Hugh Hudson, director. 1981. Warner Home
Video. [Faith]

City of Hope.
John Sayles, director. 1991. SVS/Triumph.
[Shadow]

City of Joy.
Roland Joffe, director. 1992. Columbia TriStar
Home Video. [Compassion]

City Slickers.
Ron Underwood, director. 1991. New Line
Home Video. [Nurturing]

Close Encounters of the Third Kind.
Steven Spielberg, director. 1977. RCA/Colum-
bia Pictures Home Video. [X—The Mystery]

Contact.
Robert Zemeckis, director. 1997. Warner
Home Video. [Listening]

Cry, the Beloved Country.
Darrell James Roodt, director. 1995. Miramax
Home Entertainment. [Forgiveness]

Dances with Wolves.
Kevin Costner, director. 1990. Orion Home
Video. [Openness]

Dead Man Walking.
Tim Robbins, director. 1995. Polygram. [Love]

Defending Your Life.
Albert Brooks, director. 1991. Warner Home
Video. [Love]

Educating Rita.
Lewis Gilbert, director. 1983. RCA/Columbia
Pictures Home Video. [Meaning]

Enchanted April.
Mike Newell, director. 1992. Paramount Home
Video. [Beauty]

The English Patient.
Anthony Minghella, director. 1996. Miramax
Home Entertainment. [X—The Mystery]

Field of Dreams.
Phil Alden Robinson, director. 1989. MCA
Home Video. [Connections]

Fly Away Home.
Carroll Ballard, director. 1996. Columbia Tri-
Star Home Video. [Imagination]

Forrest Gump.
Robert Zemeckis, director. 1994. Paramount
Home Video. [Play]

Fried Green Tomatoes.
Jon Avnet, director. 1992. MCA/Universal
Home Video. [Nurturing]

*From the Heart of the World: The Elder
Brothers' Warning.*
Alan Ereira, director. 1992. Mystic Fire Video.
[Reverence]

Gandhi.
Richard Attenborough, director. 1982. RCA/
Columbia Pictures Home Video. [Peace]

Good Will Hunting.
Gus Van Sant, director. 1997. Miramax Home
Entertainment. [Grace]

Grand Canyon.
Lawrence Kasdan, director. 1992. Fox Video.
[Kindness]

Groundhog Day.
Harold Ramis, director. 1993. Columbia Tri-Star Home Video. [Transformation]

Hidden in America.
Martin Bell, director. 1997. Evergreen Video. [Compassion]

Household Saints.
Nancy Savoca, director. 1993. Columbia Tri-Star Home Video. [X—The Mystery]

House of Angels.
Colin Nutley, director. 1992. Columbia TriStar Home Video. [Openness]

House of Cards.
Michael Lessac, director. 1993. LIVE Video. [Imagination]

A Human Search: The Life of Father Bede Griffiths.
John Swindells, director. 1993. Parabola Video. [Hospitality]

Il Postino (The Postman).
Michael Radford, director. 1994. Miramax Home Entertainment. [Wonder]

Jerry Maguire.
Cameron Crowe, director. 1996. Columbia TriStar Home Video. [Attention]

Jesus of Montreal.
Denys Arcand, director. 1989. Orion Home Video. [Justice]

Joe Versus the Volcano.
John Patrick Shanley, director. 1990. Warner Home Video. [Questing]

Kundun.
Martin Scorsese, director. 1997. Touchstone Home Video. [Peace]

The Last Wave.
Peter Weir, director. 1977. Rhino Video. [Imagination]

Le Huitieme Jour (The Eighth Day).
Jaco Van Dormael, director. 1997. PolyGram Video. [Being Present]

Les Misérables.
Bille August, director. 1998. Columbia TriStar Home Video. [Forgiveness]

Local Hero.
Bill Forsyth, director. 1983. Warner Home Video. [Wonder]

The Long Walk Home.
Richard Pearce, director. 1990. LIVE Home Video. [Justice]

Mandela: Son of Africa, Father of a Nation.
Jo Menell and Angus Gibson, directors. 1997. Island Video. [Hope]

Men with Guns.
John Sayles, director. 1998. Columbia TriStar Home Video. [Meaning]

Microcosmos.
Claude Nuridsany and Marie Perennou, directors. 1996. Miramax Home Entertainment. [Reverence]

The Milagro Beanfield War.
Robert Redford, director. 1988. MCA Home Video. [Unity]

The Mission.
Roland Joffe, director. 1986. Warner Home Video. [Forgiveness]

Mountains of the Moon.
Bob Rafelson, director. 1990. Carolco/LIVE Video. [Questing]

Much Ado About Nothing.
Kenneth Branagh, director. 1993. Columbia TriStar Home Video. [Joy]

My Life as a Dog.
Lasse Hallstrom, director. 1985. Paramount Home Video. [Teachers]

Nell.
Michael Apted, director. 1994. Fox Video. [Listening]

Never Cry Wolf.
Carroll Ballard, director. 1990. Walt Disney Home Video. [Connections]

The Object of Beauty.
Michael Lindsay-Hogg, director. 1991. LIVE
Home Video. [Beauty]

*Once Upon a Time . . . When We Were Col-
ored.*
Tim Reid, director. 1996. Republic Video.
[Teachers]

Paradise Road.
Bruce Beresford, director. 1997. Twentieth
Century-Fox Home Entertainment. [Unity]

Phenomenon.
Jon Turtelt, director. 1996. Touchstone Home
Video. [Transformation]

The Piano.
Jane Campion, director. 1993. LIVE Home
Video. [Yearning]

Places in the Heart.
Robert Benton, director. 1984. CBS/Fox Video.
[Hope]

Plenty.
Fred Schepisi, director. 1985. HBO Video.
[Being Present]

The Power of One.
John G. Avildsen, director. 1992. Warner
Home Video. [Teachers]

The Quiet Room.
Rolf de Heer, director. 1997. New Line Home
Video. [Silence]

Race the Sun.
Charles T. Kanganis, director. 1996. Columbia
TriStar Home Video. [Enthusiasm]

Regarding Henry.
Mike Nichols, director. 1991. Paramount
Home Video. [Transformation]

A River Runs Through It.
Robert Redford, director. 1992. Columbia
TriStar Home Video. [Shadow]

Roger & Me
Michael Moore, director. 1989. Warner Home
Video. [Justice]

Romero.
John Duigan, director. 1989. Vidmark Video.
[Vision]

Ruby in Paradise.
Victor Nunez, director. 1993. Republic Pictures
Video. [You]

Rumi: Poet of the Heart.
Haydn Reiss, director. 1998. Magnolia Films.
[Yearning]

The Scent of Green Papaya.
Tran Anh Hung, director. 1994. Columbia
TriStar Home Video. [Attention]

Searching for Bobby Fischer.
Stephen Zaillian, director. 1993. Paramount
Home Video. [Nurturing]

The Secret of Roan Inish.
John Sayles, director. 1994. Columbia TriStar
Home Video. [Connections]

Shades of Fear.
Beeban Kidron, director. 1997. Miramax Home
Entertainment. [Hope]

Shall We Dance?
Masayuki Suo, director. 1997. Miramax Home
Entertainment. [Yearning]

Shirley Valentine.
Lewis Gilbert, director. 1989. Paramount
Home Video. [Zeal]

Sister Act.
Emile Ardolino, director. 1992. Touchstone
Home Video. [Enthusiasm]

The Spitfire Grill.
Lee David Zlotoff, director, 1996. Columbia
TriStar Home Video. [Openness]

Strictly Ballroom
Baz Luhrmann, director. 1993. Touchstone
Home Video [You]

The Sweet Hereafter.
Atom Egoyan, director. 1997. New Line Video.
[Meaning]

Tender Mercies.
Bruce Beresford, director. 1983. HBO Video.
[Love]

Thérèse.
Alain Cavalier, director. 1986. Circle Films
Video. [Faith]

Thunderheart.
Michael Apted, director. 1992. Columbia Tri-Star Home Video. [Vision]

Tin Cup.
Ron Shelton, director. 1996. Warner Home Video. [Play]

Truly, Madly, Deeply.
Anthony Minghella, director. 1991. Touchstone Home Video. [Joy]

Turtle Diary.
John Irvin, director. 1986. Vestron Video. [Reverence]

Ulee's Gold.
Victor Nunex, director. 1997. Orion Home Video. [Compassion]

What's Eating Gilbert Grape.
Lasse Hallstrom, director. 1993. Paramount Home Video. [Love]

The White Balloon.
Abbas Kiarostami, director. 1996. Evergreen Video. [Openness]

Wide Awake.
M. Night Shyamalan. 1998. Miramax Home Entertainment. [Questing]

Wings of Desire.
Wim Wenders, director. 1988. Orion Home Video. [Being Present]

Zorba the Greek.
Michael Cacoyannis, director. CBS/Fox Video. 1964. [Zeal]

*E*nough, Friend.
If you want to read on,
Then go, yourself become the book
and its essence.

—ANGELUS SILESIUS

ABOUT THE AUTHORS

Frederic and Mary Ann Brussat have been covering contemporary culture and the spiritual renaissance for three decades. They are the authors of *Spiritual Literacy: Reading the Sacred in Everyday Life,* a collection of more than 650 examples of spiritual perspectives on everyday experience, which is the basis of a 26-week television series. In that book, they introduced the Alphabet of Spiritual Literacy—37 spiritual practices that are common in the world's religions.

In the early 1990s, the Brussats wrote the magazine *Values & Visions: A Resource Companion for Spiritual Journeys,* which Bill Moyers called "the most original and refreshing guide to what's truly valuable in American society." They have continued this kind of positive reviewing of new books, spoken-word audios, feature films, and videos for other religious and spiritual publications, including *Spirituality & Health* and *The Lutheran.* Each year they identify spiritual themes in more than 300 books, 200 feature films, 200 videos, and 100 spoken-word audios. They also provide discussion guides and program ideas to the Values & Visions Circles, an international network of small groups who use books and movies in a process of soul making and spiritual growth. More than 300 guides are currently available and new ones are prepared every month.

Readers can find information on the Brussats' books, discussion guides, and other projects by visiting their web site at www.spiritualrx.com. New recommendations of spiritual resources are posted every week, and a searchable database contains thousands of recent reviews. Readers can also sign up to receive free e-mail "Soul Boosters" containing quotes and practice suggestions in the format the Brussats pioneered in their two gift paperbacks, *100 Ways to Keep Your Soul Alive* and its sequel *100 More Ways to Keep Your Soul Alive.*

Frederic is a United Church of Christ clergyman with a journalism ministry. The Brussats live in New York City. They can be reached via e-mail to brussat@spiritualrx.com or by writing:

Frederic and Mary Ann Brussat
Values & Visions Circles
P.O. Box 786, Dept. RX
Madison Square Station
New York, NY 10159